D1773234

Fathering Your toddler

A Dad's Guide to the Second and Third Years

"I'll teach you about trucks, William, and you teach me about life."

Fathering Your toddler

A Dad's Guide to the Second and Third Years

SECOND EDITION

Armin A. Brott

Abbeville Press • Publishers
New York • London

For Lumpty Goose, Roo, and the Zip, who constantly remind me that there's always more to learn

EDITORS: Jacqueline Decter, Susan Costello
DESIGNERS: Celia Fuller, Misha Beletsky
PRODUCTION EDITORS: Owen Dugan, Molly Dorozenski, David Fabricant
PRODUCTION MANAGERS: Elizabeth Gaynor, Louise Kurtz

Text copyright © 2005, 1998 Armin A. Brott. Compilation, including selection of text and images, copyright © 2005 Abbeville Press. All rights reserved under international copyright conventions. No part of this book may be reproduced or utilized in any form or by any means, electronic or mechanical, including photocopying, recording, or by any information storage and retrieval system, without permission in writing from the publisher. Inquiries should be addressed to Abbeville Publishing Group, 137 Varick Street, New York, N.Y. 10013. The text of this book was set in Bodoni Book. Printed and bound in the United States of America.

Second paperback edition
10 9 8 7 6 5 4 3 2

Cover photograph by Milton Heiberg.
For cartoon credits, see page 288.

ISBN 0-7892-0850-4 (pb) — ISBN 0-7892-0849-0 (hc)

A previous edition of this book was cataloged as follows:

Library of Congress Cataloging-in-Publication Data
Brott, Armin A.
A dad's guide to the toddler years / Armin A. Brott. — 1st ed.
p. cm. — (The new father)
Includes bibliographical references and index.
1. Toddlers. 2. Toddlers—Care. 3. Father and child. I. Title. II. Series.
HQ774.5.B757 2005
6498.122—dc21 05-32876

For bulk and premium sales and for text adoption procedures, write to Customer Service Manager, Abbeville Publishing Group, 137 Varick Street, New York, N.Y. 10013 or call 1-800-ARTBOOK.

Contents

Acknowledgments 7

Introduction 9

12–15 MONTHS
Getting Off on the Right (or Left) Foot 14

15–18 MONTHS
Keeping Communication Open 50

18–21 MONTHS
Still Wild (or Mild) after All These Months 86

21–24 MONTHS
What Are Daddies Made Of? . 116

24–27 MONTHS
Off to School 137

27–30 MONTHS
Time for a Financial Tune-up 167

30–33 MONTHS
Hey, Who's in Charge Here? 195

33–36 MONTHS
Learning to Let Go 226

Selected Bibliography 258

Resources 265

Index 273

Acknowledgments

Many of the people who helped with the previous books in this series were, remarkably, willing to put up with me again. Even more remarkably, when I told them we were doing a completely revised second edition, they didn't change their phone numbers or e-mail addresses or run screaming in the opposite direction. So I'd like to thank all of those people without whose help this book wouldn't have been possible. Some helped with the first edition, some with the second, some with both.

Bob Abrams gave me his confidence and support. Justin Anderson advised on everything having to do with teeth. Sharon Braz reviewed the section on big-time communication breakdowns between partners. Gene and June Brott, my parents, also read the early versions, babysat, and were a constant source of support. Jim Cameron and the folks at Temperament Talk generously shared their work on temperament, which opened my eyes to a whole new world. Susan Costello lent her support, encouragement, patience, and editing skills. Phil and Carolyn Cowan, who have studied fathers and families for decades, met with me and helped hone my ideas. Jackie Decter guided the first version through from start to finish and made it all coherent. Celia Fuller and Misha Beletsky created the outstanding design. Dave Gould, financial planner extraordinaire, reviewed the sections on financial and tax planning and made them far more accurate and accessible. Ken Guilmartin and Edwin Gordon spent a huge amount of time with me discussing the importance of teaching music to children. Jim Levine made the connections. Amy Handy smoothed out the rough edges in the first edition, and Miranda Ottewell in the second. Louise Kurtz expertly supervised the production. The research on fathers done by Rob Palkovitz, Glen Palm, and Ross Parke was an incredible inspiration. Dawn Swanson, at the Berkeley Public Library, helped select the kids' books in the first edition. Heartfelt thanks to Liz, for her careful eye, support and encouragement, and beautiful soul; and finally, to the hundreds of dads I've relied on over the years, who bravely and openly shared their insights, thoughts, fears, worries, advice, and wisdom.

"I was just telling them that there used to be a show called 'Father Knows Best.'"

Introduction

What image comes to mind when you hear the word *toddler*? Probably that of a child, small, but not nearly as helpless as an infant, walking, falling, walking again. A child brimming with confidence and eager to learn.

Much of the same could be said about the fathers of toddlers as well. You've learned a huge amount over the year or so since your child was born, and you're really getting the hang of this parenting thing. But as confident as you are, something happens every day to remind you that there's still plenty more to learn.

Over the next two years your child will go from crawling to standing to walking to running, and from one- and two-syllable words to telling you that you don't know anything about anything. Psychologist Lawrence Kutner likens toddlerhood to a musical fugue in which "the themes of intellectual, physical, emotional, and social development intertwine."

But the focus of this book isn't really on that. Sure, we'll spend some time discussing your child's growth and identifying developmental milestones. If you want an exhaustive study of child development, though, you need look no further than your local library or bookstore.

This completely updated edition of *Fathering Your Toddler: A Dad's Guide to the Second and Third Years* is primarily about *you* and *your* musical fugue, about how fathers develop and grow over time. And that's something you can't find anywhere else. In writing this book I talked extensively with dozens of leading experts and studied the research and writings of many more. I also drew from my own experiences as the father of three, as well as from the interviews I've done with hundreds of fathers about their experiences and feelings. It is my hope that giving you access to all this wisdom and experience will leave you far better prepared to meet the challenges of being—and staying—an active, involved father.

The big question, of course, is, Why bother to be involved? Three simple reasons: it's good for your kids, it's good for you, and it's good for your relationship with your partner. We'll talk about all of this in detail throughout the book, but let me give you a small taste now.

- **The benefits for your baby**. "The evidence is quite robust that kids who have contact with a father have an advantage over kids without that kind of contact," says Norma Radin, who conducted research on fathers for more than twenty years. And these benefits are evident very early in life. In one study, Radin found that children who were raised by actively involved fathers scored higher on verbal ability tests than children raised in more traditional families by less-involved fathers. In another study, toddlers whose fathers took a special interest in child care were consistently rated two to six months ahead of schedule on tests of development, problem-solving skills, and even social skills. And there's also a strong connection between kids' math skills and the amount of contact they have with their fathers.
- **The benefits for you**. Working fathers also benefit greatly from being involved with their kids. Too many men worry that there's no real way to balance their work and family lives, and that taking an active role at home would be committing career suicide. But the truth is that men who put child-rearing high on their list of priorities are on average more successful in their careers at midlife than men who focus only on their work. Fatherhood also seems to "promote men's abilities to understand themselves as adults and to sympathetically care for other adults," says fatherhood researcher John Snarey. Men who take an active role at home are—by the time their children are grown—better managers, community leaders, and mentors. Overall, they're more concerned with the generation coming up than with themselves.
- **The benefits for your partner and your relationship**. Division-of-labor issues are right up there with money as the top marital stressor. Not surprisingly, the more involved you are and the more support your partner gets from you, the happier she'll be in her marriage and the better she'll perform as a parent. And that will make her a happier woman, which will make you happier as well and will make your relationship last longer.

How This Book Is Organized

Because babies (and their fathers) develop so quickly, the previous book in this series, *The New Father: A Dad's Guide to the First Year*, was organized month by month, a format that enabled us to capture the rapid changes that you and your baby were undergoing. But as your baby morphs into a toddler and as you gain in experience, neither of you is developing quite as quickly, and a month-by-month approach would have been too cumbersome. Instead, while we're still going through your child's and your development in chronological order, we've divided things up into three-month blocks. Each of these quarterly chapters is further divided into several sections:

What's Going On with Your Child

In this section we take a brief yet extremely important look at how your toddler is developing physically, intellectually, verbally, and emotionally/socially. In many ways your toddler's growth parallels your own growth as a father. And much of what you'll be experiencing over the next few years will be closely related to your child's development. So knowing the basics of child development will not only help you understand your child but give you a better, deeper understanding of yourself.

As you no doubt already know, children develop on very different schedules, and the range of "normal" development is quite broad. Dividing the book into three-month sections should take care of most—but probably not all—of the variations, so it might help to imagine that each chapter title is preceded by the word roughly. The first chapter, for example, would be "Roughly 12–15 Months." You might also want to keep extra bookmarks in the chapters immediately preceding and following the one you're reading. If your baby seems to be two chapters (six months or so) ahead of her age, call Oprah. If she's two chapters behind, read the special sections I've added on developmental red flags. If you're still worried, pick up the phone and call your pediatrician.

What You're Going Through

There isn't a lot of social support or any role models out there for fathers who want to be actively involved, which means that most dads don't have very many people to talk to about parenting feelings and concerns. As a result, far too many fathers end up thinking not only that they're absolutely alone in what they're experiencing but that they're abnormal as well. Chances are, however, that with very few exceptions what you're going through at any particular moment of your fatherhood is fairly similar to what millions of fathers before you have felt and millions more after you will. Just as babies develop along a more or less predictable path, so do fathers. And in this section of each chapter, we'll examine what fathers typically go through at that particular time, so you'll be able to monitor your own physical and emotional development. We'll talk about the emotional ups and downs, the joys, the frustrations, the anger, the confusion, the incredible pride, and the confidence that fatherhood brings to all of us. If what you're reading in one chapter doesn't sound like it applies to you, or there are specific issues you want to hear about, feel free to skip around.

You and Your Toddler

Besides being very important, these sections are undoubtedly the most fun. This is where you'll get the tools you'll need to get to know your child better and to create the deepest, closest possible relationship with her—even if all you have is half an hour a day. We'll deal with activities as diverse as playing games, reading, music, making art, cooking, potty training, computers, discipline, handling your child's fears, and overcoming gender stereotypes. Every one of these sections is completely different and covers age-appropriate material.

Family Matters

Although the focus of this book is mostly on you and your toddler, the two of you are still very much part of a family, which includes your partner and any other children you might have. For that reason, we've included a separate section that covers all the things that can have a major impact on everyone in your house. We'll talk about finances, family planning, nutrition, looking for preschools, finding dentists, dealing with tantrums, how your child's temperament affects the whole family, improving communication with your partner, sex, and much more. A number of chapters also include a special "You and Your Partner" section that focuses on specific topics that affect your relationship with the mother of your children.

A Note on Terminology

He and She

As the father of three daughters, I often get annoyed when I read a piece of parenting advice that constantly refers to the child in question as "he." And I'm sure parents of boys feel the same way when the situation is reversed. So in an attempt to offend everyone equally, I opted to simply alternate between "he" and "she," one chapter at a time. Of course, some sections in the book apply only to boys or to girls, and in those cases the appropriate pronoun is used. Otherwise, the terms are completely interchangeable.

You're Not in This Thing Alone, You Know . . .

Whether the mother of your child is your wife, your lover, your girlfriend, your live-in companion, your ex, or your fiancée, she plays an important role in your child's and your life—you wouldn't be a father without her. To keep from making any kind of statement about the importance (or lack of importance, depending on how you feel) of marriage, I've decided to keep referring to the mother of your child as your "partner," as I did in *The New Father: A Dad's Guide to the First Year.*

In Case You Experience a Little Déjà Vu....

This book, like child and father development, is part of an ongoing process that began with *The Expectant Father: Facts, Tips, and Advice for Dads-to-Be* and continued with *The New Father: A Dad's Guide to the First Year.* And like most ongoing processes, previously mastered skills become the basis for learning new ones. Simply put, this means that while all the information in this book is completely new, some of the topics have been touched on in a different way in previous volumes. In each case I give the exact page reference to indicate where the idea first came up. If you've got a copy of either or both these books around, you can check these references. If not, don't worry; everything covered here stands on its own.

The All-Important Disclaimer

I'm not a pediatrician, financial planner, accountant, or lawyer, nor do I play one on TV (although I do host a radio show). This means that even though all the medical, financial, and legal advice in this book has been reviewed by experts and proven to work by real people (including me, in most cases), you should still check with an appropriate professional before trying any of it out on yourself and your family.

And please be particularly careful when trying out any of the recommended games or other activities with your child. Safety should be your number-one concern. Make sure that your home is properly childproofed and never, ever leave your child alone during any of these activities—especially any that involve water or small objects. Children can drown or choke much faster than you'd think. And be sure that anything that could possibly end up in your child's mouth is nontoxic and recommended for children under three. Finally, know your child's limitations and don't push him to do anything he's not developmentally ready for. I've made every effort to ensure that the activities in this book are safe when you or another trusted adult is there to supervise. However, neither Abbeville Press nor I can be responsible for any unforeseen consequences.

12–15 MONTHS

Getting Off on the Right (or Left) Foot

What's Going On with the Baby

Physically

- In his first twelve months of life, your baby grew at an incredible clip, probably tripling his birth weight by his first birthday. This year, the growth rate will slow way, way down. In fact, he'll most likely gain only three to five pounds over the next twelve months. As he gets more mobile, he'll start trimming away the baby fat and will soon be looking less like an infant and more like a little kid.
- By the end of this period, your baby will be most comfortable in a fully upright position and can squat down and stand back up again without keeling over. Most babies take their first steps between nine and eighteen months, and once they start, they'll insist on practicing at every opportunity—sometimes holding on to one or both of your hands, sometimes unassisted. And when they're not walking, they're climbing. But even if your baby is toddling around by himself, he may still drop into a crawl if he wants to get somewhere quickly.
- Your child's favorite activity now is filling and emptying containers of all kinds (with the emphasis on emptying). He can clean out your dresser drawers, kitchen cabinets, refrigerator, and bookshelves in a matter of seconds.
- He wants to feed himself and may try to undress himself. He is especially good at removing—and losing—socks and hats.
- His fine motor coordination is greatly improved. He can turn the pages of a book one at a time and now releases objects as accurately and gracefully as

he picks them up—a skill he'll find invaluable when he learns to throw a ball. He can also draw a straight line (if you do one first) and stack two blocks, and he may occasionally use a spoon or fork to get food from a plate into his mouth as well as for banging (although most of the time he'll use his free hand to take off whatever's on the silverware and pop it into his mouth).

- He loves to play all sorts of physical games. Chase me/catch me, rolling balls back and forth, and wrestling are big favorites, and so are games that involve pouring or splashing water.
- He's trying really, really hard to turn doorknobs. If you're lucky, it'll be a few more months before he successfully puts together grasping and twisting.

Intellectually

- In his ongoing attempt to trash your home, your toddler will be picking up, rotating, dropping, tasting, stacking (then knocking over), and throwing everything he can get his hands on, thus giving him a crash course in shape, texture, taste, density, balance, and aerodynamics.
- He has a clearer understanding of his own limitations and is getting better at using tools—including adults'—to get what he wants. He'll use a stick to get something out from under the couch and will demand that you help him achieve his desire to swing on a swing all day.
- He's much better at distinguishing sizes and shapes and has a well-developed sense of how things "should be." He may occasionally put a square peg in a square hole, and if you turn a familiar object (like a book) upside down, he'll turn it right side up.
- His memory continues to improve, and he can now look for an object he hasn't seen you hide. He's also developing a sense of time, and he understands that certain things (like naps) follow others (like meals).
- He's fascinated by hinged objects—especially doors (which he'll open and close over and over and over) and books—not so much for what's in them but for the sheer feeling of accomplishment he gets when he turns the pages.

Verbally

- According to psychologist Fitzhugh Dodson, there are two phases of language learning: passive language learning (what you understand) and active language learning (what you can actually say). Most of the language learning your toddler will do over the course of the next twelve months will be passive. He understands anywhere from two to a hundred words now and will try to increase that by pointing to everything in sight and asking you to tell him what it is.

Taking a Walk—or a Crawl—on the Wild Side

On average, babies take their first steps at about twelve months. But as mentioned above, the range is pretty big, from nine to eighteen months. How early—or late—your child starts to walk depends on a number of factors:

- Genetics. If you and/or your partner were early or late walkers, chances are your child will be too.
- Birth circumstances. If your baby was born prematurely, he'll probably be a late walker. Researchers have found that very low-birth-weight, preterm infants learn to walk at an adjusted age of fourteen months. Premature babies usually catch up to their agemates by the time they're three, but the more premature the baby, the longer it takes to pull even.
- Older siblings. Having a brother or sister who's a few years older sometimes gives babies a little extra incentive to walk early.
- Medical issues. Your baby may learn to walk late if he had to go through a lot of medical intervention early in life, or if he simply got sick or had a bad fall right when he was about to take his first steps. Babies with Down syndrome typically start walking at about twenty-four months.

- By the end of the fifteenth month, he'll identify upon request his shoes, clothes, and body parts; familiar people and objects; and one or two pictures from a favorite book.
- Although he has a speaking vocabulary of fewer than ten words, he'll use them whenever he has a chance, pointing to and naming whatever he sees. Multisyllabic words may give him some trouble (peek-a-boo becomes "boo," and thermonuclear becomes "taa"), but by fifteen months he'll be stringing words together two at a time: "Bye-bye, Daddy," and, "No, baby," are among his first "sentences." He can also do some pretty good cow, dog, and cat imitations.
- He's becoming aware of the expressive function of language and has developed an uncanny ability to pick out—and endlessly repeat—the one swear word you accidentally slipped into a ten-minute-long conversation.
- His understanding of the symbolic use of words is growing. If he knows the

- Scheduling issues. Your baby has a lot going on now, including learning to speak, trying to identify everything in sight, and establishing his independence. He may simply have decided that walking isn't that much of a priority—especially if he's a fast crawler.
- Environmental factors. Slippery floors, bulky clothing, and parents who gasp every time the baby looks like he's going to fall can contribute to delays in walking.

The whole crawling-to-walking transition is full of myths. You may hear, for example, that babies who scoot or slide or roll instead of crawling develop behavior problems later in life, presumably because they missed a major developmental milestone. Or you might hear that early walking is a sure sign of genius in the making. Or you might hear the opposite, that early walkers do poorly in math and science because crawling helps develop the brain. None of it's true.

Bottom line? Your baby will learn to walk when he's good and ready, and there's nothing you can—or should—do to change his schedule. If you're worried about your baby's walking ability, be sure to read the rundown of physical development in "What's Going on with the Baby" at the beginning of every chapter in this book. If you're still concerned, schedule a visit with your child's pediatrician.

word ball, for example, he may use it when he sees a globe, a coin, an egg, or the moon. He may also call every cat, horse, goat, pig, llama, or other hairy, four-legged animal a "dog."

Emotionally/Socially

- He's becoming fiercely independent, demanding to push his stroller instead of riding in it. He'll also insist on feeding himself, but will end up with more on his face, his cheeks, the walls, the high-chair tray, or the floor than in his mouth.
- Doing things on his own isn't all there is to being independent. Your toddler wants to separate himself physically from you as well—but not for too long. Pretending to be on a scouting expedition, he'll stroll a short distance away, casually looking back over his shoulder to make sure you haven't gone anywhere. But independence is a pretty scary thing to a one-year-old, so a

second or two after you disappear from his view, he'll scamper back and cling to you for all he's worth. He'll repeat the process of going away and coming back at least until he's graduated from college.

- As he slowly becomes secure in the idea that you'll always be there for him, your child's shyness around strangers and his fear of separation should decrease.
- As those fears disappear, however, they are replaced by other, even more irrational-seeming ones: the vacuum cleaner and the neighborhood dogs that never bothered him before suddenly terrify him; he now needs a nightlight in his room; and he may refuse to take a bath, fearing that he'll get sucked down the drain.
- With all the places he has to go and things he has to do, your baby won't want to waste his precious time eating, and may reject any attempts to do so. He will also regard sleep as a major imposition and may refuse to nap.
- He's a social little creature and will clap and try to sing along with familiar songs. He also loves attention and knows exactly what it takes to get you to focus on him. Sometimes it's something incredibly cute; other times he'll throw in a cough or choking sound just for the shock value.

What You're Going Through

Wear and Tear

Being a father can be an exhausting proposition, and I'm not talking about sleep deprivation (which has probably passed for the most part by now anyway). Just trying to keep up with a toddler as he careens happily through his day can be enough to drop even a world-class athlete to his knees.

In our prefatherhood days, most of us never did anything to prepare for all the stooping (to get kids into and out of their car seats), bending (to put away hundreds of toys a day), wrestling, pushing (swings or strollers), chasing (to make sure the baby stays out of trouble), schlepping (all those extra bags of groceries in and out of the car), holding (it's fun, but it's hard to keep up for more than a few blocks), and carrying (sleeping children seem to weigh a lot more than awake ones). Not to mention all that extra laundry and housecleaning. Is it any wonder that just about every father I know has a bad back?

And let's not forget about the psychological pressures that go along with trying to be a good father, husband, friend, employer, provider, and protector all at the same time.

It's crucial to take care of yourself physically as well as psychologically. Not doing so can make it impossible for you to take care of anyone else. Here are a few things you can do:

- **Get plenty of exercise**. Thirty minutes of aerobic activity three times a week not only gets you into better shape but has also been shown to reduce stress and depression. Of course, finding the time to exercise when you have a young child around is easier said than done. So you might want to invest in a jog stroller or a child seat (or trailer) for your bicycle and take your baby along. Remember to stretch before and after your workouts, and be sure to include some special strength-building exercises for your back and abs.
- **Eat right**. Skip the fad diets and make sure you're getting a healthy balance of carbs, proteins, and fats. Go for the good ones—unsaturated and omega-3—and stay away from saturated fats and trans fats (partially hydrogenated oils). Eat more often—five small meals a day is better than three big ones. And try to drink at least eight glasses of water a day. Coffee or caffeinated drinks don't count.
- **Catch some rays**. The neurotransmitter serotonin is a natural antidepressant, and your brain produces more of it on sunny days than on overcast ones.
- **Catch some z's**. Seven to eight hours of sleep is optimal for most people. Averaging less than that is associated with a higher risk of heart disease. Interestingly, getting *more* than eight hours a night may be even worse, according to Dr. Najib T. Ayas, who led a team of researchers at Brigham and Women's Hospital.
- **Pay attention to your symptoms**. Physical pain is a sign that something's not right. So are headaches, ulcers, muscle tension, chronic depression, feeling angry even when there's nothing wrong, sleep problems, high blood pressure, sudden weight gain or loss, and an unusually short temper.
- **See your doctor regularly**.
- **Skip the quick fixes**. Alcohol and cigarettes may seem to reduce your stress, but they're only covering it up for a while. Sometimes they even make things worse.
- **Treat yourself nicely**. Take some breaks, get an occasional massage, buy yourself something special once in a while. If possible, schedule a regular time when you can be without phone, pager, e-mail, and so on. Even a few hours unplugged can feel like a vacation. If you can't spare a few hours, twenty to thirty minutes of meditating will do wonders.

- **Get some intellectual stimulation.** With all the reading you're doing with your baby, don't forget to do some for yourself as well.
- **Leave time for lovin'.** Sex is an important way to stay emotionally and physically connected to your partner. It's also an excellent stress reliever, and some research has shown that regular sex can reduce the likelihood of developing prostate problems.

A Conflict between Separateness and Connectedness

As we'll see later in this chapter, your child has been struggling to strike a balance between being dependent on you and independent from you. But your baby isn't the only one in your immediate family who's dealing with these issues.

As a parent, you're probably wrestling with an adult version of separation anxiety: a conflict between wanting to be needed by your child (wanting to keep him a baby) and wanting to push him toward independence.

The great irony here (to me, anyway) is that the attachment that we've tried so hard to achieve with our children is inextricably related to separating from them. In fact, "The task of becoming attached includes beginning to understand separateness," says Ellen Galinsky, head of the Work and Family Institute. It really seems that the stronger your attachment to the child, the more likely you are to be affected by the separation.

There are, of course, two common ways to deal with adult separation anxiety: push the baby to be more independent, or encourage him to be more dependent on you. Adopting either approach by itself will guarantee disaster for your child as well as for your family. As with just about anything else to do with parenting, the trick is to find the right balance between the available extremes. And the first step is to become aware of what might be motivating you to move in the direction you're heading.

WHY YOU MAY BE PUSHING YOUR CHILD TO BE MORE INDEPENDENT

- Your child may be quieter than you'd like him to be.
- He may not be as curious as you think he should be.
- You may be afraid that your child is too clingy or dependent and that if he doesn't start learning to take care of himself, he'll grow up to be a wimp.
- You may be afraid that your child is controlling you, that you're losing your independence, and that he's making too many demands on your time and affection. This is especially common among fathers who have a child with a "difficult" temperament.

". . . and so the princess and the prince lived happily ever after. The end. Now get some sleep. We want you to be fresh as a daisy for your first day of college tomorrow."

- If you're a stay-at-home dad or if you're especially involved, you may be afraid that besides having lost your career, you've also lost your prestige and your masculinity.

Pushing early self-reliance tends to be thought of as a "dad thing," but mothers are far from immune from trying to make their kids more independent. Either way, remember this:

- If your child seems clingy, there's probably a reason for it. Until he feels secure in your relationship, he won't be ready to separate from you.
- Learn to take pride in what he does, rather than in what you think he should do. He's your child, but he's not you, and he won't do exactly what you wish he would.
- If you feel that your baby isn't growing up as quickly as you'd like, you may end up pushing him to go places or do things he isn't ready for, says psychiatrist Stanley Greenspan. This can lead to your being even more

disappointed when the baby fails to live up to your overly high expectations, and to him feeling guilty and inadequate because he can't make you happy.

Some potential negative side effects of pushing independence on your child too much or too soon:

- You may suddenly start working longer hours, coming home later, or doing just about anything to stay away from home more.
- You might begin distancing yourself from your partner as well as the baby, feeling that you have to make up for all the time you haven't been getting for yourself since the baby came.
- You may become less affectionate with your child—especially if you have a boy.
- Your child may come to feel unloved and uncared-for, as though you're trying to get rid of him.
- You may not supervise your child as well as you should, or you might not help your child when he really does need some help. Unsupervised kids get into more accidents and suffer more injuries than well-supervised ones.

WHY YOU MAY BE SUBTLY ENCOURAGING YOUR CHILD TO BE MORE DEPENDENT

- You may be saddened that your baby is growing up so quickly. As young as he still is, he's already outgrown certain adorable behaviors and gestures, and you may almost wish that he'd stay this age forever.
- You may be afraid of being rejected or abandoned by your child. You'll get a sharp jolt of this feeling when you want to sit quietly and snuggle with your baby, but he's got places to go and things to do and would rather squirm off your lap and run away.

Although it's usually thought of as more of a "mom thing," plenty of dads have trouble letting their kids go. If you're one of them, consider this:

- Don't think the baby doesn't need you or love you. He may not show it, but he actually needs you more than ever. Your support and love let him know that growing up (which he's going to do whether you like it or not) is okay.
- Your feeling that your baby's youth has somehow been "lost" runs parallel to his feelings of exploring unknown territory. Taking pride in his independence and all the "big boy" things he can do is an important part of building his self-esteem and independence.
- You may wistfully wish that your baby would stay a baby forever, but is that

what you *really* want? To be changing his diapers for the next fifty years? I don't think so.

Here are some of the potential negatives of limiting independence:

- You might hover too much, never allowing your child to make the mistakes he needs to make in order to learn. Or, you might be overprotective and not give your child enough room to explore. As a result, he could end up lacking the confidence he'll need throughout his life to persevere in the face of adversity.
- You might limit his contacts with other people, feeling that any free time he has should be spent with you.
- You might refrain from setting limits or disciplining your child for fear of driving him away.
- You may spoil your child or become excessively aggressive in trying to win his love.

RECOGNIZING YOUR LIMITATIONS

Before Clint Eastwood (as Dirty Harry) was throwing down the gauntlet with his "Go ahead, make my day," he was advising people that "a man's got to know his limitations."

According to the research of family and parenting experts Phil and Carolyn Cowan, one of the factors that differentiates fathers from nonfathers is that fathers do a better job of discriminating between what they can and can't control. This skill—as absolutely basic as it sounds—is something that actually takes years to develop. "We heard men working on it when they discussed their struggles with wanting it all—job advancement, involved relationships with their wives and children, time for themselves—while accepting the fact that no matter how hard they tried, some things had to be put aside for the time being," write the Cowans. Men who weren't parents, however, seemed to have fewer competing roles to juggle, didn't seem to be as aware of their limitations, and were "more invested in maintaining at least the illusion of personal control."

You and Your Child

Play

The first few months of your child's second year have been full of dramatic changes, and the way he plays is no exception. Only a few months ago he depended on you to pick the toys or games he'd play with, and he could focus on only one object (or person) at a time.

But in just the past few weeks, your child has begun to assume a more active role in his own entertainment. Play is now serious business. And there's a lot more to it than just having fun: play is how your baby is going to learn about the world around him. It's how he's going to try out new skills and perfect them; it's how he's going to improve and perfect his communication, counting, large motor skills (running and walking) and fine motor skills (picking up a single grain of rice), balance, imagination, problem solving, and more.

But play isn't only for kids. Playing with your child is a great way to get to know him, see how he reacts to challenges, and check out his likes and dislikes, attention span, and natural aptitudes. So set aside some time every day—try for a minimum of twenty to thirty minutes—to get down on the floor and play with your child.

Actually, the phrase "play with" isn't completely accurate. At this age your baby is too young to play with anyone. Oh, sure, he may hand you a toy he's been using or snatch something from you, or he may excitedly want to show you what he's accomplished. But he doesn't understand sharing or taking turns or rules or the give-and-take flow of games. What he's doing is called "parallel play," which simply means playing next to someone.

This doesn't mean you can't have fun together—I'll tell you a lot of ways to do just that below. What it does mean is that you might not be able to play with your child exactly the way you'd hoped. Most dads want to interact with their children, teach them strategy, show them the best way to pass a football, hit a baseball, shoot a basket, dig a hole, ride a bike, catch a fish, fold a paper airplane, or move a chess piece. You'll be able to do all that, just not right now. Instead, you'll have to master one of the most important—and hardest—ways of playing with your child: watching.

You'll want to decide what to play with and how. And you're going to be tempted to jump in to save the day, or wrestle away a toy so you can show your child the "right" way to use it. Don't give in. Remember: your child is the real play expert. He doesn't tell you how to do your job, so don't tell him how to do his.

Offering choices ("Do you want to play with the blocks or take a walk?") and making occasional encouraging suggestions ("Can you put one more block on your tower?") is fine. And so is teaching by example, such as building a tower of your own right next to the one your child is working on. But be sure to spend at least part of your time together just looking. Once you get used to it, you'll be amazed at how much fun it is. I can't count the number of hours I spent watching my children play, marveling at how they'd overcome obstacles, trying one solution after another until they got it right, and admiring their capacity to find joy in the littlest things.

Here are some toys and activities that will keep you and your baby entertained for the next six months or so:

12–15 MONTHS

TOYS

When looking for toys, pick those that:

- Are age-appropriate. You may be in a hurry for your child to grow up, but giving him toys that are meant for older kids will frustrate him—and you. The age ranges printed on most toy boxes are pretty accurate. But remember, they're only guidelines, so use some common sense. If the box says the toy inside is for kids 12–15 months, but it introduces a skill your baby has already mastered, get something else. At the same time, if that same toy introduces a skill your baby isn't ready for, put it away and bring it out again in a few months.
- The baby can safely chew on or throw without damaging anything or anyone (soft plastic or padded blocks, for example).
- Can be washed.
- Can survive in water, like cups, sponges, boats, cars, and anything else your baby might want to bring into the bath.
- Stimulate the senses by incorporating lots of different noises, textures, and colors—the more the better.
- Encourage manual dexterity by requiring that the baby twist, turn, poke, flick, and/or snap them to get a response.
- Encourage the use of both hands: Duplo (the bigger Lego blocks), toy farms with animals, and the like are great.
- Have wheels or can easily be pulled, pushed, dragged, or shoved. Lawn mowers, buggies, strollers, wagons, and "popcorn poppers" are all good. If your child still isn't very steady on his feet, make sure to get toys that won't fall over, roll away, or collapse if he leans on them.
- Develop sorting and categorizing skills, such as containers or toy trucks for filling and dumping, nesting toys, measuring spoons, and shape sorters (although it'll be a few months before the baby will be able to get the round block in the round hole very regularly).

- Are real. Old telephones (without cords) and even that extra computer keyboard and mouse you've got lying around, for example, are more interesting to many kids than their fake counterparts.
- Bounce. Just about any kind of ball will amuse just about any kind of kid.
- Offer variety. Your child's toy collection should include a good mix of big and little, indoor and outdoor, wet and dry, noisy and quiet.

ACTIVITIES THAT:

- Encourage manual dexterity and hand-eye coordination.
  - Blowing bubbles. Try to chase them down and catch them before they hit the floor.
  - Touching games, such as "This little piggy went to market . . . " and "Round and round the garden went the teddy bear. . . ."
- Promote awareness of size, shape, color, spatial concepts (in/out, up/down, and so forth).
  - Emptying, dumping, and refilling everything from buckets to bathtubs and kitchen cabinets builds awareness of in and out.
  - Toys that nest and stack. These are great for teaching about size, as are large boxes the baby can crawl into.
- Encourage large motor skills.
  - Playing ball. For now, this means rolling a ball back and forth. Your baby will be able to heave a ball in a few months, but won't be able to catch one for another year. The first time you play ball, start just a few feet apart and increase the distance a little every time you play. By varying the speed and bounciness, you'll be teaching your baby about timing and anticipation.
  - Obstacle courses. Arrange pillows, furniture, boxes, and toys that your baby will have to go over, through, around, and under.
- Develop balance.
  - Blanket sledding. Fold a blanket in half and lay it out lengthwise on the floor. Sit your baby about two feet from one end with a pillow behind him. Then take the other end and gently pull your baby toward you. The first few times you do this, your baby will probably fall over backward (which is why the pillow is there). But it won't take long for him to develop the sense of balance he needs to stay upright. A few notes: Hardwood floors are best, but you can play this game on carpet as well. Always make sure your baby is sitting solidly before you start, and don't jerk the blanket. And never, ever do this near stairs.

- ◊ Push/pull toys such as lawn mowers and shopping carts. These are great for improving balance.
- ◊ If your baby walks well, have him try to kick a large ball. It's harder than it looks, so be patient.

♦ Teach about consequences.

- ◊ Tie a string to a favorite toy, hand the other end of the string to the baby, and ask him to get the toy. Will he pull the string?
- ◊ Have your child turn the lights or the television on and off. Does he understand the connection between flipping the switch and what happens next?
- ◊ If your child is able to blow bubbles, show him the difference between blowing softly (you get larger bubbles) and hard (you get smaller ones).

♦ Stimulate the imagination.

- ◊ Have a pretend phone conversation with your child.
- ◊ Ask him to feed and diaper one of his stuffed animals.
- ◊ Have him read you a bedtime story instead of the other way around.
- ◊ Stick out your tongue or make a silly face and ask your baby to imitate you. If he does, try picking up a toy and putting it away. He'll probably go along with the game for a little while, but as soon as he figures out that you're making him work, it's over.

♦ Are low-key.

- ◊ Take a walk around your neighborhood and talk about everything—the trees, the flowers, the difference between a pickup, a car, a motorcycle, and a garbage truck. Stop and watch a spider spin a web or an ant carry a bread crumb across the sidewalk. Try to look at the world through your child's eyes. Everything he sees or hears or smells is new and fascinating. So take your time and enjoy.
- ◊ Snuggle up on the couch and read (see pages 34–37 for more).

♦ That are really and truly fun—for your baby.

- ◊ Let's face it: most dads love to play, and it's oh-so-easy to get caught up in something you're doing and forget about your playmate. I remember getting really annoyed at one of my daughters after I'd spent a bunch of time building a gorgeous Lego skyscraper, only to have her angrily knock the whole thing down. She'd been trying to tell me for quite a while that she was tired of playing with Lego, but it just didn't register. So pay close attention to your child's mood—when he's not having fun anymore, it's time to move on to the next activity. But feel free to build all the skyscrapers you want after you've put him to bed.

15–18 MONTHS

TOYS

All of the above, plus toys that:

- The baby can pound, smack, beat, and smash. Hammer-and-peg boards and sandbox toys are always big hits at this age.
- The baby can ride on. Four-wheelers are better (more stable) than trikes. Skip the batteries (the baby hasn't been walking long enough to need a break) and forget the pedals (it's too early).
- Encourage sorting. Your baby's getting much better at putting the right block in the right hole on his shape sorter. He should also be able to stack a series of different-sized rings on a cylinder in the right order, putting the largest at the bottom.

ACTIVITIES

All of the above, plus those that:

- Encourage body-part identification.
  - ◊ Games like Where's Your Nose? or Where's Daddy's Belly Button? And don't limit yourself to people. Animals and toys have body parts too.
- Continue to encourage turning, twisting, and so on.
  - ◊ For some strange reason, all of my kids have entertained themselves for hours by locking and unlocking the doors to the car and the house.
- Continue to promote awareness of size, color, and spatial relationships. But take things up a notch if your baby is ready.
  - ◊ Have your child pour some uncooked rice or beans from one bowl to another. Then have him try to pour the same stuff into a narrow-necked bottle.
- Promote independence.
  - ◊ Let your child ask you for help before you jump in—at this age he should be able to give you some pretty clear signals. See how long it takes him, or how many tries he needs, to learn new skills. For example, watch as he figures out how to sit down on a baby-sized chair. In the beginning, he'll climb on front first. But after a few falls he'll figure out that backing on works better.
- Use real tools.
  - ◊ Let your baby sweep, push the vacuum, wipe up the floor, and shave you. An electric razor is no problem, but if you use a razor and shaving cream, you might want to leave the blade off the handle the first few

times. The lathering is the most fun anyway. Then shave one side of your face and show him the difference between smooth and scratchy.

- Stimulate memory.
  - Play your own version of the shell game. Get three identical cups (plastic yogurt or margarine containers work well) and have your child put a small ball underneath one of them. Then move the containers around and have him guess where the ball is.
  - Have a treasure hunt. With your baby watching, hide several of his toys in various parts of the house. Then ask him to find them.
- Stimulate the senses.
  - Take a "texture tour." Take off your shoes (and your baby's too) and walk around your house testing out all the different surfaces—tile, wood, carpet, vinyl. If it's safe, you can take the tour outside as well, trying out grass, sand, concrete, and mud puddles.
  - Make your own orchestra (or at least a percussion section), with pots, pans, xylophones, cymbals, drums, and wooden spoons. This game is also a great way to start introducing him to music.
- Promote art awareness. (See pages 37–41.)
- Encourage physical fitness, such as dancing to music, chasing, wrestling, and early attempts at gymnastics. For much more on the importance of physical play, see pages 209–10.

PLAYTHINGS TO AVOID FOR THIS GENERAL AGE GROUP

- Anything with springs, pinch points, sharp edges, or small detachable pieces. A good rule of thumb is that anything that can fit through a cardboard toilet-paper tube is too small and poses a choking hazard.
- Complicated things. Simplicity is the key here. Your baby doesn't need fancy attachments, cellular phones, fax machines, and the like. Busy boxes are generally unappreciated by kids this age. You can have a huge amount of fun with whatever you happen to have in your house.
- Antiques. Unless they're exceptionally sturdy, conform to today's more stringent safety standards, and aren't covered in lead paint, leave them in the attic.
- Anything that has a heating element or an electrical cord (battery-operated toys—provided that the battery can't be accessed by the child—are okay).
- Balloons and anything with small, detachable parts. These are the leading causes of toy-related fatalities.
- Audio tapes. They're great fun to unwind, but not nearly as much fun to get

back in the cassette. CDs are at least as interesting to play with (they're shinier, for one thing) and are pretty much indestructible.

- Passive toys. You want a toy that will make your child want to get up and dance, rather than one that will encourage him to sit quietly and watch.
- Gender-specific toys. There is absolutely no reason why boys can't play with dolls, vacuums, brooms, and kitchen sets, or why girls can't play with cars, walkie-talkies, and balls. In fact, one of my younger daughter's favorite activities is shooting her fifty Hot Wheels cars one at a time down her loop-de-loop track. Don't push any particular toys at your child—just make them available and try to incorporate them into your playtime. If your child sees you using them, he will want to do the same.

Technology for Toddlers

I know that your child has been walking for only a few months, but have you thought about whether it might already be time to introduce him to some of the high-tech equipment he's likely to encounter as he grows up?

A lot of parents have some legitimate questions about the sensibleness and worthwhileness (and even the danger) of starting kids on computers and/or computerized toys at such an early age. Making the right decision—assuming there is such a thing—is nearly impossible, given the heated debate among academics, software designers, and advocacy groups.

On one side, there are psychologists and other experts who claim that it's almost never too early to get children comfortable with using technology. On the other side, people with equally impressive résumés say exactly the opposite, that introducing children to technology too early can be dangerous. Here's how the arguments stack up:

THE ARGUMENTS IN FAVOR	THE ARGUMENTS AGAINST
• Our world is becoming more and more wired every day, and kids who don't have superior computer skills will be at a disadvantage as they grow up. It makes intuitive sense that a child who goes to preschool and kindergarten already knowing shapes and colors and numbers and the letters of the alphabet will have a leg up.	• Children are being pushed by their parents to grow up too fast. What they need is time to relax, enjoy life, and be a kid. Put a little more succinctly, "Young kids need to interact with their parents, not machines," says child psychiatrist Michael Brody.

THE ARGUMENTS IN FAVOR	THE ARGUMENTS AGAINST
♦ The "risks" that computers pose are way overblown, according to Warren Buckleitner, editor of *Children's Software Review*. For example: repetitive stress injuries may occur from heavy computer or video game use, but they are also caused by playing musical instruments, and by the repetitive motion of sports. "Shall we take away the violins and the tennis rackets, too?" asks Buckleitner.	♦ According to the Alliance for Childhood, "computers pose serious health hazards to children. The risks include repetitive stress injuries, eyestrain, obesity, social isolation, and, for some, long-term damage to physical, emotional, or intellectual development." (You can download a free copy of their comprehensive study, "Fool's Gold: A Critical Look at Computers in Childhood," through their Web site, www.allianceforchildhood.net.)
♦ Although computers are not nearly as social as reading, computer games are far more interactive than television, and they offer many opportunities for creativity, without all the mess of finger paints. ♦ Properly supervised (more on this below), children as young as a year can use computers to learn shapes, colors, numbers, and opposites. As they get older, computers can assist them in learning upper- and lowercase letters, recognizing words and patterns, spelling, reading, doing arithmetic, and developing reasoning skills and hand-eye coordination.	♦ Toddlers learn by actively engaging the world: touching, feeling, pushing, pulling, throwing, tasting, and so on. Computers, by their very nature, simply can't provide any of these experiences.

Technology and Special Needs Children

Although the topic of technology for toddlers is very controversial, there's one group that almost everyone agrees can definitely benefit from computer technology: children with disabilities, including Down syndrome, cerebral palsy, mental retardation, and autism.

According to the Parent Advocacy Coalition for Educational Rights (PACER), assistive technological (AT) options, including computers, software, modified keyboards, and other devices, can help disabled children learn or improve their skills in a number of important areas, including:

- social interactions, including sharing and taking turns
- communication
- attention span
- fine and large motor skills
- self-confidence and independence

If you have a child with special needs, the sooner you introduce him to AT, the better. If you're worried that relying on technology will discourage your child from learning certain skills on his own, don't be. One of the big risks disabled children face is what researcher Catherine Burke calls "learned helplessness"—where children learn to wait for their parents or other people to initiate communication, play, or other interactions. AT can help children become more empowered initiators in play and communication regardless of their age, according to Burke.

Another advantage of AT is the effect it could have on you, your partner, and the other people who love and care for your child. As PACER puts it, "With assistive technology, parents learn that the dreams they had for their child don't necessarily end when he or she is diagnosed with a disability. The dreams may have to be changed a little, but they can still come true."

PACER and Burke suggest several AT options for very young children:

- Switches, or specially adapted knobs or buttons, that enable a child to turn devices off or on, to demonstrate cause-and-effect relationships,

So will exposing a child to computers make him antisocial or keep him in front of the screen instead of doing other things all the time? Unlikely. Initially, the novelty of the computer may suck children away from other activities, but that's not all that different from what happens with any new toy. Your child or to get a toy to move. Even children with severe disabilities can use switches. For example, one can be placed near a child's head so that every time he moves in a certain direction, a mobile or other toy will start to move.

- Velcro wrist or ankle bands can be attached to bells, rattles, or other toys, if the child has trouble holding on to them without assistance.
- Augmentative communication devices allow children who can't speak, or who aren't speaking yet, to communicate. This could be anything from touch-screen computers and holders that help children keep books open to picture boards and special pointers that can activate prerecorded messages, such as "I'm hungry."

A lot of parents worry that augmentative communications technologies might actually keep their child from learning speech. But according to Catherine Burke, using augmentative communication within a spoken language framework will eliminate the problem. "We typically see children become more verbal in response to spoken language paired with signs and communication boards because they understand more about what words mean and how to use them with the people in their lives," she says.

If you think your child could benefit from AT devices, your first step should be to get in contact with the agencies in your state that provide information, services, and evaluations for special-needs toddlers and their families. Depending on the results of the evaluation, you may be able to receive AT devices and all necessary training at no charge. If your child isn't eligible for free services, they may still be covered under your health insurance policy.

If you aren't already in contact with the right agencies, the National Information Center for Children & Youth with Disabilities (NICHY) will help you find them. Contact information for NICHY is in the Resources guide (page 264).

needs a wide variety of things to play with and learn from. As long as you don't try to make the computer replace all your child's other toys, it will be just another toy on his shelf.

After thoroughly investigating the pros and cons, I came to the conclusion that it's worth a try, but only if you stick to the following guidelines:

- **Your child must be ready**. He should have a firm grasp of cause-and-effect relationships (I push the Enter key, and something happens on the screen).
- **He must be interested**. One way to increase the chances he'll be interested is to let him watch you work on your computer; another is to let him bang around on an old keyboard (if you don't have one, you can probably buy a used one at a flea market for about five dollars).
- **Never use the computer as an electronic babysitter**. You must be willing to be there, with your child sitting on your lap, every time he plays on the computer. When he's a little older, he can graduate to sitting next to you.
- **Keep it interactive**. Talk about what you're seeing on the screen, why your child is making the choices he is, and so on, just as you would if you were reading a story or playing a game.
- **Have fun**. At this age, the goal of exposing your tot to technology isn't to teach him anything, and it's not to boost his IQ or get him into an Ivy League school before he's out of diapers. It should really be just another way the two of you can play together. As with any other activity, pay attention to your child's cues. If he's bored or isn't interested, shut down the computer and go for a walk or pick up a book.
- **Don't put a computer in your child's room**.
- **Make sure you select good equipment**. Childrensoftware.com (fee based) and Superkids.com (free) both do reviews and make recommendations of software and hardware. One particularly good piece of hardware is the Comfy keybord (www.comfylandnorthamerica.com).
- **Limit screen time**. Computer games should be part of a well-balanced diet of fun activities. Chances are your child won't be interested in playing on the computer for more than five minutes at a stretch. But if he's easily mesmerized, cut him off at ten to fifteen minutes per day.

Reading

By about fifteen months, your baby will have put his passive reading days behind him, and he'll become a real participant. He'll babble along with you now as you read, and make unsolicited (but often appropriate) animal sounds. And if you pause briefly while reading a familiar story, he'll often fill in a missing word or two—usually the last word in a sentence or rhyme. Over the next few months he'll try to seize control of your reading sessions by pointing to illustrations and insisting that you identify them.

But no matter how great your baby's newfound power, the thrill of being mobile is so consuming that he'll start squirming within seconds after he sits in your lap. Don't be offended or try to limit his movements. If he wants to go, let him. He'll be back soon enough. (At bedtime, though, this situation could change, and your baby might demand book after book after book as a way to avoid having to go to sleep.)

To encourage your baby's interest in books and to give him more control over his reading material, consider making a low bookshelf for him, one where the books face cover out, so he can bring you his current favorites. Having a

Poetry for Babies?

Generally speaking, children's taste in poetry is just about as lowbrow as my own. According to researchers Ann Terry and Karen Kutiper, kids seem to like:

- poems they can understand
- narrative poems or poems that tell a story
- poems with rhyme, distinctive rhythm, strong sound patterns, and a sense of excitement
- poems about animals or familiar experiences
- limericks of all sorts

On the other hand, they don't like:

- poems with a lot of abstract or figurative language and imagery
- highly abstract poems that do not make sense to them or do not relate to their own experiences
- haiku

Having said all that, if you start introducing your child to a variety of types of poetry now, he'll eventually develop a taste for it. Here are a few suggestions to get you started:

The Owl and the Pussycat, Edward Lear
Every Time I Climb a Tree, David McCord
A Light in the Attic (and others), Shel Silverstein
Scranimals (and others), Jack Prelutsky

A lot of people are intimidated by poetry. Don't be. You don't have to be a college professor; in fact, you don't even have to be able to tell the difference between a sonnet and a couplet. All you have to do is find poems you like, read them with enthusiasm, and have fun.

baby-accessible bookshelf will also allow your child the opportunity to pull a few books down and "read" by himself.

If your baby has developed enough hand-eye coordination to turn the pages of a book without shredding them, it's safe to break out the lift-the-flap books. If you're really brave, try a few pop-up books too. But before you read either kind to your baby for the first time, go through it once yourself and test all the flaps and pop-ups; unopened (and hard-to-open) flaps can frustrate even the most eager little fingers.

Interactive books and those dealing with real-world themes are also big hits.

At this stage babies crave familiarity and will request the same two or three books over and over. For variety—as well as your own sanity—try to slip in a new one every few days. But watch out: your baby's literary tastes can turn on a dime, and the books you had to read him seventeen times yesterday will be pushed away today before you even get a chance to open them. And what gets pushed away today could be back on the A-list in a few days.

Whatever you're reading, keep these points in mind:

- **Make reading part of your child's daily routine**. And be sure to select a time when he's not exhausted and not bouncing off the walls.
- **Use a pleasant, conversational manner and be theatrical**. Adopt a different voice for each character.
- **Be interactive**. Your baby won't be interested in plot for a few more months, so don't be afraid to interrupt your reading to "discuss" what's happening in the story or the illustrations. If there's a picture of an apple tree, pretend to pick an apple or two and share it with your baby. Occasionally, it's also fun to replace a book character's name with your child's (when reading to my younger daughter, for example, I turned Goldilocks into Zoëlocks).
- **Read your baby's cues**. There's no law that says you have to read a book from beginning to end, or even that you have to finish it at all. If your baby's losing interest, offer another book or take a break.

ADDING TO YOUR LIBRARY

Keep reading your child's favorites until either he gets sick of them or they fall apart (but if the latter happens before the former, you might have to go out and buy another copy). Hopefully, you've been reading to your child for a few months, and you've probably put together a pretty good basic book collection (if you need some suggestions, you might want to take a look at the lists on pages 119–20 and 208–9 of *The New Father: A Dad's Guide to the First Year*).

As you introduce new books, keep in mind that toddlers like rhyme and rhythm and books about things and activities they know, such as animals, going to the store, getting ready for bed, and so on. They also love bold, bright colors and illustrations that contain lots of hidden objects. Here are some of my favorites for this age:

Airport, Bryon Barton
Are You There, Bear? Ron Maris
Crash! Bang! Boom! (and others), Peter Spier
The Cupboard, John Burningham
Dear Zoo, Rod Campbell
Duck, David Lloyd
Freight Train (and many others), Donald Crews
Goodnight, Goodnight (and others), Eve Rice
Goodnight Moon, Margaret Wise Brown
Have You Seen My Duckling? (and many others), Nancy Tafuri
In Our House, Anne Rockwell
Jesse Bear, What Will You Wear? Nancy White Carlstrom
Listen to the Rain, Bill Martin Jr. and John Archambault
Max's Ride, Rosemary Wells
Mommy Buy Me a China Doll, Harve Zemach
My Brown Bear Barney, Dorothy Butler
Piggies, Don and Audrey Wood
Tickle, Tickle (and many, many others) Helen Oxenbury
Toolbox, Anne Rockwell
Two Shoes, New Shoes (and many others), Shirley Hughes
The Very Hungry Caterpillar (and many, many others), Eric Carle

CONCEPT BOOKS

Animal Dads, Sneed B Collard III
100 First Words to Say with Your Baby, Edwina Riddel
Dogs, and many other photography books, Seymour Simon
Everybody Has Feelings, Charles Avery
In the Morning, Anne Rockwell
I Touch (and many others), Rachel Isadora
Slam Bang, John Burningham

Art

As soon as your child has gotten past the everything-I-pick-up-goes-directly-into-my-mouth stage, it's safe to introduce him to art. His first tools will be a crayon, a marker, or a pencil, and it all starts with scribbling. At first, the art he produces will look like a bunch of random marks on the page, which is exactly what it is. But in the same way that the random sounds your child used to make turned into babbling and then actual words, those scribbles will eventually become drawing and writing. And the way that's going to happen is just as predictable as his physical, intellectual, verbal, and social development. Here's how the sequence starts:

1. The first marks he makes on a piece of paper (or the wall, if you happen to turn your back for two seconds) will be dots—the result of banging.
2. As you encourage him and he tries to imitate you, he'll make some sweeping lines. The edges of the paper mean absolutely nothing to him.
3. He'll start making back-and-forth scribbles and may occasionally draw a single line if you make one first. He's paying a little more attention to the size of the paper.
4. He's discovering that making marks can be fun; he'll try to draw with anything he can get his hands on and will scribble so energetically that he'll sometimes wear through the paper. If he can't find any drawing tools, he'll use his fingers, often dipped in ketchup or mashed-up food.

Painting skills also evolve along a fairly predictable sequence, from simple, random marks to big swaths of individual colors to putting so many colors on top of each other that the result looks like mud. For more about art, see page 40.

GETTING READY; OR, FRANKLY, MY DEAR, I DON'T . . . Making art with a toddler can be incredible fun—and incredibly messy. Now that you've been warned, if you don't take the necessary precautions, it's your own fault:

- **Cover every surface—walls, floors, tabletops, chairs—with paper.** If you're still concerned, move the whole show outside onto the sidewalk or into the backyard, where you can just hose everything off.
- **Use an easel or tape the drawing paper right to the table.** It's far too frustrating for the baby to have to hold the paper steady and draw on it at the same time.
- **Observe the dress code.** Kids this age usually don't like to wear aprons, so have them either work naked (always fun) or wear old clothes that are okay to trash.
- **Use tiny amounts.** A thin film of paint or glue on the inside of a shallow container is fine. You can refill it as often as you need to, and if anything falls, there won't be much to clean up.

- **Dilute**. Most of the paint you get at craft stores is quite concentrated. Diluting it 25–50 percent with dishwashing liquid will help the paint wash out of the clothes later (and last longer, too). It also tends to deter kids from putting the paint in their mouths.

SO WHAT'S YOUR ROLE IN ALL THIS?

The first thing you have to do is to let go of the idea that you're teaching. At this point—and for the next few years—all you need to do is encourage and support. Here are some tips that will make doing art with your child fun for both of you:

- **Don't give too many choices**. Asking "Do you want red or green?" is okay. Asking "What colors do you want?" is an invitation to a power struggle (unless you're prepared to give in to your child's every demand).
- **Stay away from coloring books**. And don't encourage tracing or copying.
- **Don't ask what anything is**. Your child is drawing or painting because it's fun. The idea that he can create something that looks like something else won't occur to him until he's at least three years old.
- **Pay attention**. Your child's attention span ranges from about three seconds to fifteen minutes. If you notice any indications of boredom, such as walking away, crying, or eating the supplies, offer another art-related activity or shut things down for the day.
- **Don't interfere**. Showing your baby once or twice how to use a brush, pencil, or marker is okay. But telling him which colors to pick, showing him where or what to draw, or making any kind of correction is inappropriate. The object here is not to teach art or to create the next little Picasso. It's simply to introduce your child—in a no-pressure, no-expectations kind of way—to the creative process and to the idea that art can be fun.
- **Monitor your expectations**. Even if your child is the next Picasso, there's a good chance that he won't create anything remotely recognizable (except perhaps a line, a circle, or a spiral) for another year.
- **Stop caring**. The more concerned you are about the mess or about your child wasting or destroying the supplies (they love to shred paper, put glue in their hair, and use markers as hammers), the less fun you'll let your baby have. So do what you can to prepare. Then take a deep breath, and relax.
- **Praise your child**. Your praise is not for the artistic merit of what he's produced, but for the effort that he put into it. ("Wow, you worked really hard on this! Can I hang it up in my office?")

The Basics

- **Safety first.** Make sure everything your baby uses in his art projects is absolutely nontoxic, washable, and too big to be a choking hazard.
- **Drawing implements.** Large, nontoxic markers are the best bet. They come in a wide variety of sizes, colors, and scents. Ordinary crayons aren't practical at this age—they crumble and can get ground into carpets and floors. You can introduce crayons in a few months when your child is doing more controlled scribbling and less banging.
- **Pencils.** They need too much adult involvement (either to sharpen them or to make sure the baby doesn't stab himself with the sharp point).
- **Painting implements.** Use long-handled (eight inches minimum), wide (at least ⅜ inch) brushes. Little kids can't—and won't—do much with anything smaller.
- **Paper to draw, paint, or glue on.** Construction (thick) paper is the staple here. It's available at toy, art-supply, and stationery stores. Children's art projects also provide a great opportunity to start a recycling program at home and at work. Instead of tossing out all those old reports, flip them over and let your baby create on the other side.
- **Things to learn from.** At this age, your child is still exploring the world with all his senses. So give him art supplies that stimulate as many senses as possible, such as scented markers and textured papers.

Given your child's age, attention span, interest, and level of hand-eye coordination, the range of age-appropriate art projects is fairly limited. Here, though, are some big hits and the supplies you'll need:

- Drawing. Paper, markers.
- Collages. Objects that will help your baby use all his senses: smelly seeds (fennel, coriander, and so forth); anything that has an interesting shape or texture or that makes an interesting sound when touched; glue; and just about anything you might otherwise be tempted to throw away—egg and juice cartons, cereal boxes, bottle caps, bubble wrap, cotton balls (clean).
- Painting. Paint, paper, potatoes or sponges (for cutting out patterns and making prints), toy cars, sticks, or anything else that can be dipped in paint and makes an interesting mark on paper.

DISPLAY

Whatever your child creates, be sure to display it someplace—on the fridge, on a bulletin board, taped to the wall. You do not have to compliment the work very much; just having it up where he can see it himself is enough to make him feel proud of himself.

Family Matters

Separation Anxiety

Try to think about things from your baby's perspective for a second. For most of your life you've controlled everything that happened in the world: who and what came and went, how long they stayed, what they did while they were there. But in the past few months, your grip seems to be slipping. People and objects seem to come and go all by themselves. And everyone you thought you could always count on to be there for you has developed a nasty habit of disappearing just when you need them most. Even worse, people you don't know—and aren't sure you want to know—keep on pinching your cheeks, making silly sounds in your face, and trying to pick you up and take you away. The universe is clearly in chaos, and given the way things are going, you can't really be sure that the people you're most attached to will ever come back.

Welcome to separation anxiety. From your baby's perspective, the best way to restore order and put himself back in the driver's seat is to cry. "That's it," he says. "If I turn on the tears, my parents won't leave. I just know it."

DEALING WITH SEPARATION ANXIETY

Some babies get it, others don't. Kids who have had regular contact with lots of friendly, loving people often have an easier time adapting to brief separations than those who have spent all their time with one or two people. They'll be more comfortable with strangers and more confident that their parents and other loved ones will return eventually.

In an unusual but far-from-uncommon manifestation of separation anxiety, many kids about this age develop some sleep problems, almost as if they view going to sleep as yet another assault on their ability to control the world. It can also be confusing and frightening for a child to go to sleep in the dark and wake up in the light or to see you wearing one thing when you put him to bed and something else in the morning. Staying awake can seem like a surefire way to make certain that everything (and everyone) stays right where it's supposed to.

Here are some ways you can help your child manage his separation anxieties:

- **Be firm but reassuring**. Tell your baby where you're going and that you'll be back soon.
- **Don't say you'll miss him or that you're sad to be leaving**. He'll only feel guilty that he's making you unhappy. He'll also wonder why you would do something to deliberately make yourself unhappy. And finally, if you act dejected or upset at leaving him, your baby will use that as a model for how to react to separation.
- **Don't sneak away, and don't linger**. If you're really leaving, say good-bye like a man and walk out with your head up. Tiptoeing away while he's not looking will undermine your baby's trust in you, and taking twenty minutes to say good-bye or repeatedly coming back to make sure everything's okay will just make your departure harder for everyone.
- **Don't give in to crying**. If you're sure the baby is in good hands, leave—with a smile on your face.
- **Don't force**. Let the baby stay in your arms for a while longer if he needs to and don't make fun of him if he wants to bury his head in your shoulder.
- **Try to use sitters the baby knows**. If you have to use someone new, have him or her arrive fifteen to twenty minutes before you go out so he or she can get acquainted with the baby while you're there. And make sure the new sitter is completely up to speed on your baby's bedtime ritual.
- **Leave while the baby is awake**. Waking up in the middle of the night to a strange (or even a familiar but unexpected) sitter can be terrifying to a child.
- **Be patient**. Don't trivialize the baby's feelings about your leaving. You know you'll be back; the baby isn't so sure. So give him plenty of time to adjust to any new situation.
- **Play**. Object-permanence games (games such as peek-a-boo that reinforce the idea that objects and people still exist even though they can't be seen) help reassure your child that things—and especially people—don't disappear forever.
- **Establish routines**. Having a regular schedule (such as dropping the baby off at day care immediately after breakfast or reading two stories right before bed) can help your child understand that at least some things in his life can be counted on.
- **Develop a strong attachment**. Singing, playing, reading, and talking together all help build a strong, loving bond between you and your baby and help him feel more secure. The more secure he is, the less he'll worry about being abandoned.

- **Ask questions**. You'll have a better chance of finding out what your child is afraid of if you do. Most kids' biggest fear, for example, isn't the dark but being alone. So make sure your child has a favorite toy or other security object at night. And leave a light on so he can see he's not alone.
- **Give the baby plenty of space**. If you hover, he'll get the idea that you're afraid to leave him by himself and that there's actually something to fear from being alone.
- **Distract**. Encourage independence by suggesting that the baby play with his train set while you wash the dishes.
- **Relax**. Babies will pick up on your mood; if you're nervous they'll figure that they should be too.
- **Let the baby follow you around**. This builds a sense of security and confidence that you're there—just in case he needs you.
- **Know your baby's temperament**. (For a thorough discussion of temperament, see pages 108–15.) If your child has a low frustration tolerance, he won't want you to leave and may cry all day after being separated. Your slow-to-adapt child won't want you to leave either, but when you do, he'll usually cry only for a few minutes. He may cry again when you return, though, because your coming back is as much of a transition as your leaving was.

INDEPENDENCE VS. DEPENDENCE

From your baby's perspective, separation anxiety can be a real problem. But from a child development perspective, it's a positive (albeit frequently frustrating) sign, marking the beginning of your baby's struggle between independence and dependence.

It's a scary time for the baby, and you can see his ambivalence dozens of times every day as he alternates between clinging and pushing you away. At this stage, says British child-care expert Penelope Leach, "his own emotions are his worst enemy"—just when it seems that your baby should be needing you less, he actually needs you more. As the grown-up, it's up to you to help your baby make some sense of his conflicting emotions, as well as to nurture his independence while supporting his dependence. But beware: it's extremely easy to get trapped in a vicious circle of dependence and independence. Here's how it works:

IF YOU . . .	HE FEELS . . .	WHICH, IN TURN, MAKES HIM FEEL . . .
Interfere with his independence and his developing ego	frustration, anger, and hate	anxious and afraid
Interfere with his need to be dependent on you and his desire to cling	anxiety and fear	frustrated, angry, and hateful

Health and Safety Update

Now that your child is vertical and moving around on his own, he can get into a lot more trouble a lot more quickly than just a few months ago. That means that in addition to thoroughly childproofing every room in your home (which, hopefully, you've already done) you're going to need to take some extra precautions to make sure your home is a safe—and fun—place for your toddler to explore. (If you haven't childproofed, and/or you need a review of what needs to be done, check out pages 193–99 of *The New Father: A Dad's Guide to the First Year*.)

GENERAL SAFETY

- Take CPR and first aid classes. Check with your local Red Cross chapter or YMCA.
- Do a car-seat safety review. Since your baby is over twelve months and probably weighs over twenty pounds, it's time to start using an appropriate front-facing seat. (If your baby doesn't weigh twenty pounds, keep him facing backward until he does.) When you're ready to make the switch, have an expert help you. Many highway patrols, fire departments, police departments, and even some baby equipment stores do them for free. You can also find inspection stations approved by the National Highway Traffic Safety Administration (NHTSA) at their Web site, www.nhtsa.dot.gov. Finally, keep your car clean. The rule of thumb is, Don't bring anything into the car that you wouldn't want to get hit in the head with.
- Be cautious around pets—whether they're yours or not—and never leave your child alone with one. Animals may not be as responsive to your child's hugs, kisses, yanks, grabs, and pulls as you'd like them to be. If you have pets of your own, make sure their shots are up to date, their claws are

"Do you know where the fire extinguisher is, Dad?"

trimmed, and that you wash your child's hands thoroughly after he touches any pet. And be sure to play with them (your pets, I mean). Jealous animals don't always express their feelings in the most civil ways.

- Lower the temperature of your hot water heater to 120° F.
- Remember the twelve-inch rule. To keep babies from grabbing things from counters and tabletops, make sure you keep everything at least twelve inches from the edge.
- Never leave your child alone—or with another child less than eleven years old—in or near water, even if he seems to be sitting up nicely by himself in the bathtub. And while we're on the subject, be sure to dump the liquid out of any buckets or pans you happen to have standing around. About fifty children drown every year after falling into large buckets. Over three-fourths of these children were supposedly being supervised by at least one parent and had been missing for five minutes or less, according to the U.S. Product Safety Commission.
- Prevent accidental shootings. The only completely foolproof way to do so is never to have firearms of any kind in your home. But if you do, at least store them unloaded in a locked safe or gun cabinet. Keep the ammunition in a

Green Babies

People generally select the products they buy based on price, quality, availability, and brand. In recent years, though, consumers are paying more attention to how products impact the environment, whether it's their home environment or the one we all live in. One recent national poll found that 61 percent of American consumers, given the choice, would rather buy environmentally preferable products. And 42 percent of adults aged eighteen to thirty-four have actually tried a new product because they felt the product, its packaging, or the manufacturer benefited the environment. So what does this have to do with you and your baby? Plenty.

You could be concerned that the paint you used in the nursery could emit toxic fumes. Maybe you're worried about the bleaches in your laundry, and you'd prefer that your baby wore nothing but organic fabrics. Or perhaps you're concerned about how disposable diapers are impacting the environment. Whatever your concern, there are environmentally friendly alternatives out there to just about any product you're currently using.

You can find some of these products at places like Walgreens and Sears (which recently opened up special green sections), or at your local natural grocer. But the widest selection and the most resources are going to be online at places like Green Home (www.greenhome.com).

separate location, and put the keys someplace where the kids can't get to them. And just to be extra careful, put on trigger locks.

- Keep furniture far enough away from windows that your child won't be able to climb up on the sills. For upper-floor windows, install childproof safety bars that are easily opened by adults. Your local fire department should be able to recommend the best bars for your home. If you don't have bars, keep windows closed and locked any time your child is in the house. Screens are not a reliable way to keep children from falling out a window. And make sure window-shade cords are rolled up or permanently attached to the floor or wall. For your child's room or play area, consider getting cordless window coverings. Every year about a dozen babies get tangled up in cords and strangle. In some cases it might be easier to just replace your window coverings altogether. But if you really love the ones you have, you may be able to retrofit them to current safety standards. You can order free retrofit kits from the Window Covering Safety Council (www.windowcoverings.org or 800-506-4636).

- Check your child's toys. Nesting cups should have ventilation holes in case your baby gets one stuck in his throat or over his mouth and nose. Toy chests should have hinges that keep the lid from closing and vent holes in case your baby develops a fascination with Houdini and locks himself inside.
- Check for toy and baby equipment recalls. The Consumer Products Safety Commission's Web site (www.cpsc.gov) is probably the most comprehensive and up-to-date resource.
- Teach your baby to climb down stairs backward. Install safety gates at the top and bottom of stairways. Pressure-mounted gates are usually okay for the bottom, but not the top, while hardware-mounted gates are usually okay for both. However, check the manufacturer's recommendations to be sure. Stay away from accordion-style gates. The diamond-shaped holes can trap little heads or hands, and they're tempting footholds.
- Keep the National Poison Control Center phone number handy: (800) 222-1222.
- Pad the corners and sharp edges of anything your baby could run or fall into. Ensure that televisions, bookshelves, and other heavy objects can't be pulled over (or fall in an earthquake). And make sure that VCRs and DVD/CD players are high enough that your child won't be able to insert a slice of bread or a handful of oatmeal.
- Keep all automatic or self-closing doors either locked or secured in the open position. Kids can (and do) get stuck.
- Scuff up the soles of your baby's new shoes with sandpaper. Slippery shoes and slippery floors aren't a good combination.

ESPECIALLY IN THE KITCHEN

- Never leave your child unattended in his high chair. Always keep waist and crotch belts securely buckled.
- Don't give your child grapes, nuts, or hot dogs unless you've cut them into small pieces. Those three foods, plus hard candies, cause almost half of all childhood choking deaths.
- Consider keeping a playpen in the kitchen. It's nice to have a safe place to put the baby while you're cooking.
- If your baby is tall enough to reach stove knobs, take them off or buy covers for them. If oven doors are low enough, get a lock for them too.

- Use back burners as much as possible and keep handles pointed toward the rear of the stove.
- Never drink anything hot with a child in your lap, and keep hot foods away from the edges of the counter and sink.
- Put your placemats and tablecloths in storage, at least until your baby is old enough to master the party trick of yanking the tablecloth off the table without dumping everything on top of himself.
- Install locks on drawers and cabinets. As a distraction, keep at least one cabinet filled with pots, pans, measuring cups, and other safe objects.
- Keep your garbage can and recycling away from where the baby is. Three-day-old food, sharp metal cans, broken glass, and babies are not a good combination.
- Remove refrigerator magnets that are small enough to be choking hazards.
- Cover electrical outlets. They're incredibly tempting for little fingers.
- Never leave chairs or stools near counters or tables.
- Lock up cleaning supplies, chemicals, and alcohol, or put them on out-of-reach shelves.

ESPECIALLY IN THE GARAGE, BASEMENT, WORKSHOP, AND OUTSIDE

- Keep all dangerous chemicals, paints, thinners, gas, oil, weed killers, fertilizers, and so forth securely locked up.
- If you have an extra refrigerator or freezer, make sure it is locked (not just shut). It's easier than you think for a toddler to pull open the door, climb in after something particularly attractive, and get stuck inside. If the refrigerator/freezer isn't being used, take the doors off.
- Be particularly careful when backing out of the garage or driveway. Your baby might run after you to say one more good-bye or to get one more kiss, and . . .

ESPECIALLY AROUND SWIMMING POOLS

- Never let your child into the pool area without at least one adult present.
- Put a fence around the pool, although not an electrified one. (Don't laugh; I actually heard of a couple who installed an electrified fence around their pool to keep the dog out, but succeeded in electrocuting one of their children.) The fence should be at least five feet high, have no footholds, and be equipped with self-closing, self-latching gates.
- Keep furniture, plants, toys, or anything else that can be used to climb on away from the fence, and keep chemicals and cleaning tools locked up.

- Get a pool cover that is strong enough for an adult to walk on.
- Make sure you have the proper poolside safety equipment (life preserver, poles, and so on).
- Keep a phone nearby for emergency purposes.
- Be very, very careful when using air-filled flotation devices such as water wings or blow-up rings. They're sometimes advertised as being "swimming aids," but they're really toys. Most important, they are not a substitute for your supervision.
- Use plenty of waterproof sunscreen.
- If you have a wading pool, be sure to empty out the water every time you're finished using it.
- If you have a spa or Jacuzzi, water temperature shouldn't ever be above 104 degrees Fahrenheit.

15–18 MONTHS

Keeping Communication Open

What's Going On with the Baby

Physically

- As if making up for the lull in motor development of the past few months, your toddler will be a blur of activity, rushing from room to room investigating everything, often carrying something in each hand.
- Right now, her walking will still be somewhat clumsy: getting herself into motion is difficult, her legs are far apart and move stiffly, and she'll hold her arms away from her body for balance. Most of the time she'll stop by falling. But by the time she's eighteen months old, starting and stopping will be no problem (although she'll still have a tough time negotiating corners upright).
- Her balance is also improving. If she holds on to something, she can actually stand on one foot. If she's been walking for a while, she may be able to do this without holding on.
- She'll climb anything and everything and has figured out the concept of using a chair to get onto the kitchen counter. She may also have figured out how to climb out of her crib, so if you can't lower her mattress any further, at least put something soft on the floor for her to land on.
- She can crawl up stairs on her hands and knees and might walk up if you hold one of her hands. Fortunately, she's also getting used to the idea of climbing down backwards and may actually do so without having to be reminded.
- She adores ride-on toys and loves to show off her strength, often grunting theatrically as she struggles to pick up, push, or drag around the biggest things she can get her hands on.

- She may be able to throw a small ball, but can't catch. And although she'd like to kick a ball, more often than not she ends up stepping on it instead.
- She's developing a clear preference for one hand over the other, uses cups and spoons, can turn the pages of ordinary books without doing too much damage, and can possibly turn on faucets and turn doorknobs.

Note: If your child isn't walking unassisted by the end of her eighteenth month, check with your pediatrician. See "Developmental Red Flags" (page 53) for more.

Intellectually

- A lot of your child's cognitive development in this period will come from lessons she learns while playing. Climbing under, over, around, and through, she'll learn how objects look from different perspectives. Dropping food, bottles, and utensils off her high chair will teach her the sounds that different things make when they hit the floor.
- She'll continue to use trial and error to solve problems and will expand her use of tools to retrieve out-of-reach items. (If a toy is on a blanket, for example, she may pull the blanket toward her instead of walking over to get the toy.)
- She still struggles with the conflict between autonomy and dependence—refusing your requests to do even the most basic things, but wanting to keep you well within sight as she explores new places.
- Her memory is getting better, and she may remember where she left a toy a day or two before. She's also beginning to associate objects with their owners and may announce "Daddy!" when picking up one of your shoes.
- She may give you some hints that she needs a diaper change, but is nowhere near ready to work on potty training.
- She has a very short attention span and flits from activity to activity. Expecting a lot of rational thought from a child this age is a waste of time, as is giving her long explanations of whys and why-nots.
- Toddlers love routines and rituals. Establishing patterns now, such as bath-story-bedtime and park-lunch-nap, will help minimize some of the problems you're likely to encounter later on.
- She's developing an imagination. She'll crawl on the floor, pretending to be a dog, and she'll "eat" food pictured in a book. The downside to this is that if your child continues imagining things after she falls asleep (and most do), she may begin to have nightmares. Since kids can't really tell the difference between dreams and reality, nightmares at this age can be particularly frightening.

Verbally

- Your toddler continues to discover the power of language. She tries as often as possible to combine words, and she knows that phrases like "up me," "gimme ba-ba," and "book read" will get her picked up, fed, or read to.
- She probably understands about a hundred words now, although her active vocabulary is a lot smaller. Her mimicking skills, however, are moving into high gear, and she'll try to repeat any word you throw at her.
- She likes books, but is much happier to point out familiar pictures than to have you read a whole story.
- She loves singing and will join in on familiar songs wherever and whenever she can. Although far from fluent, your baby is beginning to understand the humorous uses of language. My middle daughter had the "moo-moo," "woof-woof," "quack-quack" parts of "Old MacDonald's Farm" down at fifteen months, but insisted that the chorus was "E-I-E-I-EEEEEEEEE."
- She may also sing, hum, chatter to herself, and bounce to music when she's alone.

Emotionally/Socially

- The first half of the second year may be marked by great frustration, a feeling that frequently results in tantrums. Unable to express their wants in words, kids this age often become enraged. They also "get angry both when their parents withhold help and when they proffer needed assistance," writes child development expert Frank Caplan. Overall, "they get angry because they are not big or strong enough for the tasks they set for themselves." Some tantrums, especially the ones that involve breath-holding, can be quite spectacular. (See pages 106–107 for more on this.)
- She's expressing other emotions besides frustration, with joy, love, and pleasure topping the list. Just watch as she hugs and kisses a favorite toy or how her whole body shakes with excitement when she sees you at the end of the day. At the same time, she's also learning about anger. If she can't get a toy to move, a page to turn, or a piece of food to stay on her spoon, she may just slam the whole thing down and scream.
- Most of the time, however, she's a pretty happy soul and is easily entertained. Her sense of humor is developing nicely, and she's truly amused by her own movement—sliding, dropping things, and falling down on purpose.
- She can also understand verbal humor, particularly when it deals with incongruities. For example, after emphatically refusing your lunchtime offer of a banana, a bowl of cereal, or a cheese sandwich, she may laugh hysterically if you suggest a spoonful of dirt.

- She still plays alongside, not with, other toddlers, although she may occasionally share a toy with a playmate. In fact, the only people she really wants to socialize with are you and her mother, and she'll try to get one or both of you involved in everything she does.

Developmental Red Flags

As we've discussed elsewhere, the developmental milestones you're reading about in this book are guidelines only, and the range of "normal" or "average" is relatively broad. That's why I suggested in the introduction to this book that you add the word *roughly* to each chapter title—this one would be "Roughly 15–18 months." Having said all of that, if one or more of the following statements are true about your child, call your pediatrician as soon as possible:

My child . . .

- Doesn't transfer objects from hand to hand.
- Doesn't sit on her own.
- Doesn't seem to know the difference between strangers and people she sees all the time.
- Can't follow simple directions, such as "Give me the book" or "Touch your nose."
- Speaks fewer than fifteen words. (If she can say more than fifteen, but you and your partner are the only ones who understand them, that's okay, just as long as you know what she means and she uses the words consistently.)
- Doesn't try to imitate words I say.
- Seems emotionally flat: no anger, no joy, no frustration, no delight, no fear.
- Shows little or no interest in toys or play.
- Can't push a toy with wheels.
- Doesn't stand by herself.
- Hasn't started walking.
- Doesn't make eye contact.
- Doesn't respond when I whisper.
- Doesn't turn toward me when I call her name.
- Doesn't look in the direction of something I'm pointing at.

What You're Going Through

Thinking about Sex

About 90 percent of couples have resumed having sex by the time their baby is four months old. But even a year and a half into parenthood, there's a big difference between "resuming sex" and "resuming a normal sex life," whatever that means to you. There are all sorts of reasons, with fatigue and lack of time in the top two slots. It's also important to understand that sex may mean very different things to you and your partner:

YOU MAY . . .	SHE MAY . . .
♦ See sex as a way of setting the stage for verbal intimacy.	♦ See verbal intimacy as a way of setting the stage for sex.
♦ Want sex as a way of feeling closer to her.	♦ Want sex when she's already feeling close to you.
♦ Need sex to establish an emotional connection with your partner.	♦ Need an emotional connection with you before being interested in sex.

OTHER POTENTIAL CONFLICTS

YOU MAY . . .

- Resent your partner's lack of seductive behavior, her failure to take the initiative, in addition to wishing for better sex, more often.
- Feel excluded from your baby by your partner and want to have sex as a way of reconnecting with her.
- Be embarrassed to admit that you feel too exhausted, unsure, or overwhelmed by family responsibilities to even think about sex.
- Feel guilty about what pregnancy did to her body.
- Feel guilty about the pain she was in during pregnancy, labor, and the delivery, and be afraid of having her to go through the same thing again (this is a common fear, even if you're using birth control).
- Feel that your partner prefers the baby to you if she rejects your advances.
- Find it difficult to contemplate sex—especially oral sex—after remembering all the blood from the birth. You may be feeling that she's somehow been disfigured and get turned off as a result.

SHE MAY . . .

- Complain that you don't talk to her, you aren't affectionate enough, you take her for granted, you don't understand her or her feelings. For women, sexual desire is often increased (or sparked) by feeling loved and wanted—using her definitions.
- Be withholding sex as a way of getting back at you for not doing more around the house and with the baby, or for spending too much time at work.
- Be "affectioned out" from taking care of the baby all day.
- Be too sleep-deprived to show much sexual interest in you.
- Have less interest in sex, find intercourse painful, or have difficulty reaching orgasm. Twenty percent of women suffer from one or more of these problems longer than a year after the baby, according to researcher Dwenda K. Gjerdingen.
- Not be feeling enough of a connection with you. After focusing predominantly on the baby, she may have lost track of what she and you have in common.
- Think that you find her less attractive than you used to. She also may find herself less attractive.
- Be more comfortable interacting with a child because the child expects less of her.

BOTH OF YOU MAY . . .

- Find it hard to admit to the other your basic need for support, comfort, and love. The result can often be mutual blaming and resentment, which you carry around until it boils over into a fight.
- Be reluctant to allow yourselves to get aroused. You might be afraid of being interrupted by the baby, or you might feel guilty about satisfying your own needs when you should really be doing something to take care of the baby.
- Have stopped touching each other because you're afraid that a stroke or a touch might be misinterpreted as a sexual overture. A new mother "may think her mate is obsessed with sexual desires," says psychologist Aaron Hass, "when what he really needs is reassurance that she still loves him and he has not been replaced by the baby."

SOME POSSIBLE SOLUTIONS

Getting your sex life back to normal is going to take communication, planning, and lots of patience.

- Make sure there are opportunities for verbal as well as sexual intimacy. And

The Ultimate Aphrodisiac?

Over the years I've done hundreds of interviews and led dozens of workshops with moms and dads. And by far the most frequent complaint I hear from wives is that their husbands aren't involved enough with the children. Actually, it goes a little beyond that. From her point of view, if you don't love the kids, you don't love her. From there, it's only a hop, skip, and a jump to all-out resentment.

The solution? Be an active, involved father.

"There is no more powerful aphrodisiac to a mother than to see her husband lovingly engaged with their children," writes Hass. "When your wife sees your involvement with her children, she will want to see you happy. She will, therefore, want to satisfy your sexual desires. She will be more likely to suggest that just the two of you get away for a night or a weekend so that you can have more intimate time together. She will be more open to sexual experimentation. . . . She will be more sexually creative. She will take pains to make sure the children are tucked away early in the evening so that you can have uninterrupted time together. And, of course, when your wife is happier, her own libido is more likely to assert itself."

Whew! If that doesn't make you want to quit your job and take care of your children full-time, nothing will.

while you're at it, get rid of the idea that there's always a connection between the two.

- Stop thinking about it (for a while). Spend some time getting used to being affectionate with each other in a nonsexual way.
  - hold hands
  - stroke her hair
  - kiss her when walking through the kitchen
  - give each other massages, back rubs, and so forth
  - make out
- Schedule sex—it doesn't have to be spontaneous like it was (see page 57 for more on this).
- Go on dates (see "Dating Your Partner," below).
- Go for quality over quantity. You may only be able to make love a few times a month, but make them count.

- Try to keep it regular. Your sex organs are muscles, and they need some regular working out to operate at peak capacity.
- Flirt. Remember when you and your partner were just falling in love? Recapturing some of those feelings isn't as hard as you think. When you see her getting out of the shower, tell her how good she looks; let her catch you looking down her shirt or staring at her butt; put some love notes in her wallet so she'll find them when she's at work. By the time the two of you get home, you'll be all over each other.
- Get out of the house—or at least the bedroom. Your house and your bedroom are filled with too many distractions. So have sex in the back seat of your car, or in the shower, or on top of the washing machine. You get the point.

Dating Your Partner

New parents have more than their fair share of marital problems (see pages 187–91 for more on this). One of the biggest culprits is not spending enough time together. It's awfully easy for you and your partner to get so focused on your baby and doing everything for her that you forget to focus on each other as individuals, and on the relationship. The result is that you can lose track of the interests, passions, hobbies, philosophies, and other things that made you who you are and brought the two of you together in the first place.

Perhaps the best solution to this problem is to schedule some dates. Yep, just like the good old days, before you had kids. The basic idea is the same: the two of you go out and spend a few hours together staring into each other's eyes and getting to know each other. A few of the ground rules have changed, though:

- Don't try to make up for lost time. Packing too many things into a single evening can put a lot of pressure on both of you.
- Make it clear that there are no strings attached. Either of you may be suspicious that the "date" will be used as a way of getting the other in the sack.
- If lack of sex has been an issue for you, however, you may want to schedule a date to do nothing but that.
- Don't talk about the baby. Let's be realistic: the baby is the one you and your partner are trying to get away from, the one who has consumed so much of your time that the two of you have neglected each other.

- Take turns pleasuring each other. She may not want to "go all the way," but she might be interested in trading a back rub for a somewhat more intimate kind of rub. And of course the same holds true if she's in the mood at a time you aren't.
- Just do it. Despite the exhaustion and everything else, sometimes just starting to go through the motions—touching, stroking, kissing—can be enough to get you aroused.

You and Your Baby

Dealing with Your Baby's Fears

Even though your baby's world is growing at an incredible clip, it's still a fairly small, well-managed, and—above all—safe little place. But the more she separates from you and the more independent she becomes, the scarier the world gets.

Babies may seem fairly unpredictable to us, but they are essentially creatures of habit who crave familiarity and routine. And just about everything your child will fear in her first three years of life will be the result of a break in her routines or an unfamiliar, unanticipated, or surprising event. Even seemingly minor changes to familiar objects or people can panic a child. For example, if your baby has only seen you with a beard and one day you come in clean-shaven, she might get very upset and not believe it's you. Or if you rearrange the furniture in your living room, she might have some doubts that she's really in her own home.

Separation anxiety and the fear of strangers (pages 41–43) were undoubtedly your baby's first fears. At about fifteen months, fear of the bath and fear of getting their hair washed top most kids' lists (see the chart on pages 60–63 for a list of some of the most common early-toddlerhood fears, a little about what they might mean, and a few suggestions for handling them). By the time they're twenty-one months old, most have graduated to being afraid of dogs, the dark (and associated monsters), and loud noises (sirens, vacuums, cars backfiring, and so forth)—in that order.

Many of your child's fears, writes child psychologist Selma Fraiberg, are "essentially a fear of his own impulses which are transferred to objects or phenomena outside himself. . . . Normally the fear will subside when the child has learned to control successfully the particular impulse which is disturbing him."

FIGHTING FEARS

Here are some general guidelines for helping your child deal with her fears.

TRY TO DISCOVER THE CAUSE

Starting when she was about eighteen months old, my middle daughter, who used love taking long walks with me, suddenly started crying hysterically every time I put her down on the sidewalk. After a few days, I figured out that she was afraid that the cars would hop the curb and run us down—a perfectly reasonable fear. I explained to her that cars live in the street and that they aren't allowed where people walk. That seemed to take the edge off the fear. But a few days later, when we were out for a walk, a car pulled into a driveway right in front of us, and my daughter went ballistic again. In her view, I'd been lying to her, and cars really *were* after her.

It's also important to remember that small children don't always make a distinction between animate and inanimate objects. In their minds, toilets and cars and stuffed animals and trees are as alive as they are—they just don't happen to be moving right now. Who knows, maybe they're asleep. If they are, they could wake up any second. And if they do, they might attack without warning.

Once you've figured out what's troubling your child, keep the following in mind:

- Acknowledge that your child's fears are real, by saying something like, "You're right: barking dogs can be scary." Let her know that everyone has fears and that being afraid is perfectly normal. You might want to tell your child about some of the fears you had when you were a kid.
- Read. There are plenty of excellent books about how kids triumph over all sorts of potentially scary situations.
- Don't tell her she really isn't—or shouldn't be—afraid of some thing, place, or person, or that "big kids aren't afraid of things like that." Instead, comfort her; tell her you'll always be there to help her.
- Never force your child to confront her fears (gently demonstrating that vacuums and baths really won't hurt the baby is okay, but don't push). And never laugh at or tease a fearful child; this will only make things worse.
- Be patient. Most childhood fears get outgrown within a few months.

THE FEAR	WHAT IT MIGHT MEAN	WHAT TO DO ABOUT IT
Bath/hair washing	♦ Fear of getting washed down the drain and thrown away (if soapsuds go down the drain, the hair can go too, and if the hair goes, why not the whole body?). ♦ Fear of the noise of the water. ♦ Fear of the hot water. ♦ Fear of getting things in the eyes and losing vision—if you can't see the world, you can't control it.	♦ Get a special toy that your baby can play with only in the bathtub. ♦ Have her give one of her washable stuffed animals a bath. ♦ Take baths with your baby. ♦ Show her that big things (like you and she) can't go down the drain. ♦ Have her get in one toe at a time, then a leg, then the bottom. ♦ Wash her with a washcloth instead of sticking her head under water.
Vacuum cleaner	♦ Fear of being disposed of just like the dust (similar to fear of baths, above). ♦ Fear of loud noises, of being yelled at.	♦ Have the baby explore the vacuum, and perhaps even push it around a little while it's off. ♦ Have one of the baby's toys go for a "ride" on the vacuum. ♦ Hold the baby while vacuuming but don't force her to be held. ♦ Let the baby turn it on and off, thus giving her control over the noise.
Haircuts	♦ Fear of being disposed of (same "logic" as getting rid of soapsuds).	♦ Have the baby check out the barber first, and watch a few strangers get haircuts. ♦ Take the baby (with another adult) to watch you get a haircut.

THE FEAR	WHAT IT MIGHT MEAN	WHAT TO DO ABOUT IT
Haircuts *(continued)*		• Find a child-friendly barber who has lots of experience with kids. • Learn to cut hair yourself. • Let your child cut the hair of her dolls, bears, and so on to practice. • Have her sit in your lap during the haircut. • Skip the hair washing—too many fears combined.
Monsters	• Fear of the unknown. • Fear of being separated from you. • Fear that there is something so powerful and unpredictable that even *you* (the all-powerful parent) can't control it.	• Read *There's a Nightmare in My Closet*, by Mercer Mayer. • Don't lie. Telling your baby that monsters don't exist or that they aren't hiding under her bed won't work. "Your child will simply reply that the monsters are hiding and will come out later," writes psychologist Lawrence Kutner. "He's right, of course, since his fears reside in his head, not in his room." • Write a "No Monsters Allowed" sign (or one warning of a monster-eating kid inside the room). • Have a large, sturdy toy "stand guard" over the baby's room.

(continued on page 62)

THE FEAR	WHAT IT MIGHT MEAN	WHAT TO DO ABOUT IT
Monsters *(continued)*		♦ Give the baby a magic wand or a special magic button to push that makes monsters disappear instantly. ♦ Cut down on pre-bedtime scary things (including stories, growling, and making faces). ♦ Leave on a night-light.
Sleep or the dark	♦ Fear of losing control. ♦ Fear that loved ones and loved things won't be there later.	♦ Establish a comfortable bedtime routine. ♦ Emphasize the big-kid bed. ♦ Tell her that everyone else she knows is sleeping (name them one at a time). ♦ Tell her that you—and everyone else—will be there in the morning. ♦ Leave a light on.
Scary stories	♦ Similar to monsters, night, dark.	♦ No scary stories before bed or, if the problem is severe, no scary stories at all, even during the day. ♦ Cuddle while reading. ♦ Edit or cut out the scary parts. ♦ Make sure she knows the story isn't real, although she won't fully grasp this concept for another few years. ♦ Use a night-light.
Animals	♦ Fear of the unfamiliar (not human). ♦ Fear of being eaten. ♦ Fear of being bitten. ♦ Fear of not being able to control her own impulses or live up to her parents' expectations.	♦ Read lots of books about friendly animals (the *Carl* books, by Alexandra Day, are great for this). ♦ Ease into it. Have your baby start by petting a toy dog, then have her approach a friendly real one.

THE FEAR	WHAT IT MIGHT MEAN	WHAT TO DO ABOUT IT
Animals *(continued)*		♦ Teach your baby the proper way to behave with pets: no fingers in animals' noses, and so on. Take her hand and show her the right way to pet an animal. ♦ Teach your baby to recognize inviting and hostile animal gestures. ♦ Ask pet owners if their animal is friendly before letting your baby anywhere near it. ♦ Hold your baby's hand near unfamiliar pets. ♦ Never force the baby to touch animals if she doesn't want to.
Doctors/ dentists	♦ Fear of strangers. ♦ Fear of new situations, smells, sights. ♦ Fear of pain. ♦ Fear that there's really something wrong (you wouldn't go to the doctor if there weren't, right?).	♦ Talk about the doctor, about how pediatricians love kids and want to make them feel good. ♦ Play through it (see pages 64–65)—have the baby do to her dolls or stuffed animals what the doctor will do to her. ♦ Do *not* lie—don't say there won't be shots or that the shots won't hurt. ♦ Schedule appointment for noncranky times. ♦ Switch to a same-sex doctor (don't worry about offending yours; he or she is very familiar with these requests). ♦ Read some books about going to the doctor.

CONTROL YOUR OWN REACTIONS

Thrust into a situation she's never been in before—especially a scary one—your baby probably won't know how to react. So she'll look to you for some visual or verbal cues as to how you think she should respond. In one classic study, researcher James Sorce and his associates conducted a series of experiments to see whether parents' facial expressions—happy, fearful, interested, or angry—have any influence on their children's behavior in potentially dangerous situations. Sorce placed the babies and one of their parents on opposite sides of a "visual cliff"—a long a piece of sturdy but transparent Plexiglas that traversed a dangerous-looking (to the babies, anyway) surface. He then tried to get the babies to crawl across the "cliff " to retrieve a tempting toy from the parent. The results were illuminating: of the seventeen children who saw a fearful expression, none crossed the cliff. And only two of the eighteen confronted with an angry expression did. Of the nineteen who saw happy faces, however, fourteen crossed, and so did eleven of the fifteen whose parent's expression was one of "sincere interest."

As fascinating as Sorce's studies were, they didn't really go far enough. Who's going to try to get a baby to do—or not do—something just by making faces at her? That might work in a lab experiment, but not in your kitchen. Researchers Amrisha Vaish and Tricia Striano took Sorce's experiments to the next level by adding vocal cues. They found that babies who heard encouraging words would cross the visual cliff faster than those who saw encouraging faces. It didn't even matter whether the parents were looking at the babies at all when they spoke!

Facial expressions and words aren't the only ways you'll influence your baby. When she's learning to walk, for example, she'll probably fall down twenty times a minute and get right back up without the slightest complaint. But if you gasp and lunge across the room to "save" her, she'll probably start crying, thinking that since you're scared, she should be too. In just a few years she'll be able to overreact on her own, without your help: when you were a kid, you could probably take a pretty good tumble, get right up, and forget all about it. But if you saw blood, you'd start crying.

PLAY IT OUT

One of the things infants and toddlers are most afraid of is being out of control. Letting them play through scary situations—either ones that just happened or ones they're anticipating—can help them regain that important feeling of being in charge. If your child is afraid of doctors, get her a toy doctor's kit, complete with stethoscope and syringe, so she can examine—and give shots

Watch What You Say

The words you use can have a huge influence on how your baby deals with scary situations. Here's how you can help:

- Bring up and discuss potentially scary situations in advance. Say things like, "We're going to the aquarium, and we're going to see the alligator. But I'm going to hold you the whole time, and if you don't like the alligator, we can go see the dolphins instead."
- Well-intentioned warnings such as, "Oh, there's nothing to be afraid of," usually backfire. In your baby's mind, if there really wasn't anything to be afraid of, you wouldn't have brought it up at all.
- Also, don't say things like, "Be careful, this might be a little scary." Your baby will actually think you want her to be scared.
- Don't go overboard on safety issues. Warnings like the ones you heard from your parents ("Don't talk to strangers," "Don't take candy from strangers," "Don't get into a car with strangers") can give a child a nearly irrational fear of, well, strangers.
- Think about potential mixed messages: now that you've got your baby scared away from the hot stove, do you think she's going to be happy about eating some hot breakfast cereal or, even worse, getting into a bathtub filled with hot water?
- Dump the crystal ball. Remember all those warnings we got when we were kids? "If you don't stop playing with that knife, you'll put your eye out." Or "Be careful going across that street, you're going to get run over by a truck." Well, in most cases, you didn't put your eye out or get run over by a truck. Giving your child a bunch of warnings that never come true only teaches her that she can't trust what you say. And that will make her less likely to pay attention to the rest of your warnings—even the ones she really should listen to.

to—all her stuffed animals. If she's afraid of real animals, try a small but ferocious-looking stuffed one she can tame.

EXPECT THE IRRATIONAL . . . AND TRY NOT TO LAUGH

A friend of mine told me about taking her two-year-old daughter, Arielle, to the barber for her first haircut. They'd talked things over, read some books about haircuts, given the stuffed animals trims, and everything was going fine—until the barber made the first cut. All of a sudden Arielle winced and let out an incredibly loud "Ouch"—a wail she repeated with every snip of the scissors. There wasn't anything wrong, but little Arielle, who knew that cutting her finger hurt, figured that cutting her hair would hurt too.

SECURITY OBJECTS

About half of all kids need, want, use, or demand some kind of security or transitional objects: blankets, pacifiers, toys, and so on. If your child has a security object, don't discourage her—she'll give it up only when she's ready to. Trying to break a security-object habit can make your baby feel even more needy than before, creating a pattern that may result in her using, in later years, such "adult" security devices as alcohol and drugs. So if you think your child is developing a real fondness for a particular object, go out and buy one

Coping with Nightmares and Night Terrors

As if being scared of things during the day isn't enough, many toddlers have bad dreams at night. Your toddler can't tell the difference between reality and fantasy, so a scary experience during the day or an image from a bedtime story or video can get lodged in her brain and resurface hours later, as a nightmare.

You can reduce the chances that nightmares will happen by not telling scary stories or showing scary videos right before bedtime. Having a calm, secure bedtime ritual can help too. But no amount of preparation will eliminate nightmares altogether. Here's what to do when your child has one:

- Make sure you can always hear her if she cries out in the night. Get a monitor if you need to. If a babysitter stays with your child, make sure he or she knows how to comfort her.
- Get to your child as quickly as you can and wake her gently.
- Reassure her in a calm, soothing voice that it's safe to go back to sleep.
- Take it easy. Really. Your child has an uncanny ability to read your emotions, and sensing your tension will upset her even more.
- Stay with her until she's settled down or let her know you're nearby. Reading a story is a great way to ease her back to sleep.
- Discuss the nightmare, but only if your child is open to it. If she remembers her dream in the morning, encourage her to talk about the frightening parts and to make up a happy ending to it.

or two more identical ones to keep in the closet. The first one might get lost, shredded, or so filthy that it can't be salvaged.

TALKING WITH YOUR BABY

The amount of time you spend speaking with your child is one of the biggest predictors of how well she'll do in life—intellectually, linguistically, and socially. To start with, the more live language (meaning it comes from a real live human, as opposed to the television or a video) children hear, the bigger their vocabularies. Dr. Janellen Huttenlocher, a researcher at the University of Chicago, found that at twenty months, children whose parents spoke with them a lot knew 131 more words than children whose parents didn't speak to them very much. By the time those same kids were two years old, that gap was almost 300 words. Huttenlocher tracked those same children for several more years and found that the ones who heard the most words when they were one

NIGHTMARES AND NIGHT TERRORS: WHAT NOT TO DO

- Don't let her sleep with you, especially after a nightmare. You may end up giving her the impression that she should be afraid of her own bed. This may also become a habit that is difficult to break.
- Don't tell her that nightmares aren't real. They seem real to her, and blowing them off as trivial will only upset her more.

Nightmares and night terrors (sometimes called "sleep terrors") are very different things and should be dealt with differently. Nightmares happen during the dream phase of sleep known as REM (rapid eye movement), and they usually end up waking the child. Night terrors, on the other hand, happen during a much deeper sleep phase. They can last anywhere from a few minutes to an hour. Technically, your child is asleep the entire time, even though her eyes will be wide open. When it's over, though, she won't remember anything. But while it's going on, it'll scare the hell out of you.

It's going to be tough, but if your child is having a night terror, don't wake her up. You can try to comfort her by stroking her head or putting an arm around her shoulders, but that may make her more upset. So just stay nearby to make sure she doesn't hurt herself, until she slips back into a more peaceful sleep.

and two scored higher on IQ and language tests. And when they were in the third grade, the children whose parents talked with them a lot still had greater language skills than the ones with less chatty parents.

Unfortunately, far too many parents talk *at* their children instead of talking *with* them. If you've got any old videos around from when you were a baby, you can see exactly what I mean. Chances are there's at least one scene that sounds like this:

> *Dad or Mom*: Can you say elephant, Jimmy? Elephant? Come on, Jimmy, you know how to say elephant, don't you? E-le-phant. You said it this morning, remember? You know what an elephant is, don't you? And where does an elephant live? In the zoo, right? Can you say zoo? ZOOOO. What else lives in the zoo? Bears, right? And monkeys. What do bears say? Do they say "grrr grrr"? Sure they do, Jimmy. And what does an elephant say? Can you say elephant, Jimmy? Jimmy? Elephant?

Even if you don't have any old family videos around, you can see the same scene live anyplace parents are likely to try to show off how smart their kids are. But no matter where they happen to occur, they all have one thing in common: Little Jimmy doesn't say a word. Thanks to Dad or Mom's constant chattering, he couldn't even if he wanted to.

And that's a problem. When you don't let your child respond to what you're saying, you're not giving her the opportunity she needs to hear the rhythm, the give-and-take nature, of speech. Here's what you can do to help your child develop her vocabulary and her conversational abilities.

- **Get down on your hands and knees**. Having a clearer view of your mouth will help your baby see how sounds are produced.
- **Explain**. Label everything you can, talk about what you're doing ("I'm taking your dirty diaper off. Now I'm wiping your butt. Now I'm putting a clean diaper on you"). And tell her where you're going and what you're going to do too. If you're going to open a door, turn on the light, or ring a doorbell, tell her. Besides building vocabulary, you're also giving her lessons in cause and effect, and in sequences.
- **Expand**. If your child says, "Truck drive," you say, "Yes, the truck is driving by." Or if she says, "Juice gone," say "That's right, the juice is gone, because you spilled it on the floor."
- **Prompt**. When your child points to something she clearly doesn't know the word for, tell her what it is. If she tries to pronounce something but makes a "mistake" ("baba" for bottle), say something like, "Good job! That is a bottle."

Raising a Bilingual Toddler

If you and your partner are fluent in different languages and you want your child to grow up knowing both, it's not too late. The most important thing is to compartmentalize the two languages. What I mean is that you should speak to your child in the language you know best, and establish some clear boundaries—English only with Daddy, Russian with Mommy, French with the babysitter—and stick with them. This will help your child keep the languages separate. Since you're living in an English-speaking country, it will help to have other people around who speak the non-English language. You might also want to get foreign-language children's books, tapes, DVDs, etc., so your baby can start learning the culture as well. Learning two languages at the same time will probably slow down the pace of your child's spoken-language development. But by the time she starts school, she'll have caught up and will be completely bilingual.

- **Don't make corrections**. Instead of correcting grammar or pronunciation mistakes, repeat the word or idea in a new, grammatically correct sentence.
- **Sing**. Nursery rhymes are great (see page 102 for some suggestions). But feel free to change the lyrics. For example, I'd sometimes replace the words to "London Bridge" with, "Zoe's climbing up the stairs, up the stairs, up the stairs. Zoe's climbing up the stairs, in her PJs."
- **Don't talk so much**. As odd as it might sound, the best way to improve your child's ability to communicate is to talk less and listen more. (My grandmother always said we have two ears and only one mouth to help us do exactly that.) After you say a sentence or two, stop talking for a few seconds and let your baby get in a few words. If she doesn't respond, say something else and give her another chance to get in on the conversation.
- **React**. Whenever your baby makes a sound, whether it's a word or a delighted squeal, say something. Babies who don't get responses to their conversation starters stop trying after a while.
- **Stay away from yes or no questions**. Your baby is just discovering the word no, and she'll be looking for any opportunity to use it. So instead of "Do you want to go for a walk?" try something like "Do you want to go to the park or the swimming pool?"
- **Watch for some interesting word associations**. A friend once told me that whenever she recited "Wee Willie Winkie" to her son, she'd make a knocking gesture in the air during the "rapping at the windows" part. One

day she was talking to the baby about wrapping birthday presents, and she was surprised when the baby smiled and made the very same knocking gesture. (Get it? *rap/wrap*.)

- **No baby talk**. Babies imitate what they hear. And even though sentences like "does widdole baaaabee want wa wa in her ba ba?" sound cutesy-wootsie, they don't challenge your child, and they may actually slow down her language development. New research by Janellen Huttenlocher shows that speaking in complex sentences (sentences with multiple nouns, verbs, or clauses) sets a much better example and may improve children's language skills. So speak clearly and normally.

Signing with Your Toddler

A few decades ago, researchers began to notice that children whose parents were hearing-impaired and who taught their children to sign were able to communicate before they were nine months old. Children with two hearing parents don't usually have much to say until after their first birthday. If you think about it, using the hands to communicate makes a lot of sense. After all, babies have a lot more control over their fingers and hands than they do over their tongue and mouth. And they start waving good-bye and pointing at things they want long before they can say "bye-bye" and "gimme."

If you haven't started teaching your child sign language, there's no reason not to start right now—especially if your child is getting frustrated that you can't understand what she wants. (Of course, if you've already started, there's no reason to stop.) Be aware, though, that once your baby realizes she can use words to communicate, she may refuse to sign.

There are two major baby signing systems out there. They're similar, but there are some important distinctions (there's more information on both in the Resources Guide, page 264):

- Joseph Garcia's *Sign with Your Baby* is based solidly on American Sign Language (ASL). His philosophy is that if you're going to the trouble to teach your baby a language, you might as well go with a real one. A baby who knows some ASL will be able to communicate with babies (and deaf people of any age) anywhere.
- Linda Acredolo's and Susan Goodwyn's *Baby Signs* is also based on ASL, but it's more flexible. Their theory is that since your baby isn't going to be using sign language all that long, it's best to make it as easy to learn as possible. So parents are encouraged to modify the ASL signs as they see fit and to invent their own.

Sign with Your Baby and *Baby Signs* are both designed to be started with babies as young as six months old but will work just fine for toddlers. *My Baby Can Talk!* (www.mybabycantalk.com) has a line of signing-related products and activities that are specifically intended for older kids.

Nutrition Update

BALANCED MEALS? GOOD LUCK!

Getting your baby to eat a balanced diet is one of the most frustrating tasks you'll have during her second year of life. For a week, it may seem that no matter what kind of delicacies you prepare, she won't eat anything but plain rice and soy sauce. Then, all of a sudden, she'll refuse to eat rice and won't be satisfied with anything but macaroni and cheese. Believe me, this happens all the time.

Part of the problem, of course, is that you and your baby haven't agreed on what, exactly, a balanced meal is—and you won't for quite a few years. Fortunately, you don't have to. In a classic study, Dr. Clara Davis allowed a group of year-old babies to choose freely from a sampling of foods (which carefully omitted high-sugar foods, candy, cookies, and soft drinks). She found that on a day-to-day basis the babies' diets were indeed out of balance. But over the course of a few months—a far more critical time frame—their diets were actually quite well balanced.

Still, having a kid eat nothing but bananas for two weeks at a stretch (as my middle daughter did) can be a little disconcerting. The only time this kind of eating truly is a problem is if the baby has absolutely no fruits or vegetables for more than a week—a situation that's probably more your fault than the baby's. If this happens, call your pediatrician; he or she may be able to suggest some alternate sources of those crucial nutrients.

Overall, you probably won't be able to do much to change your baby's eating habits. But if you're really worried, here are some suggestions that might help:

- Give the baby the same foods you eat. Unless your pediatrician says otherwise, you don't need baby food anymore. Just cut up regular food into bite-size pieces and stay away from very salty or spicy dishes. A lot of times your child may turn up her nose at whatever's on her high-chair tray and lunge for whatever's on your plate instead.
- Save liquid for later in the meal. If your baby fills up on milk or water, she'll be less interested in trying a new food.
- Introduce a wide variety of foods—even if the baby won't touch any of them.

"Because I'm *a* sovereign, *and a sovereign is* allowed *not to eat his spinach if he doesn't want to."*

- Serve small portions—roughly a tablespoon of each kind of food for every year of age. Large servings can be a little intimidating .
- Keep a log of what the baby eats over the course of a week—just to see how she's doing.
- Don't give up after only one try. It can sometimes take as many as twenty tries before your baby will agree to take a taste.
- Give her some silverware. For some reason, babies often find that the sense of accomplishment they get from skewering their food on a fork makes it taste better. The fork also enables them to fling the food farther across the room than with a bare hand.
- Don't make a huge battle out of it.
- Don't beg; it will just give your baby an inflated view of her own abilities to control you.
- Don't punish the baby for not eating what you serve.
- Don't expect the baby to eat the same amount every day.
- Go along with the craziness; let the baby knock herself out.
- Don't use dessert as a bribe (for more on this, see page 181).
- Be sure to read "Food and Your Child's Temperament," on page 184.

Weaning Your Child from the Bottle (and/or Breast)

At this point in her life, your child is probably less interested in drinking from a bottle (or nursing, if your partner has continued to do so), and more interest in imitating you by drinking from a cup. If she's started to wean herself, great. If not, you should get the process going now.

As mentioned earlier, if your baby fills up on liquids, she may lose interest in the solid foods she needs for that all-so-elusive balanced diet. In addition, babies who feed from bottles are more susceptible to ear infections and/or tooth decay. Finally, it's easy for bottles to become security objects (see page 66), and some experts believe that overdependence on the bottle can interfere with physical and mental developmental milestones and advise giving it up entirely by eighteen months.

If your baby is still nursing, she's already gotten most of the health benefits. She also may start (or may already be) using the breast as a comfort or sleep aid, thus delaying development of her ability to comfort herself or fall asleep by herself. Tread lightly on this one. If your partner wants to nurse for a bit longer, that's fine. Besides providing some nutritional value for the baby, nursing can also provide a lot of emotional value to both baby and mom.

Here's how you can start the weaning process:

- **Phase out the bottles.** Start by replacing midday bottles with cups. Then, over the course of a few weeks, eliminate the morning bottle altogether, followed by the right-before-bed bottle.
- **Cut back on milk.** Your baby shouldn't be drinking any more than 24 ounces of milk (unless your pediatrician says otherwise). If you're giving her more than that, replace the excess milk with bottles of water. Reducing the amount of milk your baby drinks will increase her food intake, which should reduce her desire for the bottle.
- **Be patient.** Trying to wean your child in a day from bottle or breast will be a traumatic experience for everyone involved.

Open Wiiiiide: Taking Care of Those Pearly Whites

Hopefully, you've been cleaning your baby's teeth at least once a day since they started coming in. If you haven't, start now. There's not much to it, really. All you need is a toothbrush and sixty seconds. Skip the toothpaste until your baby is able to spit—most toothpastes have fluoride, which can upset your baby's stomach if swallowed.

If your baby will let you brush her teeth, do it for a total of one minute—thirty seconds (about as much time as it takes to sing the "ABC" song all the way through) on the top, thirty on the bottom.

Not all babies are so cooperative. Although they love to put things in their mouth, they aren't nearly as happy to have anyone else put something in there, unless it's edible. So if your baby won't let you brush her teeth, make sure she's around when you're brushing yours, and give her a toothbrush of her own to play around with—even if it's an adult size one—but keep an eye on her the whole time so she doesn't run around with it in her mouth. The combination of wanting to imitate you and chewing on the toothbrush will probably get her teeth pretty clean. If that doesn't work, try making it more fun: she brushes your teeth, and you brush hers; sing her favorite song while you brush her teeth, and so on.

One important reminder: Never put your child to sleep with a bottle or sippy cup of milk, or even a breast. Any kind of sugar, including lactose, which is in milk, will cause tooth decay.

Looking for Mr. Goodbrush

Unless your child needs dental work, your child's dental exams probably won't last any more than a minute or so until she's three. Still, like most new things, the first trip to the dentist can be a scary experience. So start preparing your toddler several weeks in advance. Tell her you're going to a special doctor who is going to count her teeth and take some pictures of them. You might also want to check out of the library one or two books on going to the dentist. Though you shouldn't ever lie to your child about what is going to happen at the dentist's office, make a special point to stay away from words that might frighten her, such as *drill*, *needle*, *shot*, and *pain*. And save all of your personal dental horror stories until she's a teenager.

If your dentist is pretty child-friendly or you belong to a family practice, bring your child along on one of your routine exams. The dentist will probably let her ride up and down in the chair a few times, give her a sugar-free lollipop and a couple of stickers or a toy, and maybe take a very quick look at her teeth. That's it. See you both in six months. After three or four visits like that, your child may actually look forward to seeing the dentist. And the fact that you (and maybe your partner and any older siblings) are seeing the same dentist will reinforce the positive experience.

If your dentist doesn't see children, if his office might be scary to a little one, or if your child won't let him anywhere near her head, find a local pediatric dentist. At my daughters' dentist, the waiting rooms are filled with toys and bowls of fruit. The furniture is all bright colors and kid-friendly patterns. In the examining room there are televisions mounted on the ceiling so the kids can watch videos while their teeth are being cleaned. And in the Xray area, kids sit on a horse—complete with saddle and stirrups—instead of a regular chair. What I want to know is, where were all the pediatric dentists when I was a kid?

Despite all the attempts to distract her, your child may still scream, squirm, and try to escape. Don't be embarrassed. Any good pediatric dentist and her staff see the same little show a hundred times a day.

Some dentists think it's a good idea to have parents in the examining room with their children; others think it's a rotten idea. Fortunately, you know your child better than anyone, so you know whether you need to hold her hand or do everyone a service by waiting in the car.

Diagnosing Food Allergies or Intolerances

Correctly diagnosing food allergies and intolerances is tricky, even for professionals. (The difference between an allergy and an intolerance is subtle, but very important: allergies generally begin in infancy and get progressively worse with each encounter with the offending food. Intolerances don't.) Since trace amounts of the most common triggers are present in many foods, pinpointing the single offending ingredient is extremely difficult. Casein (a milk protein), for example, is sometimes found in tuna and even in nondairy ice creams. Chili recipes often include peanuts, and just try to find a packaged product that doesn't contain corn, or at least corn syrup.

If you suspect your toddler is allergic or has an intolerance, but her reactions aren't severe, keep a diary of everything she eats and all her symptoms for at least two weeks. This may seem like a real pain, but the diary will help you and your pediatrician identify the source of the problem.

Because the only proven way to treat food allergies and intolerances is to avoid the offending foods, your pediatrician may, after reviewing the diary, prescribe an elimination diet. These diets typically last two weeks and include only the least allergenic foods possible (see page 76). If the symptoms don't improve after a few weeks, you can assume your child doesn't have a food allergy. But if the symptoms do improve, other foods are introduced, one at a time, a few days apart. If a reaction occurs, the new food is eliminated again and reintroduced after the symptoms have subsided (to make sure the first reaction wasn't just a coincidence). Because most allergies (except those to peanuts and fish) are eventually outgrown, however, many doctors recommend reintroducing previously eliminated foods every three months or so.

Elimination diets may sound simple, but don't start one without your doctor's supervision. Too many parents misdiagnose food allergies and intolerances and eliminate too many foods—and given that your toddler's eating repertoire

MOST ALLERGENIC FOODS	LEAST ALLERGENIC FOODS
♦ Egg whites	♦ Rice
♦ Wheat and yeast	♦ Oats
♦ Milk and other dairy products	♦ Barley
♦ Fish	♦ Carrots
♦ Tree nuts (almonds, walnuts)	♦ Squash
♦ Citrus fruits	♦ Apricots
♦ Berries	♦ Peaches
♦ Tomatoes	♦ Pears
♦ Chocolate	♦ Apples
♦ Peanuts and soybeans	♦ Lamb
♦ Shellfish	♦ Veal

may be fairly limited, that could be a real problem. For more information on food allergies and intolerances, see the Resources Guide (page 264).

Dealing with the Disappointment of Disability

One of the major themes in this book is the constantly evolving need to deal with the disparity between the way you dreamed your child would be and the way she actually is. A lot of the differences between reality and expectation have to do with choices and interests—the child choosing to join a motorcycle gang instead of going to medical school like you wanted her to, or having no interest in sports or in living out your dream to win an Olympic medal in the luge.

In most cases, parents manage to get past these things, and they learn to accept their children as they are. But what happens if your child can't live up to your expectations or hopes because she's disabled or chronically ill?

You're likely to feel a wide range of emotions, from shock, disbelief, and denial to depression, anger, ambivalence at having a child at all, resentment at having to spend so much time and money on treatment, and even wishing that your child had died. Many of these more negative feelings will be immediately followed by profound guilt at ever having had the thought in the first place. Whatever your feelings, having a disabled child may do serious damage to your self-esteem.

Mothers and fathers react to a child's disability differently. Mothers typically worry more about the emotional strain of caring for a retarded child, how they'll have to reorganize their life around the child, and whether that will make them neglect other members of the family, according to researchers Jaipaul Roopnarine and Brent Miller.

Fathers tend to worry more about practical things: the cost of providing care, and whether the child will be able to function in school. Dads also tend to be more concerned with their disabled children's (especially boys') social status and employment prospects, says fatherhood researcher Michael Lamb. Some fathers with disabled children feel inferior, says Lamb. They get less pleasure out of their disabled children, and "they end up with fewer reminders of their own value." Overall, Israeli researcher Malka Margalit and her colleagues found that fathers of disabled children derived less satisfaction from family life, perceived fewer opportunities for independence and personal growth and intellectual and recreational activities, and had less confidence in themselves than fathers whose children were not disabled.

How (and how well) you and your partner cope with a handicapped or chronically sick child depends on a fascinating collection of factors.

- **When you become aware of the problem**. The earlier the problem comes to light, the easier it is for parents to begin to cope. It's harder for parents to acknowledge a problem with a child who seemed perfect for a while.
- **How obvious the handicap is**. Fathers, according to Michael Lamb, generally feel more scrutinized by society, which makes them particularly sensitive to any perceived "imperfections" their child might have.
- **Birth order**. Fathers tend to be more involved with firstborn children who are handicapped than with ones born later.
- **The type of disability**. Physical or mental handicap seems harder for parents to adjust to than chronic illness.
- **The gender of the child**. Sadly, since a lot of parents (especially fathers) have higher expectations for their sons than their daughters, they may react more negatively to a boy's handicap than to a girl's. Families with a mentally retarded son, for example, have more problems than families with a retarded daughter.
- **The couple's relationship with each other**. Couples who are more content and who have more social support are more likely to have favorable reactions to disabled kids than those who aren't as stable, according to Roopnarine and Miller.
- **How the father's parents respond**. Acceptance of the disabled child by the father's parents had a big influence on how well the father himself accepted the child.
- **Whether you join a support group or not**. Men who get involved with

Coping with the Death of a Child

Losing a child is every parent's worst nightmare, something no one who hasn't experienced it can possibly imagine. It can bring up grief, anger, denial, and even feelings of guilt at not having been there enough or inadequacy at not having been able to prevent the death.

Researcher Kim Wendee Schildhaus studied how couples adapt to and cope with the loss of a child and keep their marriage alive. She found that, as in most areas of parenting, men and women cope with the loss of a child differently. Women had two basic needs: one was to focus on the surviving children, if any; the other was to use support systems. Men did what men usually do: they tried to ignore their feelings and dove headlong into their jobs. The rationale for that kind of approach, as several of the men I interviewed said, is that since they'd failed in their societally approved role as protector of the family, they knew they could at least succeed at being a breadwinner. Unfortunately, that isn't an effective way of coping with grief—either in the short or the long term. "Grief will change you," advises Amy Hillyard Jensen, author of *Healing Grief*. "But you have some control over whether the changes are for better or worse."

Men are brought up to be tough, strong, competent, knowledgeable, and in control of their emotions. Weakness—especially tears—is discouraged. Anger and frustration are okay, but sadness and pain are not. This kind of socialization is very effective in a lot of ways. But when we face an emotional upheaval such as the loss of a child, too many of us have no idea how to react.

Instead of acknowledging our grief and dealing with it, we ignore it. Instead of getting help, we pull away from the people closest to us.

other fathers of handicapped kids feel less sadness, fatigue, pessimism, guilt, and stress, and have more feelings of satisfaction and success, fewer problems, and better decision-making abilities than dads who don't join groups, according to researchers Patricia Vadasy, Rebecca Fewell, and their colleagues.

There's no question that having a handicapped child puts a lot of stress on the entire family. Conflict, tension, and even divorce are more common in families with a disabled child. That's why it's especially important that you and your partner get as much support as possible and that you communicate with each other constantly. When one parent backs off, that leaves the other parent

The results can be dangerous. "If feelings are left buried, they cause prolonged turmoil, bitterness, family problems, and even ill health," writes author William Schatz. Researchers at the University of Aarhaus in Denmark found that parents who lose a child are far more likely than other parents to commit suicide or die in an accident. In the case of mothers, the likelihood of dying of cancer or infectious disease is also higher.

Besides being devastating to the parents, losing a child can also destroy the marriage itself. But it doesn't have to. Kim Schildhaus identified a number of factors shared by couples who adapted to their loss and stayed together. These couples:

- Accept different ways of grieving and allow each other space in the relationship without making judgments. Men and women should accept each other's individual style.
- Believe in and utilize a support network, asking for help when it's needed, accepting when it's offered.
- Focus on other children.
- Focus on their work and career.
- Agree that the death of their child was the most tragic loss imaginable, and that the thought of losing their spouse too is unbearable.
- Develop new friendship networks that include other parents who've lost children.
- Get therapy.
- Keep the memory of the deceased child alive.
- Communicate with each other.

with twice the burden. If your friends are able to step in, that'll certainly help. But you absolutely must explore every other possible resource.

Start by getting some couples therapy. Then check with your child's pediatrician, parent support groups, and your local school district. In addition, About.com (specialchildren.about.com) has a good collection of resources, and *Exceptional Parent* magazine (www.eparent.com) provides information, support, and resources for parents and families of children with disabilities.

Your child's disability will undoubtedly have an impact on how you treat her. You may respond by being overprotective, or you may be more lenient and lax with setting limits and enforcing them. Try not to do this if you can. Naturally, you'll need to adapt to your child's individual disability, but use this as a rule: As with any child, if you treat her as though she's weak and fragile, she'll grow up thinking of herself in exactly those terms.

Keep in mind that having a disabled child is not an entirely negative experience. Most families get great pleasure out of raising a handicapped child, and many even go out of their way to adopt one. In addition, several studies have shown that handicapped children can actually have a positive effect on families, says Lamb. At least one researcher found that some fathers in particular reorder their priorities to put their family first, discover new values, and experience personal growth as they adapt to their children's disabilities.

You and Your Partner

Communication

One of the most common traps new parents fall into is that they stop communicating—or at least change the way they do it. Half the time these changes are permanent, according to researcher Jay Belsky. Here are some factors Belsky and several other researchers have identified as contributing to the problem :

- "A new child deprives a couple of many of the mechanisms they once used to manage differences," says Belsky. For example, a couple that had disagreements about who did what around the house might solve the problem by getting a housekeeper. But with a baby around the house, strained finances might not allow for a cleaning person, which means you'll have to deal with the once painless who-does-what disagreements.
- The lack of spontaneity. Before your baby was born, if you wanted to go to a movie or just sit around and talk, you could just do it. But now, as parents, you don't have that luxury. If you want to go out, you have to get a sitter a day or so in advance, make sure the baby is fed, and be back at a certain time.
- Physical exhaustion. Your baby may now be sleeping through the night, but having a child around can be incredibly tiring. So even if you and your partner stay home together, there's a better than even chance you'll be too tired to stay awake for an entire conversation.
- There's a general decline in intimacy-promoting activities such as sex, getting together with friends, and so forth.
- With so much time and energy focused on the baby, you and your partner may find that your pool of common interests is shrinking fast.
- There's a lot less time and money left to pursue individual interests and

activities outside the home. As a result, many new parents find that their communication skills have "rusted." They don't have nearly as many new things to talk about, and they've lost (partially, at least) the ability to hear and understand each other.

- If you or your partner has left the workplace, you've lost a rich source of conversational topics; there are now a lot fewer stories to tell about people at the office.

Here are some things you and your partner can do to keep (or get) communication on track:

- Get a family calendar. This can keep double-booking and scheduling miscommunications to a minimum.
- Set aside at least fifteen minutes a day to talk about things other than the baby. It's harder than you think. See "(Re)Learning to Talk," below, for more.
- Go out on dates (with your partner, of course). Spending time alone with your partner is absolutely critical to the long-term health of your marriage. Get a sitter if you can, or ask friends or relatives to step in. You might also want to set up an informal babysitting cooperative with a few other parents

"They're playing the blame *game."*

in your neighborhood; they need to get out as much as you and your partner do.

- Do something special for each other. But be flexible and understanding. If you've made surprise plans, and your partner is too exhausted, it doesn't mean she doesn't love you. Try again another night, or put the "surprise" on the calendar.
- Schedule sex. It sounds terribly unromantic, but just having the big S on the calendar may actually make it more fun. And anyway, if you're still interested, this may be the only way it's going to happen. Weekdays may be out, but if you use your weekends wisely, you should still be able to rechristen every room in your house.
- If your partner is at home with the baby during the day, try to give her some time every day when she can be completely alone and doesn't have to take care of anyone but herself. If you're the primary caretaker, do the same for yourself.
- Don't blame the baby for your troubles. Too many couples interpret their communication problems as a sign that the baby pushed them apart and that they shouldn't have become parents.
- Talk to other people. Talk to other couples with kids to find out what they've been through, what works, and what doesn't. You might also join a new parents' or new fathers' group.

(RE)LEARNING TO TALK

"I get the picture sometimes of two people who may be very much in love and very much together, having private dreams that shape their lives, but not letting each other know the content," writes fatherhood researcher Phil Cowan. Frequent, open, and honest communication is "the key to an effective transition from couple to family," he adds. But because so many couples seem to forget how, let's go over the basics:

- **Open your mouth**. Although many men have been socialized into thinking that we don't have strong feelings or emotional needs, this obviously isn't true. Nevertheless, many men are reluctant to talk to their partners about their needs and feelings, fearing that they'll seem weak in the eyes of their partners and will be letting them down.
- **Now close your mouth and open your ears**. One of the most widespread stereotypes about men and women is that women are more open than men about discussing their feelings and emotions. If your partner is a natural talker, great. But plenty of new mothers need some gentle, supportive encouragement. "A great deal of needless suffering goes on

because mothers and fathers are ashamed to express feelings they have that seem 'unmotherly' or 'unfatherly,'" writes Phil Cowan. So encourage her to talk, ask her about her deepest feelings about the baby, tell her you love her, reassure her that you'll be there for her.

- **Speak the same language**. Sounds silly, but it's not. Some of the biggest communication breakdowns come because people don't (or can't or won't) agree on the definition of some very basic words. For example, does the word *love* mean the same thing to you and your partner? Do the two of you show your love for each other in the same way? Probably not. Men commonly express love for their partners and other people by doing things for them (which may be how the whole "good provider" thing got started). Women, however, are more likely to express their love verbally. Unfortunately, most people want to be spoken to in their own language. Consequently, what you do may not be loving enough for your partner, and what she says may not be enough for you. Learning to express—and accept—love differently is like learning a new language. Granted, it's a little more complicated than high-school French, but it can be done.

Here are some ground rules for putting your newly polished communication skills to work:

1. **Schedule a special time and place for your discussions**. Let's face it: if you can't have sex without a calendar, you won't be able to have a serious conversation without one either.
2. **Tell her what's on your mind**. Tackle one issue at a time, and stay away from phrases like "You always," "You never," or anything else that's guaranteed to put a quick end to your conversations.
3. **Ask her to tell you what she heard you say**. Just saying, "I understand what you're saying" isn't enough here. It's important to have your partner tell you in her own words what you've just told her.
4. **Confirm for her that she heard you correctly**. Tell her again if she didn't.
5. **Go back to step 2, but switch roles: she talks, you listen**.
6. **Listen—really carefully**. Most people use the time in a conversation when they aren't talking to plan out the next thing they want to say, the next killer point that will score big and maybe win the argument. The problem with that is that scoring isn't worth much in a marriage—at least one that you want to last. And while you're busy plotting, your partner is saying something that you really should hear.
7. **Learn to compromise**. Understanding each other's concerns is a great

place to start, but it doesn't do much good if you can't figure out how to bridge the gaps.

8. **Get professional help if you need it.** Set up a monthly or quarterly appointment with a marriage counselor to give you and your partner a safe place to discuss your relationship, differences, problems, worries, and so forth.

FIGHTING CAN BE A GOOD THING . . .

Parenting approaches are the source of just about as many marital spats as money and division of labor. Naturally, you should avoid having huge fights in front of your children. (Kids are scared and confused when their parents yell at each other, and researchers have found that the angrier the parents, the more distressed the children.)

But this doesn't mean that whenever the kids are around, you and your partner always have to see eye to eye (or at least seem to). In fact, just the opposite is true: "Children of parents who have regular and resolved fights have higher levels of interpersonal poise and self-esteem than those whose parents have chronic unresolved fights or those whose parents appear not to fight at all," writes psychologist Brad Sachs.

Children can also learn plenty from watching their parents disagree—provided they do it civilly. Seeing you and your partner handle your disagreements respectfully will encourage your children to do the same. It may also help them learn some negotiation and bargaining skills that will come in handy when trying to convince others of their point of view. So let your child see you and your partner squabble about easily resolvable things, and schedule weekly or, if necessary, daily meetings away from the kids to discuss the bigger issues.

Big or small, if you do ever have a disagreement in front of your child, pay close attention to how you make up afterward. "It is probably useful for young children to observe how adults renegotiate their relationship following a squabble or moments of hostility," says columnist Lilian Katz. "These observations can reassure the child that when distance and anger come between her and members of the family, the relationship is not over but can be resumed to be enjoyed again."

GO AHEAD, GET ANGRY

Don't go too far out of your way to avoid fighting with your partner. As odd as it sounds, a little spousal fighting now and then may actually be good for you. Internalizing your anger for long periods can cause all sorts of problems, including ulcers, high blood pressure, and depression. And if you don't let off a little steam now and then, your anger can come out in more subtle ways. "The phone message that we forget to deliver to our partner, the medicine we forget to give to the baby, the check we forget to deposit," writes Sachs, "can all be passive aggressions directed against our spouse when we're afraid of what we're feeling."

18–21 MONTHS

Still Wild (or Mild) after All These Months

What's Going On with the Baby

Physically

- No longer content just to walk forward, your toddler can now walk backward and sideways. He may even be able to run. (Well, sort of. It really looks more like a clumsy speed walk.) And as his ability to balance on one leg at a time improves, so does his ability to climb stairs.
- He can kick a ball without stepping on it and can, at long last, throw overhand.
- He can draw a pretty good straight line, brush his teeth, and even wash and dry his hands (although he may not want to).
- As his hand-eye coordination improves, your toddler loves piecing things together. He does simple puzzles (in which each piece fits in a separate hole) and can build some pretty impressive towers, five or six blocks high. He'll also put blocks, Duplo, or Lego pieces together to make long, straight walls. There's still room for improvement; when hammering, he finds it nearly impossible to keep the head of the hammer straight, and more often than not it lands sideways.
- He's getting really good at undressing himself. But his dressing skills are still largely confined to not squirming for a few seconds and allowing you to slip something on him. He may be able to put his shoes on, but they'll often end up on the wrong feet.
- He's experimenting with using forks and spoons, but not the way you'd hoped. He holds his fork in one hand, picks up a piece of food, and pushes

it onto the tines with the other. His liquid handling skills are getting better, though: he can pour water from one container to another without spilling much, and can drink from a cup without completely drenching himself.

- He's doing better at turning the pages of a book, but may still tear them.

Intellectually

- Although he's made major intellectual advances over the past eighteen months, your toddler is still a fairly egotistical little creature, believing that he is the source of all action. Child psychologist Selma Fraiberg beautifully describes the typical toddler's attitude toward the world: "The magician is seated in his high chair and looks upon the world with favor. He is at the height of his powers. If he closes his eyes, he causes the world to disappear. If he opens his eyes, he causes the world to come back. . . . If desire arises within him, he utters the magic syllables that cause the desired object to appear. His wishes, his thoughts, his gestures, his noises command the universe."
- Despite his self-centered view of the world, your toddler is becoming aware of the ownership of objects. He can (but may not want to) distinguish between "mine" and "yours."
- His sense of object permanence is becoming more sophisticated, and he now anticipates where objects "should" be. If a ball rolls under the couch, for example, he'll run to the back of the couch, knowing the ball will be there soon. And as you pass the gas station down the block from your house and turn onto your street, he'll begin to get excited, knowing he'll be home soon.
- Your toddler is developing a mind of his own and is increasingly negative and contrary: the first word out of his mouth in any given situation is usually "no," he'll refuse to do almost anything you ask, and he deliberately dawdles when he knows you're in a hurry. For a toddler to do just the opposite of what you want him to do "strikes him as being the very essence of his individuality," writes Selma Fraiberg. In the right mood, though, your toddler may be able to follow two-stage directions, such as "put down that crystal vase and back away from the table."
- He still has some difficulty with time concepts: "now," "later," "yesterday," and "tomorrow" mean nothing to him. But he can now identify several colors by name, and he recognizes himself in the mirror.

Verbally

- At about eighteen months, your toddler's passive vocabulary (the words he understands) will start growing by a word or two every day. At around twenty-one months, his active vocabulary (the words he can say) will kick into overdrive, and he'll learn as many as five new words per day. Once he can say fifty to sixty words (not including animal sounds, or air-raid siren and airplane imitations), he'll start experimenting with two-word (and possibly three-word) sentences such as "Up me" or "Down me."

- He now makes a serious effort to repeat what you say, using a kind of shorthand. For example, if you say, "No, you can't pour your milk on the floor," he'll probably reply, "Pour milk floor." Language expert James Britton has found that toddlers repeat the words that carry the most information, while omitting the less important ones.
- He's learning about "what" and "why" and will frequently ask you to identify unfamiliar (and sometimes quite familiar) objects. And when you're reading to him, he'll name every object or character on the page.
- Kids this age are beginning to grasp the concept of pronouns and can make subtle distinctions: "Don't hit him" is different from "Don't hit her."
- For the first time, your toddler is capable of engaging in "conversation." Instead of responding physically to your questions (by going somewhere, pointing to something, or doing something), he may use words.

Emotionally/Socially

- He still has some trouble telling the difference between inanimate objects and people, and treats other toddlers accordingly—poking, hitting, biting, and pushing them. This kind of behavior is usually not hostile, though; he's just learning some valuable lessons about actions and reactions.
- Although he's expressing some interest in interacting and socializing with other kids, your toddler prefers to play alone, pausing once in a while to defend his property rights or to snatch something away from a "playmate." He may even hide his toys so other kids won't be able to play with them. Despite his seeming lack of interest, he's learning a huge amount by imitating his friends (they, presumably, are also learning from him).
- He loves cuddling and will hug and kiss you (and his favorite toys) frequently.
- If they haven't already, this is about the time when girls discover their vaginas and boys their penises. Boys may even get, albeit rarely, an erection. This is absolutely normal for kids this age, and every attempt should be made not to make a big deal of it (see pages 231–32 for more on this).
- He knows what he wants, and you'll see plenty of tantrums when he doesn't get it.
- Your toddler may exhibit an early interest in toilet training by occasionally

letting you know when he has a wet or soiled diaper. But it's going to be a while before he's ready to use the toilet.

What You're Going Through

A Fear of Being Rejected by Your Baby

One of these days, you're going to run to comfort your crying child. Oh, you've done it before, but this time it'll be different. This time, instead of running to meet you, your child will see you and scream, "No! I want Mommy!" or "I hate you," or "You're a bad daddy!" There's not really anything I or anyone else can say that will make you feel any less rejected or despised when those horrible words pop out of your child's mouth. The first time (and the tenth and the twentieth) my older daughter said something like that to me, I nearly cried. And those feelings came flooding back as each of my other children went through the same phase.

Remember, though, that your child has no idea that he's hurting you with words. Feelings are still something new to him, and he may just be experimenting to see how you'll react. Rather than withdraw completely or punish your child (even subtly) for wounding you, here are a few other approaches:

- Acknowledge that your child is upset. Say something like, "You're really mad, aren't you?"
- Reassure him that you love him.
- During a calm moment much later, talk with him a little about how it feels when your feelings are hurt. But don't go on too long about this; the last thing you want to do is put your child in charge of your self-esteem (or to make him feel as though he is).
- Try some sarcasm. Saying, "Yep, you're right. I'm the world's worst father, and everyone hates me," may shock your child so much that he'll rush to your defense.

Eventually, you'll learn to ignore (or at least pay less attention to) your child's slings and arrows. And you'll find that things have a way of coming full circle. When my middle daughter was about eighteen months old, she went through a stage when she wouldn't let me put her down. In fact, she wouldn't let anyone else—my wife included—come near her. On one occasion, after I'd been carrying her around for about eight hours straight, my legs and shoulders had gone completely numb and I needed a break. So I told my daughter I was going to take her to Mommy for a while, and did exactly that. The handoff went

"I know what you're going through. I, too, spent several years as a small child."

fairly well, but the moment I turned to walk away, my daughter shrieked, "Daddy! Help me, Daddy! Save me!"

Why Bother Anyway?

At some point in his life, every father asks himself whether his priorities are in the right order, and one of the biggest issues he'll think about is whether he's spending enough time—or could it be too much?—with his family. On pages 92–93 I'll talk about the pluses and minuses of fatherhood. But for now, let me give you some very compelling reasons to stay (or get) as involved as possible.

IT'S GOOD FOR YOUR CHILD

- He'll have better friendships. Three-year-olds who have positive relationships with their fathers have better friendships when they're five. The more negative the father-child relationship, the worse the quality of the kids' friendships.

- He'll be cooperative and self-reliant. Children whose fathers regularly look after them during infancy and the toddler years are more self-disciplined and have better social skills than those whose fathers spend less time alone with them, according to Kay Margetts, a researcher at Melbourne University in Australia.
- He'll have an easier time separating from Mom. From the time your child is eighteen months old until he turns three or so, you—and only you—are gently helping him safely and securely separate from the intense dependency he has on his mother. "Healthy though dependency on their mother is for children at the beginning of their life," says child psychiatrist Kyle Pruett, "they will not experience, let alone practice, their own competence and mastery skills if they do not strike off in search of their own physical and emotional autonomy."
- He'll develop better problem-solving skills. The combination of a father's more interactive play style and his less immediate support in the face of frustration helps kids adapt to new situations or things, explore the world more vigorously, stick with difficult tasks longer before giving up, and become more competent problem solvers, says Pruett.
- He'll be smarter. Sons of nurturing fathers score higher on intelligence tests than boys whose fathers are less involved. And children of both genders who grow up without involved fathers have more trouble solving complex math problems than kids whose dads are involved.
- It sets a good example. By being involved, you're demonstrating that both men and women can nurture. It shows young boys that being an involved father is something to aspire to when they grow up, and it shows young girls that they should expect their future husband to be an involved father as well.
- Your child will have fewer problems as a teen. The biggest predictor of whether a girl will take up sports or be physically active is having a father who plays with her (wrestling, playing ball, shooting hoops, whatever) when she's young. Adolescent girls who are involved in sports are less likely to drop out of school, get pregnant, develop eating disorders, put up with abusive relationships, smoke, drink, or develop breast cancer as adults. I know your child isn't even two yet, but hey, it's never too early to start thinking about these things.
- He'll be a more empathetic adult. Several long-term studies have found that how compassionate adults (men and women) are and how well they are able to experience others' feelings depend more than anything else on how involved their fathers were during the toddler years.

Benefits and Costs of Fatherhood

I realize that it may sound like I'm telling you that being an involved dad is wonderful and fantastic and incredible every single minute. Well, it's not. The truth is that being a dad, just like anything else, has its ups and downs. It can be the greatest thing you'll ever do, and it can be the most frustrating. It creates opportunities for growth and fun, but interferes with others. Below I've summarized many of the benefits and costs associated with being an involved dad. It's based in part on fatherhood researcher Rob Palkovitz's findings as well as my own interviews with hundreds of fathers. We'll talk more about some of these themes in later chapters.

BENEFITS

- You're extending the family line, passing on your name and your genes; your children are your legacy.
- You gain satisfaction from watching children grow and develop. You know that your teaching has made a difference in their lives, and you find joy in their accomplishments.
- A sense of pride. You feel that what you're doing is right, that you've achieved something meaningful by investing in your children's development. This feeling comes whether or not you get compliments from others on how great a dad you are or how great your kids are.
- You receive love. In a sense this is your compensation for being an involved dad. You get to be needed, loved, admired, and appreciated, and it feels great.
- It's an opportunity for personal growth—in maturity, self-discipline, role-modeling, and emotional expressiveness.
- You experience a shift in perception, an expansion of your sense of self. You're less goal-oriented, less driven, and more interested in the family.
- It's fun. Your kids give you all sorts of excuses to express joy, to experience life as a child again, to play and do things you'd never do without a child (go to a park or the zoo, collect baseball cards, go to G-rated movies . . .).
- It's a chance for continued learning. You may develop skills and interests you never had before, just to keep up with your kids. You can also brush up on some of the subjects you'd forgotten long ago or learn some of the ones you never got around to in the first place.
- It gives life meaning. Having kids may give purpose and direction to an otherwise ordinary life.
- It may enhance your marriage. Some men feel that having kids makes their marriage better, giving Mom and Dad a shared focus in life and in their children's accomplishments. Not surprisingly, a lot of women agree.

COSTS

- Time. For some men, time is a metaphor for freedom or the opportunity to focus on themselves. Having kids requires giving up freedom to do what you want while you're with them. You may have to give up activities that brought you pleasure. (Although the opposite can be true: I rekindled an interest in martial arts when my middle daughter started taking karate.) You also may spend a lot of time thinking about your children when you're not with them.
- Sacrifice. You may have to defer satisfying your own goals and dreams, putting off career advancement or continued education in order to be the good provider. This tends to be much more common among men who became fathers young.
- Lifestyle. You'll probably live in a different place, drive a different car, take different vacations, and maybe even have a different job than you would have if you hadn't had children.
- Finances. Again, a more common worry among younger dads. It costs a lot to raise a child these days.
- Marital closeness. You'll probably spend less private time with your partner. There'll be less time for physical and/or emotional intimacy, or even to talk over important issues.
- Energy. There's the sleep loss of early fatherhood, then the physical exhaustion of chasing a baby around, then more sleep loss when you start worrying about a sick child or drugs and alcohol and sex and friends and grades.
- Potential. All that time and energy you put into being a father is time and energy you could have devoted to writing a book, directing a movie, painting a masterpiece, inventing a cure for cancer . . .
- Loneliness or isolation. This is especially common for stay-at-home dads, who don't usually have a support network or group of other guys they can get together with to discuss fatherhood, babies, or even the latest football scores.
- Lower self-esteem. Again, especially common among stay-at-home dads. Some of these men feel that because they aren't working, they aren't productive members of society anymore. And some worry that spending so much time with their children has made them overweight and less intellectual, and might even have shaved a few points off their IQ.
- Kids grow up and don't need you as much. A lot of the meaning in your life will come from your relationship with your kids. If that relationship changes or gets strained, as it is likely to do as your child grows up and seeks independence, you may mourn the loss of meaning.
- You get spread out. All the demands on your time and energy leave you feeling like there isn't enough of you left.

IT'S GOOD FOR YOUR PARTNER AND YOUR MARRIAGE

- You'll be more committed to making your marriage work. Men think about marriage and family differently than women do. For men, "family" tends to mean a mother, a father, and some kids. As a result, once a man becomes a father, he also becomes very committed to keeping his family together. That way of thinking explains, to some extent, why after divorce men remarry sooner and more often than women. Women, however, can imagine themselves parenting without a man around and still consider themselves part of a family. That goes a long way toward explaining why about 75 percent of divorces are initiated by women.

IT'S GOOD FOR YOU

- You'll be less depressed. Constance Hardesty and her colleagues found that low levels of paternal involvement can lead to depression. In other words, higher levels of involvement may promote mental health in men.
- You'll have a longer, healthier life. Involved fathers suffer fewer accidental and premature deaths, less-than-average contact with the law, less substance abuse, fewer hospital admissions, less depression, and a greater sense of well-being overall, according to Joseph Pleck and other researchers. (For more on your health, see page 142.)
- You'll be a more effective parent. Researcher Mary De Luccie did a fascinating study of 177 firstborn boys and girls in an attempt to figure out what made dads get involved and feel satisfied. She found that it was a kind of loop: fathers who were warm and firm with their kids felt they were doing a good job and thought they had good relationships with their kids. That, in turn, made them want to get even more involved. It just keeps getting better and better.

You and Your Baby

Play

As your baby gets closer to his second birthday, three major play-related developments occur, usually in rapid succession:

- He learns to play with others his own age.
- He learns to play alone.
- He learns to tell the difference between what's pretend and what's real.

Issues for Adoptive Fathers

Adopted children and their adoptive fathers develop in very much the same ways as biologically related fathers and kids.

Perhaps the biggest adoption-related issue at this stage is whether and how to tell a child that he's adopted. The consensus seems to be to hold off for a while, at least until the child is six. Before then, most children aren't capable developmentally of understanding what adoption means, and they haven't got a clue about how conception and birth really work. (They may be able to tell you that babies come from mommies' tummies, but don't really get how they got there in the first place.) Adoption expert Gordon Finley tells a great story about a family with a three-and-a-half-year-old adopted child that went to the airport to pick up a newly adopted infant. "For a long period after," he writes, "whenever the family passed an airport, the oldest would point to the airport and talk about how that is where babies come from."

Many—but certainly not all—adoptive parents experience feelings of inadequacy at not having been able to produce their own children. By the time their children reach the toddler years, though, most adoptive parents have put aside their feelings about infertility, and they've shelved their fantasies of having a biological child. Instead, they're "coming to see themselves as they really are, the eminently entitled and very 'real' psychological parents of their adoptee," writes Finley.

But the thought of telling your child about the adoption can bring all the negative feelings about adoption back—the infertility, self-doubt, conflicts with your spouse. Throw in a little fear that the birth parents might change their minds and you might lose the child, and you can see why this could be a very stressful time.

PLAY WITH PEERS

If your child has been thinking of himself as the center of the solar system, he certainly considers you and your partner to be nearby planets, orbiting around him contentedly. But just recently he's realized that there are other objects floating around out there. And some of them seem to be stars—just like him.

A few months ago, your baby would have completely ignored a child playing nearby, unless the other child snatched one of his toys. But at the ripe old age of eighteen months or so, he's suddenly paying very close attention. He's not quite ready to actually play with other children, but he's extremely interested

A Few Equipment-Buying Tips

- Make sure anything you buy for use by your child can be easily used. For example, if you have a mini basketball hoop, make sure the child—not just you—can hit a few jumpers. If it's too high, he'll get frustrated and quit.
- Chairs should be wider at the bottom than at the top to reduce the chance of their tipping over. They should also be low enough so that the baby can get up and sit down without having to ask for help.
- Tables should be high enough to fit comfortably above your child's knees while he's sitting on his chair.
- Be aware of your attitude about gender roles. Toddlers naturally gravitate toward gender-appropriate toys, although gravity is helped along by parents, who generally discourage boys from playing with dolls and girls from playing with trucks, and who tend to furnish kids' rooms along gender lines: ballerina bedspreads and frilly curtains for girls, Spiderman bedspreads and dinosaur curtains for boys. In later chapters, we'll talk more about gender stereotyping and what you can do to avoid it.

in everything they do. Researcher Kim Whaley found that when a baby is in a room with his parent and another child, he pays more attention to the other child than to the parent. It's at about this age that toddlers start to realize that they may have more in common with each other than with their parents.

It's going to be a while yet before your baby has mastered the art of sharing. But there are a few things you can do to help him grasp the concept:

- Show him how it's done. If you're peeling an orange for yourself, give him half and tell him what you just did (something as simple as, "Daddy's sharing his orange with Bobby").
- Talk to him about what belongs to whom (Daddy's cell phone, Mommy's laptop, Aunt Ida's alligator purse).
- Have duplicate toys. If your baby has regular play dates with another child, there'll be a lot less fighting if each one has the same toy.

PLAYING ALONE

Ordinarily, being ignored isn't considered a compliment. But if you and your baby are together, and he wants to spend some time playing by himself, consider yourself praised: if he wasn't absolutely sure he could count on you to be there in an emergency, he'd never take his eyes off you.

The capacity to be alone is a critical sign of emotional maturity, says English pediatrician and psychoanalyst D. W. Winnicott. And as usual, your role as a father needs to be adjusted in response to your child's growth and development. "Toddler learning now depends in part on the freedom a child is given to explore the environment," says Kim Whaley. "There is now a shift from adult as participant to adult as audience."

One very important thing you can do is minimize the amount of time your child spends cooped up in a playpen. The more time he's in it, the less time he'll be out exploring. Of course, safety should always be a priority, and if your baby is in the playpen to keep him from doing something dangerous, let him stay there.

Although your child may be playing alone, he'll often accompany himself by singing, humming, laughing, or squealing. The bottom line is that he's just begun to discover some of the wonderful things his spry young body can do, and it feels incredibly good. And anything that makes him feel good enough to squeal is certainly worth doing again.

PRETEND PLAY

Toddlers come prewired with a healthy imagination, and you should encourage your child's pretending any way you can: play imitation games, act out stories with your child and his toys, pretend to take a nap and use him as a pillow, or write a script and film your own movies. As it turns out, toddlers who do a lot of pretend play are more creative when they start school, have more advanced language skills, are less impulsive and better able to tolerate frustration, are better at sharing, and frequently become leaders in their peer groups, according to Yale psychologists Jerome and Dorothy Singer. So the next time your toddler starts talking into a carrot as though it were a telephone, grab a piece of broccoli and get in on the conversation.

Making Music

"In general, the more you and your child have become actively involved in music . . . the more your child's attention span and appetite for music will increase," writes music educator Edwin Gordon.

Even if you haven't done much more than sing a couple of lullabies or leave the radio on a few hours a day, you'll notice that your baby has become a much more active music listener than he was in his first year. He clearly recognizes familiar songs and tries to sing along. At this age, he won't be able to get more than a note or two—usually the last one in the song or phrase—the "O" in "E-I-E-I-O," for example. But he's delighted to be able to do even that.

By the time he's about two and a half, he'll add the first few notes and an occasional short phrase in the middle of a song as well (all of "E-I-E-I-O," perhaps, or maybe even "Yes, sir. Yes, sir. Three bags full"). And by his third birthday, he'll be putting all the pieces together and doing entire songs.

Here are a few things you can do to encourage your child's musical development:

- **Sing**. If you haven't done so already, make singing part of your everyday routine. Since your child is taking a more active role in singing, select songs that are short and repetitive, and change your focus from singing *to* your child to singing *with* him. If you can't think of any songs, set the words of a favorite book to music; make up a melody if you have to. Encourage him to make up his own songs and have him teach you the words or melody. Don't expect perfect pitch from your toddler. Although a few kids this age are able to sing in tune, most can't.
- **Go for variety**. Toddlers respond to the mood of the music they hear. Scary music will frighten them, happy music will get them onto the dance floor, and slow or sad music will slow them down. Look for music with dramatic changes—fast and slow, loud and soft, high and low, stop and start. The original *Fantasia* is wonderful for this. If you'd like a little help selecting music, several companies produce sets of developmentally appropriate tapes that are aimed at children but that you'll like too. A few are listed in the Resources guide on page 264.
- **Let him make his own music**. He already knows plenty about percussion instruments, but if you have a guitar around the house, let him strum the strings while you finger the chords. Or get a few easy-to-blow whistles.
- **Forget the ulterior motives**. Despite what you might hear about the Mozart effect, music isn't going to make your baby any smarter. But it's a great way for the two of you to spend time together having fun.
- **Watch**. Just a few months ago, your baby's arm and leg movements seemed almost random. But now, just before his second birthday, he has adopted his very own, unique rhythmic "gestures"—shaking, wiggling, half-crouching, or bouncing up and down—that are different from those of every other child his age. As before, your child's movements—which now come in groups of three to seven "pulses"—may not seem to have much to do with the music he's hearing. They are, however, definitely in response to the music and are internally very consistent, meaning that you can almost set your watch by the pulses.
- **The way your child moves to music is an expression of some primal part of his personality**. So let him do what he wants—don't tell

A Few Fun Educational Activities for Kids This Age

Of course, just because your child is starting to take an interest in other kids, enjoys being alone, and is developing an imagination, that doesn't mean that your days of playing together are over. Not even close. Your baby still needs you. Here are some fun activities you can do together:

- Games that emphasize letter, number, color, or size recognition. Shape sorters are excellent for this. So are matching games. Cut postcards in half and have the baby match the halves. Or, in a more advanced version, match playing cards.
- Games that involve digging, pouring, building, and destroying. The more your child does these things, the more he's learning about how different materials respond or how the same material might respond in different situations. If he's playing at the beach, for example, he'll be able to make steeper mountains out of wet sand than dry.
- Games that emphasize abstract thinking. Get a bunch of identical containers with tops (plastic yogurt containers work very well) and put in a variety of items: sand, rice, Cheerios, water, and so on. Then shake the containers (or have the baby do it himself) and ask him to guess what's inside.
- Take a nature walk. Pick up things and discuss them. You'd be amazed at the variety of stuff there is just lying around, and at the variety of educational opportunities. (Picking up a leaf, for example, can spark a great discussion about how nutrients get from the root of the tree to the leaves and about the difference between deciduous and evergreen trees.) Activities like nature walks also encourage observation skills, and you'll probably find that your child is spotting a lot more interesting things than you are.
- Cook. Make simple edible recipes together, or just make some Oobleck—a kind of moldable dough that kids love to play with. (Mix together 1 pound of cornstarch, 1½ cups of cold water, and some food coloring until smooth. That's it.) Besides teaching all sorts of great things—measuring, textures, how things change shape and form when heated or cooled—cooking with your child will subtly teach him some valuable lessons about men's and women's roles in society. But best of all, it's a lot of fun. (See pages 215–20 for more on cooking with kids.)
- Build a fort out of chairs and blankets. Learn about structure, balance, privacy, light, and dark.
- Relax. Don't forget to build some downtime into your schedule. Read, draw, do puzzles, or even just watch your tropical fish swim around.

Thinking Music

Ever since you were just a few years old, you've been able to summon up images of objects or people, or imagine words and sentences or entire conversations without actually speaking a word. That's what thinking is. In music, the same basic process is called *audiation*. "To audiate is to hear and comprehend music that is not physically present, just as to think is to hear and give meaning to language, the sound of words not physically present," write Richard Grunow, Edwin Gordon, and Christopher Azzara. Just as you can't develop as a person without thinking, "without audiation, no musical growth can take place," they add.

Sound complicated? It really isn't. Think of all those times you haven't been able to get a particular melody out of your head, or the times you've taught someone else a song without looking at the music or listening to the CD. That's audiating.

One of the best things you can do to help your child build his audiating skills is to expose him to music without words. Because language development receives so much emphasis in our culture, the words of a song may distract your child from being aware of the music itself. In the case of kids with limited language skills, the words can actually slow down musical development. If a child's language "has not developed well enough to sing the words of the song," writes Gordon, "she may not attempt to sing the song at all."

Please remember that as important as it is to expose your child to music, having the stereo going twenty-four hours a day isn't necessary or helpful. Learning to listen to and appreciate silence is important too. It is during periods of silence that your child has the opportunity to exercise his developing powers of audiation by remembering, thinking about, and experimenting with the music he has already heard.

him how to move, show him new routines, or move his arms or legs for him. That's the surest way to stifle his budding self-expression.

Keep on Reading

DEALING WITH BOREDOM

After reading the same book six times at a single sitting (or several hundred times over the course of a few months), you might find yourself less than completely enthusiastic about reading it again. If (when) this happens, spice things up by making some deliberate mistakes in the text, just to see if your baby is on the ball: switch characters' names, say "in" instead of "out," and so forth.

YOUR ATTENTION, PLEASE

The average almost-two-year-old's attention span is about three minutes, so try to get in at least three or four reading sessions each day. But be prepared: the range varies enormously. When my oldest and youngest daughters were this age, they could easily spend an hour listening to me read, but at the same age the middle one wouldn't sit still for more than thirty seconds at a stretch. Please also remember that attention span is not an indication of intelligence. Despite her seeming indifference, my middle daughter still ran around the house most of the day demanding to be read to and still managed to memorize at least as many books as her seemingly more attentive peers.

ADDING TO YOUR LIBRARY

If your child is still interested in the same books that you've been reading to him for the past year, don't worry. And don't push him to give up old favorites. This doesn't mean, though, that you can't slip in a few new titles every once in a while. Big hits for this age group include books that introduce numbers, sizes, shapes, colors, opposites, and special concepts (up, down, in, out), and discuss body parts. Here's a short list of some of my developmentally appropriate favorites for this age:

Across the Stream (and many others), Mirra Ginsburg
Can't You Sleep, Little Bear? Martin Waddell
Caps for Sale, Esphyr Slobodkina
Each Peach Pear Plum, Janet Ahlberg and Allan Ahlberg
Fuzzy Yellow Ducklings, Matthew Van Fleet
Golden Bear, Ruth Young
A Good Day, a Good Night, Cindy Wheeler
Holes and Peeks (and many others), Ann Jonas
How Do I Put It On? Shigeo Watanabe
I Can, Helen Oxenbury
Jump, Frog, Jump, Robert Kalan
Little Gorilla, Ruth Borenstein
Lunch, Denise Fleming
Mouse Paint, Ellen Walsh
Owl Babies, Martin Waddell
Peekaboo Kisses, Barney Saltzberg

Planting a Rainbow (and many others), Lois Ehlert
Quiet Night, Marilyn Singer
Ten, Nine, Eight, Molly Bang
Where Does the Brown Bear Go? Nicki Weiss
Who Hops? Katie Davis

CONCEPTS
Becca Backward, Becca Frontward: A Book of Concept Pairs, Bruce McMillan
Cold Little Duck, Duck, Duck, Lisa Westberg Peters
On Market Street, Arnold Lobel
One Wolly Wombat, Rod Drinca and Kerry Argent
Piggies, Don and Audrey Wood
White on Black, Tana Hoban
(For more concept books, see pages 34–37, 152, and 206.)

POETRY AND RHYME
A Child's Garden of Verses, Robert Louis Stevenson
Jamberry, Bruce Degen
Rainbow in the Sky, Louis Untermeyer, editor
Wake Up, Big Barn! Suzanne Tanner Chitwood
(For more poetry books, see pages 34–37, 152, and 206.)

Family Matters

Tantrums

WHAT CAUSES THEM

In some cases as early as twelve months, but most frequently between fifteen and eighteen months, almost all kids begin having regular tantrums.

One of the major causes of tantrums is the frustration that results from the child's inability to use his limited verbal skills to express his specific needs and wants. Generally speaking, the more verbal the child (hence the better able to explain his needs), the less he'll be frustrated and the fewer tantrums he'll have. Many kids, however, are also frustrated by their body's inability to respond to their mind's rather sophisticated requests or desires.

Either way, frustrations build up over the course of a day or two until the child finally is no longer able to control himself and explodes. He may scream,

"Rachel! *If you can't even stay focused on spreading* peat *moss, how do you expect to get into* law *school?*"

cry, throw himself on the floor, kick, bite, or even hold his breath until he passes out. Just to put this into perspective, consider this: nearly 15 percent of twelve-month-olds and 20 percent of twenty-four-month-olds have two or more tantrums per day.

Besides frustration, of course, a variety of other factors may account for tantrums:

- Your child is trying to assert himself. He may feel he's lost your attention and will do whatever it takes to get it back.
- Your toddler wants to explore and wander all over the place. You want to keep him safe and alive, which sometimes means restricting his movements.
- He may be frightened at how angry his frustrations make him, and may be trying to attract your attention, hoping you'll help him regain control over his life and emotions.
- Illness, hunger, exhaustion, or overstimulation.
- Too much discipline. You may have set too many limits, or laid down too many rigid or inconsistent rules.

- Not enough discipline. You may have imposed too few rules or established erratic or inconsistent limits. Tantrums may be, in a sense, a plea for more effective limit setting.
- Imitation. Do you get upset when you don't get what you want?
- It works. If it's been successful in the past, it might just work again. . . .
- Temperament. Low-frustration-tolerance, slow-adaptability kids (see pages 108–15 for a discussion of temperament) are much more susceptible to tantrums. This susceptibility can also result in parent-child personality clashes.
- Family stress. Divorce, separation, or even a major change in work schedule or lifestyle can be tough for kids to deal with.

WHAT TO DO ABOUT TANTRUMS

When your child is in the midst of a tantrum, he is no longer a member of the human race. So reasoning, shouting, hitting, and punishment will have little if any effect. Here are a few things that may work to minimize the tantrum and its effect on everyone:

- Don't panic. That's exactly what your child is trying to get you to do. If you get upset and rant, you'll only make things worse.
- Use humor. Say something completely silly. If that doesn't work, get down on the floor and thrash around in your own tantrum. This may snap out of it by showing him how ridiculous a tantrum looks.
- Walk away (assuming that the baby is in a place where he can't hurt himself or anyone around him). In many circumstances, no audience equals no performance.
- Stand firm. If the tantrum is the result of some disciplinary measure, tell your child that the rule still stands and will continue to do so until he calms down.
- Explain. Say things like, "I know you're upset because you really wanted to read that story. . . ."
- Time out. If things are really getting out of hand, put the child by himself someplace and explain (privately) that he won't be able to be with other people until he calms down. Again, the no-audience-equals-no-performance theory applies here. Limit time outs to one minute per year of age.
- Protect your child. Kicking, swinging, and throwing things can hurt not only other people but the child as well. Holding him firmly but calmly often calms an out-of-control kid.
- After the tantrum, reassure the child that you're still there for him, that you

still love him, and try to figure out what caused the problem. But do not reward him for stopping.

WHAT NOT TO DO

- Don't shout. Any big reaction proves that the tantrum was the right approach.
- Don't try to argue with a kid who's in the middle of a tantrum. You'll be wasting your breath.
- No physical punishment. Another waste of time, since your child isn't usually in control of the tantrum anyway.
- Don't give in. Doing so offers kids conclusive evidence that tantrums do, indeed, work.

Public Tantrums

Sometimes I'm absolutely convinced that my children subscribe to some kind of special, underground newsletter filled with super-secret techniques they can use to drive adults nuts. And I'm sure one of the most popular features is "Tantrums in the Produce Section, and Twenty-five Other Surefire Ways to Embarrass Your Parents into Giving You What You Want NOW!" Besides the techniques described above, there are a few special ways of handling public tantrums:

- Speak softly. Bend over and whisper in your child's ear that if he doesn't stop right now, you're going to leave immediately. If that doesn't work, pick your child up and do what you said you'd do.
- Isolation. Take the child to the bathroom, outside, to the car—anywhere you and he can be more or less alone.
- Ignore the audience. You'll be mortified at what your child is doing—and even more mortified at what spectators will think you're doing to him. If your child is particularly theatrical, he's liable to attract quite a crowd. Given that you're a dad, there's a good chance that everyone who walks past you and your screaming toddler will offer some absolutely brilliant piece of advice. A lot of them don't even have children. If the peanut gallery gets overly aggressive or hostile, Brazelton suggests that you ask for volunteers to take over for you. You'll be amazed at how fast the crowd will disperse.
- Consequences. When you get home or to some other private place, tell your child that since he had a tantrum, he won't get dessert.

Breath-Holding, Passing Out, and Other Spectacular Variations

Starting at about eighteen months, babies who have finished in the top 10 percent of Tantrums 101 are invited to get advanced training, this time in how to scare the hell out of their parents by holding their breath and passing out.

The bad news about breath-holding is that it is incredibly frightening (how could a child's turning blue and keeling over not be?). But the good news is that besides taking ten years off your life, it isn't all that dangerous. What usually happens is that the child starts to cry, takes a huge breath—and holds it. If he holds it long enough, he may lose consciousness, but the moment he does, he'll start breathing immediately and will usually recover within thirty to sixty seconds.

Somewhere between 1 and 20 percent of children have at least one breath-holding episode. The frequency peaks at around two years of age, and most kids will outgrow them by age four or five. In a small number of cases—if, for example, your child seems drowsy for ten to fifteen minutes after coming to, or if he turns blue while unconscious instead of *before* — he could be having a true seizure. For that reason, the first time your child has a breath-holding episode, take him to see his pediatrician. Again, it's probably nothing to worry about, but it's worth letting the doctor know.

So why do kids really hold their breath? "When all else seems to fail in battling for control," says temperament researcher Jim Cameron, "holding one's breath becomes the ultimate stronghold—no one can make you breathe."

Breath-holding is more common among active, intense, slow-adapting-

HOW TO PREVENT TANTRUMS

There's nothing you can do to prevent tantrums completely. But there are a few preemptive steps you can take that should greatly reduce the frequency and severity of these little outbursts:

- Be a reliable source of help and support.
- Know—and pay close attention to—your child's temperament (see below). This is extremely important to do and will help you in every interaction with your toddler. Don't try to force an irregular child to be regular, or a slow-to-warm child to warm quickly.

to-change toddlers (see pages 112–115 for more on this). According to Cameron, "The more energetic they are, the less they want to stop what they're doing or to shift to things you want them to do." In addition, since active kids spend more time practicing large motor skills (running, crawling, and so on) than other kids, the joy of doing these things is greater. They also may be a little behind in verbal skills, making it harder for them to argue with you.

In some cases, advanced tantrum throwers may opt for banging their heads against something or screaming so intently that they make themselves vomit. Just about all you can do to keep these episodes from happening is to try to avoid the kinds of confrontations that precipitate them. But there's no guarantee that even that will work. If your child has started holding, or trying to hold, his breath, or has added head banging or vomiting to his repertoire, start with the dos and don'ts listed on pages 104–5 and add the following:

- Give him extra time to adjust to change. Instead of one ten-minute warning, give notice at ten, five, three, and one minute.
- Don't react intensely to your child's reactions. If your child has vomited, clean him up as matter-of-factly as possible. The bigger your reaction, the more likely your child will make breath-holding or vomiting a regular part of his routine. Also, don't become overly permissive out of fear of triggering another episode.
- Talk, talk, talk. Encourage your child to use words. As frightening as these fits are, they won't last forever. The more verbal your child becomes, the faster they'll fade.
- Do not attempt to "shock" your child back to reality by slapping him or throwing water in his face. Instead, hold your child.

- Give your child plenty of opportunities throughout the day to let off steam—physical play, running around, and so forth—as well as some occasional periods without rules (or with as few as possible).
- Encourage your child to talk about the things that make him angry. And be supportive and empathetic when he does.
- Make sure your child gets enough food and sleep. Shortages of either can make kids cranky and more susceptible to having tantrums.
- Think carefully before you say no. Is what you're rejecting really that big a deal? Giving in—perhaps partially, with some conditions or time

limits—can give kids more control, thus reducing the "need" to throw a tantrum.

- Compromise as much as possible. Offering a firm "Two more minutes" gives the child a lot more control than insisting that he immediately do what you want him to do. But following your two-minute warning with a five-minute warning and then not going anywhere for fifteen minutes after that tells your child that you're an easy mark.
- Avoid yes/no questions and open questions ("Which pair of socks do you want to wear?"). Give choices instead: "Do you want the red ones or the blue ones?"
- Compliment good behavior regularly. Tell your child you understand that doing some things is hard and frustrating, but that you appreciate his efforts.
- Give clear, concise warnings. "Daddy and Mommy are going out later, and Grandpa will be baby-sitting. We'll be there when you wake up." Or, "Five more minutes, then we have to start cleaning up." I've found that setting a timer helps a lot: "When the buzzer goes off, we'll have to . . ."

Temperament

You've been watching your child grow and learn for more than a year now, and you've seen him develop a unique personality and his very own way of reacting to the world. Actually, "develop" might be the wrong word. If you think back to when your child was just a few months old, there's a good chance that you'll see that the way he is now—how loud, sensitive, curious, active, independent, emotional, and moody—is pretty much the way he's always been.

About fifty years ago a husband-and-wife team of psychiatrists, Stella Chess and Alexander Thomas, developed a theory that children are born with a set of fundamental behavioral and emotional traits that they called "temperament." The way your child's temperamental characteristics blend together make him different from every other child, and they determine whether he'll be "easy" or "challenging." You've got a unique temperament too. And the "goodness of fit" between yours and your child's goes a long way toward setting the tone for your relationship with each other.

Over the decades, temperament theory has been expanded and refined by many researchers. Some even disagree completely with Chess and Thomas and suggest that what makes up a person is more "nurture" than "nature." Either way, it's important that you accept your child's (and your own) temperament. After this paragraph, you'll find a brief overview of what each temperament trait is all about, followed by a quiz (based on the rating scale suggested by the Center for Human Development in Oregon) to help you determine the traits that best fit your child. Then on pages 112–15 you'll find a thorough discussion of each characteristic.

1. Approach/Withdrawal: How your child reacts to new experiences: meeting new people, tasting new foods, going to sleep in a new place, and so on.
2. Adaptability: Similar to Approach/Withdrawal, but deals with your child's longer-term reactions to changes in routines or expectations, new places, or new ideas.
3. Intensity: Your child's overall volume level, when both happy and unhappy.
4. Mood: Your child's general outlook—wildly excited, serious, or something in between—over the course of a typical day.
5. Activity level: Your child's overall preference for active or quiet play and his overall energy level throughout the day.
6. Regularity: The day-to-day predictability of your child's basic biological functions: hunger, sleep, and filling diapers. Each should be rated on its own scale.
7. Emotional Sensitivity: How your child responds emotionally to a situation. This trait has two subcategories: one for sensitivity to his own feelings, and one for sensitivity to others' feelings.
8. Sensory Awareness: How sensitive your toddler is to pain, touch, taste, smell, hearing, and sight. Each category is rated on a separate scale. Note: It's quite possible for a child to be highly sensitive in some areas and insensitive in others.

For Readers of The New Father: A Dad's Guide to the First Year

If you read the previous book in this series, you already know a little about your child's temperament. But don't skip this section. The nine basic temperament traits we covered in that volume are very similar to the ten presented here. The difference is that because your child's emotions are so much more sophisticated than they were a year ago, I've taken the advice of the folks at the Center for Human Development in Oregon and divided the Sensitivity category into two related but separate categories: Emotional Sensitivity and Sensory Awareness. So spend a few minutes going over the trait descriptions and take the test on pages 110–11. Again, because your child is far more sophisticated than a year ago, the rating system is too.

9. Distractibility: The ease with which your toddler is distracted by all the things going on around him.
10. Persistence: Similar to Distractibility, but goes beyond the initial reaction and concerns the length of time your child will stick with something—even when the task gets hard.

TRAIT		RATING	
APPROACH/WITHDRAWAL	Outgoing	1 2 3 4 5	Slow-to-warm
What is your child's first and usual reaction to new people, situations, places?			
ADAPTABILITY	Easy-going	1 2 3 4 5	Strong-willed
Does your child adapt quickly to new ideas, new places, changes in routine or schedule?			
INTENSITY	Mild reactions	1 2 3 4 5	Dramatic reactions
How loud or physically dramatic is your child when expressing strong feelings?			
MOOD	Happy-go-lucky	1 2 3 4 5	Serious, displeased
Is your child primarily an optimist or a pessimist? Lighthearted or serious?			
ACTIVITY LEVEL	Calm and slow-moving	1 2 3 4 5	Wild and quick-moving
Is your child a "wiggler" or a watcher? Does he jump up and dance to music, or does he rock in place?			
REGULARITY			
Hunger	Wants food at same time every day	1 2 3 4 5	Irregular eater
Sleep	Tired on schedule	1 2 3 4 5	No schedule
Toileting	BMs at same time every day	1 2 3 4 5	Try and guess
Does your child normally eat, go to bed, wake up, and have bowel movements at the same time every day?			
EMOTIONAL SENSITIVITY			
Own feelings	Unaware of emotions	1 2 3 4 5	Feels emotions strongly
Others' feelings	Doesn't notice others' feelings	1 2 3 4 5	Highly sensitive to others' feelings
Does your child often get upset over nothing, or does he rarely get upset even when circumstances suggest that he could? Does your child feel sympathy or empathy for others?			

TRAIT		RATING	
SENSORY AWARENESS			
Pain	What nail in my foot?	1 2 3 4 5	EEEOOWWWWHH!!
Touch	No reaction to contact	1 2 3 4 5	Easily irritated or pleased by contact
Taste	Can't make subtle distinctions	1 2 3 4 5	Notices tiny variations
Smell	Doesn't notice odors	1 2 3 4 5	Human bloodhound
Hearing/Sound	Noise is no problem	1 2 3 4 5	Sensitive to sounds
Vision/Lights	Visually sensitive	1 2 3 4 5	Visually insensitive
DISTRACTIBILITY	Not easily diverted	1 2 3 4 5	Easily diverted
Is your child very aware and easily distracted by noises and people? Can you distract him from upset feelings by redirecting his attention?			
PERSISTENCE	Hard to stop	1 2 3 4 5	Stops easily
Does your child stick with things even when frustrated? Can he stop an activity when asked to?			

After you've evaluated your toddler, take a quick look at your own temperament and see how the two of you compare.

The Ten Temperament Traits of Toddlers

APPROACHING TODDLERS

- are the opposite of shy
- lack fear in potentially dangerous situations
- may be friendly with strangers
- separate easily from parents; may get lost in crowds or stores
- may be impulsive
- approach new situations with great interest

WITHDRAWING TODDLERS

- are usually shy
- need time to get used to new stuations
- say they don't like things before even trying them
- may be picky—eating only certain foods, playing only with certain toys
- usually have difficulty separating from parents
- show fear in seemingly safe situations
- hesitate before investigating strange sounds
- stand back and watch when first entering a playground

FAST-ADAPTING TODDLERS

- are usually fairly compliant
- fall asleep easily and wake up happy
- tend to go with the flow when faced with something new
- may lack assertiveness
- like change and may get easily bored
- may give into peer pressure later in life

SLOW-ADAPTING TODDLERS

- often refuse to go along with almost anything
- need time to adjust to transitions and new ideas
- like to follow their own agendas, and can be bossy and stubborn
- may be quick to anger and slow to get over being angry
- get "locked in" on what they are doing
- protest loudly against taking medicine
- may have trouble getting to sleep in unfamiliar places

LOW-INTENSITY TODDLERS

- are hard to read—they have emotions, but it is difficult for others to notice
- may seem apathetic
- are sometimes mistakenly viewed as uninvolved, low in motivation or intelligence

HIGH-INTENSITY TODDLERS

- wear their hearts on their sleeves—you know exactly what they are feeling all the time
- shout instead of speaking and may scream so loudly it hurts your ears
- have intense reactions—good or bad—to new toys

POSITIVE-MOOD TODDLERS

- are rarely bothered by anything
- can be described as happy-go-lucky
- may lack seriousness
- may be easily taken advantage of
- tend to trust easily
- expect goodness/success

NEGATIVE-MOOD TODDLERS

- cry often and easily, and frequently seem angry, depressed, or disappointed
- may be skeptical and expect the worst
- extend trust slowly
- complain when given a bath
- don't like traveling in a car or stroller

LOW-ACTIVITY TODDLERS

- may take a long time to complete tasks
- may avoid activities that require a lot of physical energy
- may dislike active games
- may nag parents to entertain them
- absorb a lot of information by watching quietly

HIGH-ACTIVITY TODDLERS

- are often extremely active—running wildly, talking incessantly
- are usually *not* clinically hyperactive
- may be aggressive during play
- are often fidgety or restless
- may, however, be able to sit quietly in front of video or TV for an extended period
- have to be watched carefully to prevent accidents

(continued on page 114)

The Ten Temperament Traits of Toddlers *(continued)*

HIGHLY REGULAR TODDLERS

- may be easy to potty train
- love regular eating and bedtime schedules and resist changes to the routine
- are so regular you can almost set your clock by them

IRREGULAR TODDLERS

- may be difficult to potty train
- have bedtime struggles due to irregularity in sleep patterns
- may not be hungry at meals, but want food at a different time every day
- have highly irregular sleep/nap patterns

EMOTIONALLY INSENSITIVE TODDLERS

- rarely display emotions
- can be "instigators" who like to start a little trouble now and then
- can be budding con artists who enjoy manipulating a situation to their advantage
- can have what seems to be a mean or cruel streak
- are often oblivious to others' feelings
- don't seem bothered by others' insensitive behavior

EMOTIONALLY SENSITIVE TODDLERS

- tend to be fearful
- get upset when teased
- are sensitive to how others are treated
- seem particularly tuned in to others' feelings
- may worry a lot
- may cry easily
- may be "people pleasers"
- get their feelings hurt easily

LOW-SENSORY-AWARENESS TODDLERS

- may have dull senses
- can miss a lot of things going on around them—they just don't seem to notice
- can have excellent concentration and aren't easily distracted

HIGH-SENSORY-AWARENESS TODDLERS

- may have sharp senses
- may be distracted by sensory input
- can be picky, finicky, or particular
- sometimes complain about things others don't notice, such as temperature changes or itchy clothes

LOW-DISTRACTIBILITY TODDLERS

- tend to stick with tasks until they are completed
- often have terrific memories
- may become caught up in their own world, not noticing things going on around them
- can be excellent naggers who challenge their parents' ability to not give in
- when upset, can be calmed by only one or two people

HIGH-DISTRACTIBILITY TODDLERS

- have short attention spans
- notice things easily
- may have trouble concentrating on complex tasks
- may leave belongings scattered everywhere
- tend to be forgetful
- when learning something new, will stop when hearing people or sounds

---

HIGH-PERSISTENCE TODDLERS

- rarely give up on difficult tasks
- take on challenges well beyond their skill level
- sometimes persist at things that are unimportant
- may tend to do things the hard way because they don't like to ask for help
- may take things too seriously
- may be perfectionists
- may have long attention spans
- may want to stick with a game long, long, long after you're ready to quit

LOW-PERSISTENCE TODDLERS

- are frustrated easily, even by simple tasks
- may throw tantrums in response to frustration
- if interrupted, won't return to original task
- may get angry and give up
- may demand help from parents, grandparents, and other caregivers
- may struggle to master self-care skills such as toilet training and dressing
- tend to stick with things they are naturally good at, and can look highly persistent when not frustrated
- tend to "let go" easily
- won't play in the playground for more than five minutes at a stretch

21–24 MONTHS

What Are Daddies Made Of?

What's Going On with the Baby

Physically

- Now that your toddler has fairly good control over her legs, she's going to use them all the time. She runs (but still has some problems slowing down and turning corners), jumps forward with both feet, kicks a ball without stepping on it, rarely falls anymore, stands on her tiptoes, climbs and goes down stairs by herself (holding on to a railing), can push herself along in a toy car, and may even be able to pedal a small tricycle. Just about the only thing she can't do with her legs is use them to get herself started on a swing.
- She really wants to dress and undress herself but may not be quite able to do the job alone. Clothes that have larger head openings and looser pants legs will relieve some of her frustration.
- And she hasn't forgotten about her arms and hands: she draws nicely controlled straight lines, can fold paper if you show her how, throws a ball into a basket, makes beautiful mud pies, spends hours opening and closing screw-top containers, can turn doorknobs (so watch out), puts together more complex puzzles, and still has time to stack, pile, tear, and pour anything she can get her hands on. She can even unzip her pants (but can't zip them up) and put her shoes on (but can't lace them).
- She especially loves to pick up and examine tiny things, and her hand-eye coordination is good enough now that she can successfully maneuver a bobby pin or a fork into an electrical outlet. This is an excellent time to go through your house to make sure it's properly childproofed.

Intellectually

- Although time still doesn't mean much to her, she's learned about sequences (first we'll put on your shoes, then we'll go for a walk), and can differentiate between "one" and "many" (although she'll probably say "two" for anything above one).
- She knows all about bigger and smaller now, and she's expanding her knowledge of spatial concepts—stuffing herself into boxes, climbing (or being held) as high as possible, pouring things back and forth. She also knows the difference between circles, squares, and triangles, and can even identify objects and people from upside-down pictures.
- She now thinks through possible solutions to problems instead of physically acting them out. For example, if an object is out of reach, she won't jump up to get it and probably won't try to knock it down with a stick. Instead, she'll bring a chair over, climb up, and grab what she wants.
- She's learning to tell the difference between animate and inanimate. She spends a lot of time staring at and comparing objects that move by themselves (dogs, people, fish) and those that need some outside intervention (blocks, bikes).
- She still has a tendency to regard everything—animate or not—as her personal property.
- She also deliberately imitates your every activity (sweeping, washing dishes, brushing teeth), but only while you're there with her.

Verbally

- Your child is using longer, more complex sentences and is beginning to use language in situations where she once used emotions: she'll ask for desired objects by name and may say, "Change my diaper," instead of crying.
- She also delights in the power that naming objects gives her, and labels everything she possibly can. She's also discovering some of the "W-H" words (where, what, who, why, when) and may use them to jump-start conversations.
- She likes nursery rhymes, and if you pause for a few seconds, she'll fill in the last word of a familiar couplet ("Hickory, dickory, dock / The mouse ran up the _____"). And if you're reading a familiar book and make a mistake, she won't let you get away with it.
- She's tightening her grasp on pronouns, correctly using "I," "mine," "his," and "hers." But she may get confused when trying to use two pronouns in the same sentence: "I want to do it yourself," for example.

Emotionally/Socially

- The contrary, negative, temper-tantrum phase is passing, and your toddler is getting more cheerful and more cooperative. She'll come when you call her and may even put away some of her toys (if you ask really, really nicely and make it worth her while by turning it into a game).
- Nevertheless, she's still easily frustrated, often to tears, by the internal conflict between independence and dependence. She still walks away from you but comes flying back for reassurance that you're still there; she truly wants to please you by doing the "right thing," but she still needs to test your limits by disobeying.
- Perhaps as a result of this conflict, your toddler is also developing a lot of fears of things she may have loved before: night, dogs, bugs, vacuum cleaners. She may also be getting more fearful of things that she was only slightly afraid of before: loud noises, big trucks, and people (especially doctors). See pages 58–66 for more on fears.
- She's getting more and more curious about other people, especially babies, and may play with them for a few minutes. But you're still at the top of her A list.
- She may be getting a little bossy and likes ordering people around ("Go away!" "I don't like!" and so on).
- She's developing a wider range of emotions: she's now quite affectionate with her friends, family, stuffed animals, and even pictures in books. She loves to "baby" her toys (and even parents), covering them with blankets and putting them to "bed." Her whole body lights up when you praise her and her feelings are genuinely hurt when you criticize her.

What You're Going Through

Your Changing Identity

There's an old saying in the Talmud that a man has three names: the one his parents gave him at birth, the one that others call him, and the one he calls himself. A person's identity, according to the rabbis, is a rather amorphous thing. What the rabbis don't talk about is that all three of those names are subject to change over time—especially the one you call yourself. The way you view yourself today may have nothing to do with how you'll see yourself tomorrow.

This point is nicely illustrated by what family researchers Phil and Carolyn Cowan call the "pie chart." Over a period of nearly two years, the Cowans asked a large number of men to draw a circle and divide it up into sections that reflected how important each aspect of their life actually felt—not simply the amount of time they spent in the role.

Over the duration of the study, "Men who remained childless showed a significant increase in the 'partner/lover' aspect," said the Cowans. "New fathers, however, were squeezing 'partner/lover' into a smaller space to accommodate the significant increase in the 'parent' piece of the pie."

As the parenting slice grows, other things happen too. Here are a number of ways that the men in my research (and several other studies as well) said fatherhood changed them (we'll talk about the emotional changes fatherhood brings on pages 170–72).

- **Confidence and pride**. Having a close relationship with your child helps build her confidence and self-esteem. It also helps build yours. Being able to stop your child's tears, making her laugh, or knowing how much she idolizes you can make you feel incredibly competent, and the pride you feel when you see all the great things she can do becomes confirmation that you're doing pretty well at this whole fathering thing. For a while, at least, your child is going to share all your tastes—in music, literature, movies, art, career, politics, and food (as long as it's not too spicy). A lot of these things will change as your child grows up. Still, I can hardly describe the feeling of pride I get when my kids start discussing Hitchcock movies with my adult friends, belt out a few Janis Joplin lyrics, or pop in a CD of Elgar's cello concerto while they're doing their homework. But beware. Confidence and pride are often made of a pretty thin veneer: any misbehavior—especially public—can suddenly make you feel you feel as though you've failed as a father. (See page 140-41 for more on this.)
- **Patience—and a better sense of humor**. Things are going to go wrong whether you like it or not, and you have two choices: take everything seriously and try to change the world, or roll with it and have fun. Learning to laugh at yourself can rub off in other areas and may also make you more understanding of the mistakes other people make.
- **Flexible thinking**. At this point it's almost impossible to tell the difference between your child's needs, your needs, and your partner's needs. In a perfect world they'd mutually reinforce one another. But on this planet, the three often compete for your time and energy. As you get more experienced as a parent, you'll get better at preparing for the future and coming up with contingency plans. You'll also learn the incredibly valuable skill of being able to see a variety of different points of view at the same time. For example,

"How do you expect me to parent if you won't child?"

most new couples say that having children brought them closer together. At the same time, though, they say that they devote so much time to their children that they hardly have any left for each other.

- **A return to childhood**. Having kids gives you a great opportunity to reread all those great books from when you were a kid and disappear back into the world of *King Arthur* and *The Hobbit*. It also gives you a rare chance to say words like "poop" and "pee" in public again. As film director Tim Burton put it after he became a father, "I'm rediscovering the joys of burping and farting, yes, and the humor therein."
- **Creativity**. A lot of parents suddenly get inspired to create. A. A. Milne (who wrote the *Winnie the Pooh* books) and J. K. Rowling (of *Harry Potter* fame) are just two who wrote for their kids. If you're giving your child music or art lessons, you might develop a talent you never thought you had or get hit with the urge to perform at school talent shows.
- **Reordered priorities**. Having kids contributes to a heightened awareness of others' perspectives, says Rob Palkovitz. A lot of guys admit that they were somewhat selfish and self-centered before having kids. This isn't necessarily a negative thing—it's simply an acknowledgment that having

people depend on us and putting their needs before our own isn't something that comes naturally to most of us before we become parents. What's especially interesting is that, according to Palkovitz, getting married doesn't trigger this same realization.

- **Changed values**. Becoming a father will make you take a long, hard look at your fundamental beliefs and values. Things you may have thought were harmless when you were younger, such as not caring about money or material possessions, having promiscuous sex, and even experimenting with drugs, look completely different now that you've got a family to support. You'll start seeing the world in different terms. You may have thought about issues like pollution, terrorism, energy policy, interest rates, AIDS, poverty, and even cloth vs. disposable diapers before, but now, instead of being abstract things that happen to other people, they're possible threats to your child and your family. Having children may also help you clarify a lot of your beliefs. Teaching your child to say that the guy you didn't vote for in the last election is a jerk is one thing. But try explaining to your child—in terms she can understand—what war is, what the death penalty is, why some people are rich while others live on the street. You might find yourself changing your mind about a few things now that they affect your family.

  In 1998, NPR radio host Terry Gross did an interview that illustrates this beautifully. Her guest, T. J. Leyden, works for the Simon Wiesenthal Center at the Museum of Tolerance, fighting racism and anti-Semitism. But what made the interview riveting was that Leyden used to be a neo-Nazi and a white supremacist and had spent a lot of time recruiting teens to commit racist violence. What caused his dramatic turnaround? When his second son was four years old, Leyden heard him repeat some of the racist, anti-Semitic things he'd been spewing, and he was shocked. It was then that he decided to change.

  Interestingly, older fathers report less of this kind of soul-searching than younger fathers. This is largely because older men come into fatherhood already feeling more mature and having had more of a chance to hone their philosophy of life.

The Ambivalent Father

Over the course of my writing career, I've written only a few things that I'm not sure I want my kids to see, and this section is one of them. But you can read it if you promise not to tell them. Throughout this book (and the others in the series) we've talked a lot about the joys, anxieties, fears, and intense feelings of love that are all part of being a father. If you're like most men, the experience—despite the ups and downs—has been overwhelmingly positive, and you wouldn't trade it for anything. In fact, being a dad has become such an integral part of your life that you probably can't imagine not being one.

But one day, completely out of the blue, you may look at your child and realize that the intense love you felt just the day before has been replaced by a numb, hollow feeling. And the delight you took in raising and being part of her life has been supplanted by complete and utter ambivalence. You're feeling overburdened and underappreciated, and you can hardly remember the last time you had a conversation with someone who knows more than forty words. You feel like chucking this whole dad thing and starting a new life somewhere else, as far away from your kids as you can get.

Most of the time these feelings of ambivalence last only a few minutes or a few hours. Sometimes they go on for days or even weeks. But no matter how long they last, one thing is pretty much guaranteed: the instant after the ambivalence starts, you'll get hit by feelings of guilt, guilt for having felt the ambivalence in the first place. And it'll stick around long after you've fallen back in love with your child. After all, goes the internal monologue, if I'm not a completely committed father 100 percent of the time, I must not be cut out for the job at all.

Most mothers are quite familiar with this little ambivalence/guilt pattern. But because they are generally more willing to discuss their worries and concerns with other mothers, they learn rather quickly that it's perfectly normal. They still feel bad about it, maybe even scared, but at least they know they're not alone.

We as fathers aren't alone either, but we rarely ever learn this lesson. If we have a few other fathers with whom we can talk things over, we're incredibly lucky. But it's still pretty unlikely that we'll actually talk to them about this. It's already hard enough to ask for advice about diaper changing, discipline, or nutrition. Having ambivalent feelings is a serious weakness, perhaps a character flaw (or at least it sure seems like one). And we're certainly not going to expose any weaknesses or character flaws to another man, who would just laugh anyway.

Hopefully just reading this section has been enough to convince you—at least a little—that your changing feelings toward your children are completely normal. If you're still worried, though, or if you need more reassurance, force yourself to spend a few minutes talking to someone about what you're feeling—a close friend, your clergyman, your therapist, even your partner (it's going to be harder to talk to her, but at least she'll know exactly what you're going through). And remember this: you're going to have these feelings dozens of times throughout the course of your fatherhood. So get used to dealing with them now.

You and Your Baby

Identifying Your Parenting Style

So you've been a dad for almost two years now, and you've probably noticed that the way you parent is quite a bit different from the way your parents managed. You may also do things much differently than your friends and perhaps even your partner. Sure, everyone has a unique parenting style. But according to Diana Baumrind, a sociologist at the University of California at Berkeley, almost all of us fall into one of three basic categories: authoritarian, permissive, or authoritative. The chart below describes these three styles as well as their relative advantages and disadvantages. (There is a fourth category, the neglectful parent, who rejects or ignores his child and sees her as an inconvenience. However, since neglectful parents aren't likely to be reading this book, I'm leaving them out of the discussion.)

Discipline and Your Parenting Style

As you might guess, authoritarian, permissive, and authoritative parents have different ways of disciplining (or trying to discipline) their children.

Naturally, we all slip in and out of each style from time to time, but almost everyone has a dominant mode. As you can see from the chart on pages 128–29, the authoritative approach is by far the most successful—in terms of discipline as well as family harmony. Moving away from either the authoritarian or permissive style isn't easy—there's a good chance that you parent the

AUTHORITARIAN PARENTS . . .	PERMISSIVE PARENTS . . .	AUTHORITATIVE PARENTS . . .
♦ Value obedience as a virtue and favor punishment whenever there's a difference between the parent's wants and the child's behavior. ♦ Yell, command, order, blame, bribe, and threaten.	♦ Try not to exercise control and don't encourage the child to respect standards and rules. ♦ Are tolerant and accepting of the child's impulses, and use as little punishment as possible. ♦ Plead, hope things turn out okay, and often give up and do nothing.	♦ Exert firm control but don't overload the child with restrictions. ♦ Use reason as well as power to achieve their goals. ♦ Make requests, give incentives, negotiate, and establish consequences.

way you do because it's what you (and your parents, and theirs) grew up with. But here are a few tips that will help you start the process:

- **Divert**. This is far and away the most successful method of getting a child two and under to stop misbehaving. And it'll keep on working fairly well for another year—especially when it's used in conjunction with the other approaches in this section. By diverting your child's attention early, you'll eliminate a lot of problems before they have a chance to develop. You won't feel the need to punish your child, and she won't feel that she's a failure.
- **Be clear**. Let your child know exactly what kind of behavior you expect.
- **Set reasonable limits, explain them, and enforce them**.
- **Be consistent**. Your child will learn to adapt to inconsistencies between you and your partner. If you allow jumping on the bed but she doesn't, for example, the child will do it when she's with you and won't when she's with your partner (see pages 84–85 for more on dealing with disagreements). But if you allow jumping one day and prohibit it the next, you'll only confuse your child and undermine your attempts to get her to listen when you ask her to do something.
- **Compromise**. Kids can't always tell the difference between big and little issues. So give in on a few small things once in a while (an extra piece of birthday cake at the end of a long day might avoid a tantrum, or you might extend your child's bedtime so she can spend some time with a relative who's in town for the day). That will give her a feeling of control and will make it easier for her to go along with the program on the bigger issues (holding hands while crossing the street, for example).
- **Be assertive and specific**. "Stop throwing your food now" is much better than "Cut that out!"
- **Think ahead**. If you find yourself butting heads with your child at certain times (such as when it's time to leave the park and go home) or places (grocery stores are toddler favorites for meltdowns), give her plenty of warning and remind her of the behavior you expect.
- **Give choices**. Kathryn Kvols, author of *Redirecting Children's Behavior*, suggests that if your child is, for example, yanking all the books off a shelf in the living room, you say, "Would you like to stop knocking the books off the shelf or would you like to go to your room?" If she ignores you, gently but firmly lead the child to her room and tell her she can come back into the living room when she's ready to listen to you.
- **Cut down on the warnings**. If the child knows the rules (at this age, all you have to do is ask), impose the promised consequences immediately. If you make a habit of giving six preliminary warnings and three "last"

warnings before doing anything, your child will learn to start responding only the eighth or ninth time you ask.

- **Link consequences directly to the problem behavior**. And don't forget to explain—clearly and simply—what you're doing and why: "I'm taking away your hammer because you hit me with it," or "I asked you not to throw that egg up in the air and you didn't listen to me. Now you'll have to help me clean it up."
- **No banking**. If you're imposing punishments or consequences, do it immediately. If you punish a child at the end of the day for something (or a bunch of things) she did earlier, she won't associate the undesirable action with its consequence.
- **Keep it short**. Once the punishment is over (and whatever it is, it shouldn't last any more than a minute per year of age), get back to your life. There's no need to review, summarize, or make sure the child got the point.
- **Stay calm**. Screaming, ranting, or raving can easily cross the line into verbal abuse, which can do long-term damage to your child's self-esteem.
- **Get down to your child's level**. When you're talking to your child—especially to criticize—kneel or sit. You'll still be big enough for her to have no doubt who the boss is.
- **Don't lecture**. Instead, ask questions to engage the child in a discussion of the problematic behavior: "Is smoking cigars okay for kids or not?" "Do you like it when someone pushes you down in the park?"
- **Criticize the behavior, not the child**. Even such seemingly innocuous comments as, "I've told you a thousand times," or "Every single time you . . . ," give the child the message that she's doomed to disappoint you no matter what she does.
- **Reinforce positive behavior**. We spend too much time criticizing negatives and not enough time complimenting the positives. Heartfelt comments like, "I'm so proud of you when I see you cleaning up your toys," go a long way.
- **Play games**. "Let's see who can put the most toys away" and "I bet I can put my shoes on before you can" are favorites. But be sure not to put away more toys or to put your shoes on first—kids under five have a tough time losing.
- **Avoid tantrums**. See pages 102–8 for some tips.
- **No spanking**. See pages 130–31.
- **No shaking**. It may seem like a less violent way of expressing your frustrations than spanking, but it really isn't. Shaking your baby can make her little brain rattle around inside her skull, possibly resulting in brain damage.
- **No bribes**. It's tempting to pay a child off to get her to do or not do

something, and once in a while you'll probably give in to the temptation in the interest of keeping the peace. But don't do it too often. The risk—and it's a big one—is that your child will demand some kind of payment before complying with just about anything.

- **Be a grown-up**. Biting your child or pulling her hair to demonstrate that biting or hitting is wrong or doesn't feel good will backfire. Guaranteed.
- **Offer cheese with that whine**. Tell your child that you simply don't respond to whining and that you won't give her what she wants until she asks in a nice way—and stick with it.
- **Set a good example**. If your child sees you and your partner arguing without violence, she'll learn to do the same. If she sees you flouting authority by running red lights, she'll do the same.

Discipline and Temperament

Not every approach to discipline works equally well with every child. And one of the best ways to improve your chances of finding the right one for your child is to take her temperament into consideration. As we discussed in the previous chapter, you can't change your child's temperament. But by understanding it, you'll see why certain things you're doing aren't working, and you'll be able to come up with some new ways of guiding your child's behavior that will work with her temperament instead of against it.

To start with, never punish your child for doing something that's probably rooted in her temperament. For example, if you have a very slow-to-warm child, don't criticize her for not cheerfully saying "Hi" and "Bye-bye" to everyone she sees. She'll only end up feeling that there's something wrong with her for being shy. So instead, encourage her to wave to people instead, and compliment her when she does.

Here are some more temperament-specific discipline tips, some of which were suggested by Jim Cameron:

- Your energetic, slow-adapting toddler needs to have some areas in which she can practice her assertiveness. She needs limits that are clear and consistent but reasonable and flexible (you may have to state the rule a few times, but she'll come around eventually). Too many limits will result in battles of will; too few will result in your being afraid of her all the time. It's especially tough for your child to follow instructions in the evening, so as bedtime approaches, start getting her calmed down by reading or watching a video instead of wrestling.
- Your highly active toddler may seem as though she never stops moving, and asking her to slow down often makes her go even faster. Expecting her to

"Sure I'm bad. I'm a prisoner of my genes!"

sit still, with her hands crossed on her lap, will never work. But you'll have much better luck if you give her something to play with while she's sitting, such as some clay to knead, a book to read, or something to draw with.

- Your slow-adapting child is likely to argue with you about everything you ask for, and it's awfully easy to interpret her dawdling as rebellion or an attack on your authority. If you respond immediately with anger, your child will resist even more. So instead, give her several firm warnings, starting well in advance. Parents of slow-adapting kids sometimes just give in out of frustration or lash out with severe punishments, feel guilty, and become overly permissive again. "For slow adapting children, loss of control over their own world [getting sent to their rooms] is the most effective punishment there is," says Cameron.
- Your moderate-activity, moderate-frustration-tolerance child has lots of tantrums. She wants something, you hold your ground, and off she goes . . . . Her goal, of course, is to get you to give in. Don't. (See pages 102–8 for more on handling and preventing tantrums.)
- Your moderate-activity, fast-adapting child needs to know exactly what the rules are and where the lines are drawn. Too many limits, and she'll be frustrated by the lack of freedom. Too few, and she'll run wild.

PARENTING STYLE The parents . . .	AUTHORITARIAN (THE BOSS) ♦ Are frequently uncompromising, dictatorial, strict, and repressive. ♦ Attempt to shape, control, and evaluate the behavior and attitudes of the child according to an absurdly high (and often theologically motivated) standard. ♦ Rarely explain the rules.
As a result, the child . . .	♦ Learns to obey out of fear of punishment. ♦ Learns to lie or hide misbehavior in order to avoid punishment. ♦ Is less independent, takes on less responsibility, and does worse in school. ♦ Is so used to being controlled that she does not develop self-control, and as a result can often be unruly and uncooperative when parents aren't present.
The power . . .	♦ Is with the parent.
Life at home can be . . .	♦ Tense ♦ Rigid ♦ Oppressive
The parent-child relationship	♦ Cold, rigid, and based on fear. ♦ Verbal interchange between parent and child is discouraged. Instead, children are taught to blindly accept the parents' word as the way things ought to be.

PERMISSIVE (THE SERVANT, THE BYSTANDER)	AUTHORITATIVE (THE GUIDE, THE LEADER)
♦ Are often passive, weak, inconsistent, and yielding. ♦ Consult with the child too much about family policies and give too many explanations for rules. ♦ Don't ask the child to take on many household responsibilities. ♦ Allow the child to regulate her own activities as much as possible. ♦ May be under stress and don't have the energy to enforce rules.	♦ Are approachable, reasonable, and flexible. ♦ Attempt "to direct the child's activities but in a rational, issue-oriented manner," says Baumrind. ♦ Don't regard themselves as infallible or divinely inspired.
♦ Is subtly encouraged to control others. ♦ Is left to follow her own wants and instincts and can become self-centered and demanding. ♦ Has less impulse control and is less responsible, less self-reliant, and less independent. ♦ Doesn't do as well in school and has more social problems. ♦ Doesn't learn to cooperate or to consider the needs of others or of the group.	♦ Is encouraged to think and to be a participant in the family. ♦ Learns to take on more responsibility with age. ♦ Becomes more independent. ♦ Gets good grades in school. ♦ Is able to focus on the needs of the group.
♦ Is firmly in the hands of the child.	♦ Is shared appropriately between parent and child.
♦ Chaotic ♦ Uncontrollable ♦ Wild	♦ Relaxed ♦ Orderly ♦ Consistent
♦ Distant and often marked by resentment and manipulation. ♦ Parents make few demands for mature behavior and without limits the child can feel unloved and uncared for.	♦ Close, respectful, and marked by sharing and communication. ♦ Parents encourage "verbal give and take, and share with the child the reasoning behind the policy." ♦ Encourages the child's independence and individuality. ♦ Recognizes the rights of both parents and children.

Spanking

A recent survey by *Child* magazine found that only about 4 percent of parents think that spanking is an acceptable form of discipline. Nevertheless, nearly a quarter of parents of toddlers admit that they sometimes resort to spanking (and that doesn't include all the parents who spank but don't admit it).

The big question, of course, is, "Does it do any good?" If you want to attract your child's attention in a hurry, the answer is yes. But if you're interested in producing any positive, long-term effect, the answer is a resounding no. In fact, there's plenty of evidence that the long-term effect of spanking children is quite negative. Researchers have found that adults who say they were slapped or spanked as children are more likely to suffer from anxiety disorders and alcoholism than adults who were never slapped or spanked. In addition, children who get spanked are more likely to suffer from poor self-esteem and depression, and have a greater chance of accepting lower-paying jobs as adults. While this may not be a direct cause-and-effect relationship, there is clearly some correlation between being spanked and poor self-esteem.

Overall, as you might expect, spanking children does little more than teach them to resort to violence and aggression as a way of solving their problems—not exactly the message most parents want to get across to their kids.

- Your irregular, withdrawing child is, not surprisingly, tough, and your expectations are the key. Expecting your child to stay in her room at night is fine, but expecting her to stay in her bed or to go to sleep right away is a waste of time. And expecting her to eat dinner is reasonable, but expecting her to eat everything on her plate every meal is not. The key here is to make repeated and firm requests for compliance. And try not to take your child's initial "deafness" as a personal affront.
- Your highly distractible child may also ignore you, but for different reasons. Get down to her level and look her straight in the eye. Tell her in simple terms exactly what you want her to do and ask her to repeat it back to you.

One special note: whatever your child's temperament, don't use food as a behavior management tool—either by bribing her or by forcing her to eat when

I still remember very clearly a scene that took place a few years ago at a bus stop not far from my house. A rather agitated woman was trying to keep her two kids—about five and seven years old—from fighting: "How many times," she said, smacking the older child, "do I have to [smack] tell you [smack] not to hit [smack] your brother [smack]?" Any guesses about where that little boy learned to hit his brother?

Author Doug Spangler suggests that fathers who spank their children are sending some very specific messages:

- It's okay to hit another person.
- It's okay to hit another person who is smaller than you.
- It's okay to hit someone you love.
- It's okay to hit someone when you feel angry and frustrated.
- Physical aggression is normal and acceptable under any circumstances.
- Daddy can't control himself or his temper.
- Fathers are to be feared.
- Children must always be quiet around their fathers.

When it comes to punishment—and just about everything else—parents treat boys and girls very differently. Parents of boys, for example, are more likely to report discipline problems than parents of girls. And boys are far more likely to be spanked, while girls are more likely to be sent to their rooms.

she's not hungry. Children two to five who throw regular tantrums over food are three times more likely to be overweight than kids who don't, according to a 2004 study of children in the San Francisco Bay Area.

Family Matters

The Old College Try

We all know it's going to cost a ton of money to send a child to college. By the time your child graduates from high school, a degree at a state college or university will probably set you back more than $75,000, including room, board, tuition, and basic expenses. A private school degree will cost about $250,000.

Looking at all those zeros—and thinking you're going to have to write a check for the whole thing—is enough to make anyone panic. But take it easy.

You'd never pay cash for a house, right? So why should you consider paying cash for an education that costs about the same? Fortunately, there are a number of excellent ways to finance your child's education, none of which involves having to sell a kidney on the black market.

Traditionally, parents have opened savings accounts in their children's names as a way of putting money aside for the child's education. However, as counterintuitive as it sounds, start by putting as much money as you can into your own retirement accounts. Doesn't make sense? Consider the following:

If you were paying attention to the flight attendant before taking off on your last airplane trip, you know that if those oxygen masks drop from the ceiling, you're supposed to put yours on first, then your child's, right? The idea is that if you can't breathe, you certainly won't be able to help anyone else. Financial guru Eric Tyson once told me the same basic thing about money: take care of your finances first—especially your IRA, 401(k), 403(b), SEP, Keogh, or company-sponsored retirement—and your whole family will be better off.

But that still doesn't clear up the problem of how feathering your own personal retirement account instead of starting a college fund in your child's name will help put him through college. Well, here's how it works:

- Money you invest in your retirement accounts is often at least partially tax-deductible and always grows tax-free until you start withdrawing it. The dollars you invest in an account in your child's name are after-tax dollars, and interest and dividends may be taxable as income or capital gains.
- Plenty of financial-aid options are available: student loans (usually available at below-market rates), grants, fellowships, work-study programs, and so on. But you'll need to qualify. College financial-aid departments assume that about 35 percent of assets held in your child's name will be used for educational expenses each year. However, they assume that only a max of 5.6 percent of your assets (which includes just about everything you own except your retirement accounts) will be available. It's pretty obvious that the less money you have in your child's name, the more financial aid you'll be able to get.
- If you'll be over fifty-nine and a half by the time your child starts college, you may be able to withdraw money from your IRA or other retirement account without incurring any penalties.

Once you've maxed out your retirement opportunities, you can start earmarking money specifically for your child's education. There are two basic options:

- Taxable savings, such as mutual funds, stocks, savings bonds, cash, and money market accounts.

- Nontaxable (or tax-deferred) savings, such as Coverdell ESAs (sometimes called Education IRAs), trustee accounts, and 529 plans.

I'm not going to discuss the taxable options here because, generally speaking, you'll end up with less money. And within the nontaxable category, the 529s are by far the best option for most people, so I'm going to focus on them. The primary reasons are that there are no income restrictions, you can contribute a lot more money, and you have complete control. There are two drawbacks to 529s. First, that if you don't use the money for education, you'll get hit with a nice tax bill along with a penalty. Second, the money has to be spent on higher education only—not on high school.

If you anticipate needing money for high school expenses, you might want to consider a Coverdell Education Savings Account (ESA). Like 529s, ESAs (formerly known as Education IRAs) grow tax free. However, there are very strict eligibility and contribution restrictions. They're also considered the child's asset, which will affect her ability to qualify for financial aid.

Every state offers its own 529 program, which is managed by a large financial services company—Vanguard, Fidelity, Merrill Lynch, and the like. You can choose any program you wish, but there could be some advantages to going

If You're Planning to Pay 100 Percent of Your Child's College Expenses

Despite all this sound financial wisdom, you may still be intent on paying cash for college. If you've got the money—and the desire—to do so, immediately disregard the above advice and start socking money away into an account in your child's name (with you as custodian). That way, you may be able to save at least a little on taxes: until he's fourteen, the first $750 or so of your child's interest and dividends won't be taxed at all. The next $750 will be taxed at the child's rate, which is around 10 percent. Anything over $1,500 gets taxed at your rate. After she's reached the age of fourteen, however, all her income gets taxed at the rate for a single adult.

Whether you decide to include your child's income with yours or file a separate return for her will depend on your specific financial situation. For example, if your child's earnings will bump you into a higher tax bracket, it's probably worth enduring the annoyance of having her file her own return. So check with your accountant to make sure you're doing the right thing for your family.

with the one in your own backyard: contributions may be deductible from your state taxes, some states match contributions, and some penalize you for using another state's plan. You can find out more about your 529 options from the College Savings Plan Network at www.collegesavings.org.

Wills and Trusts

By this time, hopefully, you've got your life insurance situation under control. If not, put this book down right now and call your insurance agent. And while you're waiting for him to call back, you might want to review the section on insurance in *The New Father, A Dad's Guide to the First Year*, pages 258–64.

Knowing that your partner and kids will be financially secure in the event of your death should make you breathe a little easier. But don't relax completely—there are a few other things you have to worry about. For example, if, God forbid, you and your partner are killed tomorrow, who's going to take care of your kids? Who's going to make sure they get the kind of education and upbringing you want them to have? And who's going to get all your stuff?

The answers to these and other horrible but important-to-consider questions are up to you. They're outlined in a will or a trust, or both. Unfortunately, about

Wills

ADVANTAGES

- It's a lot cheaper to prepare a will than a trust.
- You can distribute your assets exactly as you want.
- There is an automatic limit on how long someone has to challenge the terms of your will (varies from state to state). According to some estimates, one in three wills is contested, so this limit could be a very good thing.
- Creditors must make claims within a certain amount of time (again, varies from state to state).
- The activities of your executors, guardians, and trustees are supervised by the court.

DISADVANTAGES

- Probate. This is the name for the process through which everything in a will must go before it is completely straightened out. Probate can easily last as long as eighteen months. And until it's over, your heirs won't have access to most of the assets of your estate.
- Court fees, attorneys' fees, executor fees, accounting fees, and so forth can eat up 3 to 7 percent (or more) of the estate.
- In most cases, probate files are public records. This means that anyone can go down to the courthouse and take a peek at your will.

Living Trusts

ADVANTAGES

- The potential costs and time delays of probate are largely avoided. After your death, your survivors should have control over your assets within a few weeks, without involving the courts.
- The trust document is not public, so no one can see it unless you show it to them.
- A trust can be revoked or changed at any time.
- Assets are distributed as you wish—either directly to your heirs upon your death or gradually over time.
- A living trust allows you to directly manage your assets when you're able, and ensures that they'll be managed according to your wishes if you become incapacitated or incompetent.

DISADVANTAGES

- Trusts generally cost more and take longer to set up than wills. It will also probably cost you a few dollars to transfer ownership of your assets from you personally to the trust. However, all the probate-related expenses that wills require can come to about the same amount as the cost of setting up a trust.
- Improperly prepared, a living trust can cause some serious problems. If the IRS feels that your trust was not properly executed, your estate could wind up in probate—the very situation you were hoping to avoid.
- Since all your assets are transferred during your lifetime from your name into the name of the trust, you are giving up personal ownership in a lot of what you own. This can be tough psychologically.
- Trusts may not reduce your tax liability.

half of all parents with young children don't have either a will or a trust. If you die intestate (meaning without a will, trust, or other document that tells how you want your assets distributed), the details will be handled according to the laws of your state. In most cases, this means that a judge will appoint a guardian for your estate and another one for your children. Chances are, neither of these guardians will be the one you would have chosen.

So which is better? A will? A trust? Actually, the answer may be both. As a new parent, you absolutely, positively need a will to designate a guardian for your child. You can also use a will to distribute your assets, but many experts feel that setting up a revocable living trust is a better alternative. However,

Doing It Yourself

Without ever having gone to law school or earned a degree in accounting, you can probably write a will or set up a living trust by yourself. There are quite a few excellent books and software packages on the market that can take you through the whole process. Several excellent ones are listed in the Resources guide.

But don't be fooled. No lawyer can throw together a will or a trust in five minutes, and neither can you. It will take hours and hours of serious work and education. So if you have a lot of money or a complicated financial situation, or if you just feel more comfortable having a professional take care of things for you, your local or state bar association can give you referrals for attorneys in your area who specialize in wills and trusts. You should also talk to a good tax or probate lawyer if you aren't absolutely sure whether you need a will or a living trust or some other instrument.

because of the time and expense involved, many decline to take advantage of the living trust alternative. Some of the advantages and disadvantages of wills and living trusts are listed on pages 134–35.

As Long as You're Thinking about Depressing Things . . .

- Consider a durable power of attorney. This document (which you may need an attorney to help you prepare) gives someone you designate the power to manage your affairs if you become incapacitated. You can include a health-care directive, which covers such topics as whether or not you want to be kept on life support, if things ever come to that.
- Consider making some gifts. You and your partner can each give away a cumulative total of $1 million during your lifetime without owing any gift tax. This has the effect of reducing the size of your estate as well as the amount of estate taxes that your heirs will have to come up with later. (Estate taxes, by the way, are usually due and payable within nine months of death.) If you have a very large estate, there are a number of other ways to use gifts to reduce or eliminate estate taxes. But the IRS rules are a little complicated, so be sure to check with your accountant or financial adviser.

24–27 MONTHS

Off to School

What's Going On with the Baby

Physically

- Your two-year-old is beginning a yearlong energy spurt and will spend a lot of time "thinking with his feet"—galloping around almost aimlessly, spending a few seconds engaged in some activity or other, then moving on to something else. Sometimes his desire to investigate outstrips his physical abilities, so make sure you keep an eye on him at all times.
- He's quite comfortable with his body and its capabilities; he can run without falling down, walk up and down stairs by himself, balance on one foot for a second or two, jump off a low step, and rock or march in time to music.
- He likes to walk by himself and may resist any attempt to carry him or put him in his stroller.
- His hand-eye coordination is getting much better, and he's now able to use his blocks to build structures that are more complex than towers: houses, forts, horse corrals, long walls.
- He still loves piling and stacking and pouring, and turns pages—and doorknobs—with ease. He can screw on the tops of jars and may even be able to open childproof containers.
- Nevertheless, he still has some problems using one hand independently of the other. "If he holds out an injured finger for bandaging, he tends also to hold out his matching uninjured finger," write child development experts Louise Bates Ames and Frances Ilg.

- As recently as six months ago, your toddler could only focus on things pretty much right in front of his face. Now he's developing peripheral vision. He's also becoming aware of faraway objects such as planes, birds, and distant houses.

Intellectually

- At this stage of his development, he's not able to separate the goal of his actions from the process of achieving it. In other words, *how* he does something is just as important as *what* he does. For example, if he decides to make a painting, he's not just interested in being creative. He's equally interested in making a mess and exploring the feel of the paintbrush on paper. And if he clambers to the top of a climbing structure, it's as much because he likes climbing as to conquer Everest.
- Your child may still push, yell, and grab, and may occasionally bite or hit. But as frustrating as aggressive behavior is to you, try to remember that he's not doing it to be mean or deliberately to cause harm.
- For at least the next year, your child's primary concern will be satisfying his own needs and wants. The fact that your back is killing you and you need a break is of no concern to him if he wants you to lift him into the air for the 327th time. And he's outraged that you're tired of reading him the same book over and over.
- He's quickly mastering quantities—especially "more" and "all gone"—and has a good understanding of cause and effect ("I push the button that Daddy keeps telling me not to touch, and his computer screen suddenly goes black. Cool."). He's got some spatial relationships down, too (under, over, next to, front, back), but he's still working on time. He understands "in a minute" and possibly "today," but "tomorrow," "next week," "last year," and even "yesterday" don't mean much.
- His feelings of power over his surroundings are reinforced by his burgeoning language skills. "He behaves as if the words give him control over the situation . . . as if he controls his own exits and entrances by means of the magic utterance," writes child psychologist Selma Fraiberg. Now that he can say, "Bye-bye," he doesn't mind quite as much when you leave him alone. And he's more cooperative about going to bed when he's the one telling you, "Night-night."

Verbally

- Until now, your child learned about his world physically: he had to touch, feel, or taste things before he could truly understand them. But from here on out, language—questions, answers, explanations—begins to take over as his primary means of acquiring information.

- Your toddler uses 20 to 100 words, his favorites being "again" and "no." But he most likely understands 200 to 500 words, and that number is growing every day. This means that unless you want your toddler to understand your private talks with other adults, you'd better start s-p-e-l-l-i-n-g.
- He's now using adjectives ("I'm a good boy") and verbs ("I go to the store"), but makes some adorable and completely logical mistakes when trying to use past tense ("I drinked milk," or "I runned fast").
- Ames and Ilg have found that despite your toddler's quickly increasing knowledge of the language, he talks mainly to himself; second most to you and other familiar adults; and little if any to other children. Most of what comes out of his mouth is self-initiated (as opposed to being in response to something you've said).
- *Note: Some two-year-olds speak in short, three-to-five-word sentences. Others still speak one word at a time. Unless your child doesn't understand simple questions and requests, there's nothing to worry about.*

Emotionally/Socially

- The first few months of the third year are usually happy ones for both toddler and parents. He's having fewer tantrums and is generally more cooperative than even a few months ago.
- He's becoming much more aware of other people and will gleefully point out every child who walks by and announce, "Baby!" And although he's still not playing with other kids very much (you're still his favorite playmate), he's getting more content to play alongside them, often engaging in the same activity.
- He's getting good at identifying other people's emotions. He knows when you're happy and will laugh with you. He knows when you're sad and will try to cheer you up.
- He already had a rather short attention span, but thanks (in part, at least) to his widening peripheral vision, he's even more distracted than before—after all, there are so many interesting new things crossing his field of view.
- He's still learning a lot about life by imitating you, so be on your best behavior and don't even bother telling him to, "Do as I say, not as I do."
- After playing with their genitals for a while, boys and girls are now establishing a budding gender identity, identifying with (and becoming more attached to) the parent of the same sex.
- He may tell you in advance when his bowel movements are about to occur,

Developmental Red Flags

As before, it's important to remember that the range of "normal" or "average" is a big one. That said, you should call your pediatrician if one or more of the following is true about your two-year-old. My child:

- Doesn't recognize himself in the mirror.
- Doesn't imitate.
- Isn't using two-word sentences.
- Doesn't seem interested in people or things he knows.
- Can't (as opposed to won't) understand basic directions, such as "Give me the book."
- Can't identify familiar objects in pictures or books.

indicating that he's finally ready to begin potty training (see pages 145–49 for more on this).

What You're Going Through

Taking Pride (and Dialing Down Your Disappointment) in Your Child's Accomplishments

One of the best things about being a parent is that it gives you a chance to go back and do all the things you loved to do as a kid, all the things you missed out on, and all the things you did but want to do again. It's like having a second childhood.

The problem is, however, that some parents forget whose childhood it really is and act as though what the child does is somehow a reflection on them. This is especially true if we've fallen into the incredibly common trap of expecting our children to live our unfulfilled dreams and do as well as—or better than—we ever did. You might, for example, want your child to do or like or excel in the same things you did when you were that age. Or you might want your child to do or like or excel in some of the same things you weren't so successful at when you were a kid.

Part of the reason for this is a fear of failing, a fear that the parent hasn't done a good enough job or that he hasn't adequately prepared the child to be a good citizen. "The child acts as a mirror for his parents," according to the Group for the Advancement of Psychiatry. "If his behavior expresses positive aspects of the parents—if he is loving, happy, intelligent, creative—his parents feel that these qualities are reflections of themselves. They feel satisfied with what they have done thus far and more able to go on successfully." At the same time, though, if your child doesn't do well, doesn't live up to your expectations, or gets into trouble, you may feel that you've failed. Your little shot at immortality, at having the world recognize your true greatness, isn't working out quite the way you wanted.

Researchers Barbara and Philip Newman agree. "Parents may experience intense emotional reactions to their child's behavior," they write. "They can make you feel warm, joyful, and proud. They can make you feel furious, guilty, and disgusted. . . . It's one thing if someone else's child is rude or selfish. But if your own child is rude or selfish, intense feelings of anger, disgust, or embarrassment may be stimulated. You may feel pleased by the successes of a neighbor's child, but the success of your own child gives rise to the peculiar parental emotion called 'gloating.'"

Trying to live your life through your kids is a rotten idea for everyone. As with everything else in your life, your child is going to turn out differently than you'd planned. Taking his failures (including his failure to act like you want him to) too personally, setting your expectations too high, or pushing him to be someone he's not (you, for example) puts way too much pressure on him. Wanting to make your child part of whomever you wish you could have been isn't a bad thing to do—it can expose him to all sorts of great opportunities you never had. The key is not to get upset if your child doesn't want to be you. He needs to know that being himself is okay, and he needs the freedom and encouragement to develop into the person he's supposed to develop into. Those are things only you can give him.

The bottom line is that the more realistic your expectations, the better off you'll be. So relax. No matter how well or badly your child does, his successes and failures are *not* a referendum on your parenting skills. You had your turn. Now move over and let someone else have a clear shot at being a child.

Gender Roles

A few months ago, we talked about how easy it is for parents to fall into the trap of treating boys and girls differently. Given that kids learn most of what they know from adults, it shouldn't come as much of a surprise that this kind of gender-based double standard works just as well the other way. In other words, kids treat men and women differently.

"Children learn the different roles that males and females play with children before the age of three," writes researcher Beverly Fagot. "And once this difference has been learned, the children will react to adults outside the home on the

Go to the Doctor—Before It Kills You

One of the most damaging messages we send to our children is that "big boys don't cry"—men don't complain when they're in pain. You can do your part to make sure that stupid idea doesn't creep into the next generation by starting to take better care of yourself now. Unfortunately, when it comes to health care, most men (myself included) are idiots. We don't get regular checkups, we don't do much in the way of preventive care, we ignore symptoms, and we don't get medical attention until the pain is unbearable (or, more likely, until a woman in our life insists). Overall, men are 66 percent less likely to visit a doctor than women, and we make only about one-fourth the number of physician visits for diagnosis, screening, or test results. Twenty-five percent of us say we'd wait as long as possible before seeking help for pain or illness, according to a recent study by the Commonwealth Fund. Nearly 40 percent would hold off for at least a few days, and 17 percent would wait a week. When (if) we finally do seek medical attention, we frequently sabotage our doctors' effectiveness by canceling follow-up appointments and not finishing prescriptions.

The results of all this negligence are startling: for every 100 women who die between the ages of forty-five and sixty-four, 170 men die. Men are twice as likely to die from heart or liver disease, 18 percent more likely to die of a stroke, and 45 percent more likely to die of cancer. And the situation is getting worse. In 1940, women outlived men by an average of 4.4 years. Today, that difference is nearly 7 years.

And once you get to the doctor, will he actually save you? Not necessarily. Almost 70 percent of men over forty who visit the doctor aren't even asked whether they have a family history of prostate cancer, despite the fact that prostate cancer kills about as many men every year as breast cancer kills women. In the past year, 40 percent of men over fifty—who should be getting a prostate exam every single year—weren't even screened by their doctors, 60 percent weren't screened for colon cancer, and half had neither a physical nor a blood cholesterol test. Going to the doctor also won't do much about the fact that four times as many men commit suicide as women, that the victims of violent crime are 75 percent male, that 98 percent of the people who work in the most dangerous jobs in this country are men, and that 94 percent of people who die in the workplace are men. And going to the doctor won't help men discuss private medical issues such as sexual dysfunction, which is often a symptom of a far more serious physical problem—clogged arteries, high blood pressure, or diabetes.

Bottom line? Go to the doctor. You should be having a complete physical at least every two years, and should be screened for prostate and colon cancer every year.

basis of this learned differentiation." Fagot found that in preschool classrooms, kids "elicited many kinds of play behavior from the male teachers; but when children needed materials or needed some caretaking, they approached female teachers."

So what can you do? Basically, just be a good role model. If you are a full participant in your home, and you love, nurture, and care for your children, they—boys and girls alike—will come to realize that men can be parents too. Studies have shown that the more responsibility dads take for household tasks and child care, the less likely their kids will be to have rigid gender roles later in life. Second, make sure your children get the message that men and women and boys and girls are not locked into any particular roles or futures because of their gender. Your children should be free to dream of becoming whatever they want to. This means that besides telling our daughters that they can grow up to be doctors, we need to tell our sons that they can grow up to be nurses (an idea one of my kids had a big problem with, even though the father of one of her best friends was, indeed, a nurse anesthetist).

So if your daughters (like mine) demand Matchbox cars for their birthdays, tear the heads off their Barbie dolls, and refuse to be in the same room with a tutu, let them alone. And if your son wants to play with dolls or wear your partner's nail polish or lipstick, let him alone. A friend who has a particularly gentle, sweet little boy once confided that she was worried about her son's lack of physical aggressiveness and was concerned that he might be gay.

Forcing your child into a particular type of behavior—either to conform with or buck gender stereotypes—can scar him for life. One fun way to dispel some of the myths about gender roles is to listen to *Free to Be, You and Me*. It's more than thirty years old but still widely available on CD, and has some very funny—and subtly educational—bits about gender.

You and Your Toddler

Sleeping Like a Baby?

On average, two-year-olds sleep eleven hours every night and take one two-hour nap during the day. Two-and-a-half-year-olds cut back to ten and a half hours at night and one and a half during the day. Of course, those are just averages; the range is from nine to thirteen hours total per day.

Starting at about two years of age, a lot of toddlers start having sleep problems. Sometimes it's a question of separation anxiety: your child may not want to go to sleep because it means that you'll be leaving him alone. In other cases the issue is that there's so much cool stuff happening in his world that he resents anything that interferes with his desire to explore. Also, there's apparently a clause in the toddler Code of Conduct that requires them to test every rule you make. They'll come up with one clever excuse after another to keep them out of bed: "One more story," "Tummy hurts," "Night-light on," and so on.

The problem here is that getting enough sleep is critical for toddlers—even more than it is for adults. Researchers used to think that the brain rested during sleep, but recent brain imaging shows that the brain is very active at this time, sometimes even more active than when awake. Not getting enough sleep can cause problems with memory, behavior, creativity, attention, and cognitive functioning.

Practicing good sleep hygiene and having regular routines are the best defenses against sleep problems. This means making sure that your child's bed is used only for sleeping—no reading, no games. The bedroom should be as quiet and as dark as possible (a night-light is okay if your toddler needs one).

Most people have bedtime routines, but they're also a good idea at nap times and first thing in the morning, especially if your toddler isn't a morning person. Sleep routines should involve some quiet time, reading, singing songs, or just cuddling and talking about your day. Whatever it is, the routine should be something the child looks forward to.

Keep in mind that it's perfectly normal for your toddler to wake up five or six times during the night. Usually he'll just take a look around, and if everything is where it's supposed to be, he'll go back to sleep. But if things have changed, he may be up all night. For that reason, it's best to put your child to bed when he's awake. Still, as a precaution, you should have a middle-of-the-night routine. (Nightmares require a different approach. See pages 66–67.)

When my oldest was about two, she started getting up in the middle of the night and wanting to play or chat. I took her down to her room, but she'd reappear a few minutes later. We went back and forth four or five times before she finally collapsed. After a week or so of this I told her that she could sleep anywhere she wanted, just as long as it wasn't in my room. As if to prove a point, she elected to sleep on the floor just outside my door. After a few nights of stumbling over her on the way to the bathroom, she eventually gave up and went back to her own bed. She's slept like a rock ever since.

Is it possible for a child to get too much sleep? Generally speaking, the answer is no. Toddlers have a very Zen approach, dropping off when they're tired. It is possible, though, for a toddler to sleep so much during the day that he's not tired enough to fall asleep at night. Combine that with an early wake-up time and you end up back at square one, with not enough sleep.

Potty Training: The Real Thing

Looking at your toddler and thinking back at how much he's grown and developed over the past two years can be a bittersweet experience. On one hand, you love how big and independent he's become. On the other, you sometimes miss his younger, more dependent days. But no matter how fondly you recall your child's infancy, there's one part of his childhood that you probably can't wait to put behind you: changing diapers.

So is your child ready to be toilet-trained? As basic as it seems to us adults, toilet training is actually a pretty complicated process that requires physical and intellectual maturity. How can you tell if he's ready? If most or all of the following statements are true for you, you're good to go. My toddler . . .

- Seems interested in what my partner, I, or others do in the bathroom.
- Likes to do things "myself."
- Often wakes up dry from a nap, or can at least stay dry for a few hours at a time.
- Doesn't have overnight bowel movements.
- Is curious about what's in his diapers.
- Knows the words our family uses for bowel movements and urination (limit the vocabulary to words you won't feel embarrassed to say in public).
- Gives indications that he's aware he's filling his diaper—could be grunting, grimacing, going off to a private corner, or actually coming right out and saying so.
- Indicates that he's uncomfortable in wet or dirty diapers.
- Can and will follow directions.
- Is physically able to pull his pants up and down by himself.
- Has bowel movements at about the same time every day.

If most of the above statements are not true of your child, check back in a few weeks. Trying to toilet-train a child who's not ready can actually extend the process.

READY, SET, GO!

Typically, toilet training happens in this order: overnight bowel control, daytime bowel control, daytime bladder control, overnight bladder control. Here's how to get the process going:

1. Leave a potty seat on the floor in the bathroom. Tell the child the little one is for him, the big one is for grown-ups. Put a stuffed animal on your child's seat, just to give him a preview. Twins (and greater multiples) often want to use the bathroom at the same time, so get each one his own seat.

2. After a week or so, have the child sit on the potty seat in his clothes while you sit on yours (clothed or otherwise). You might want to read a story to keep him there.
3. After another week, ask the child a few times a day if you can take his diapers off so he can sit on his special toilet. You sit on your toilet as well and tell him that you, Mommy, Grandpa, Grandma, and everyone else he knows do this every day. My younger daughter loved this stage and would sit on her potty seat for a few minutes shouting "Peeeeeeee!" (but without actually peeing).
4. A week later, take off the child's dirty diaper and dump the contents into the toilet while he's watching. Emphasize that just like there's a special place for everything else, the toilet is the special place for urine and BM, and that that's where grown-ups put theirs. Do not flush in front of the child (see opposite page).
5. Let the baby run around naked during the day for ten to twenty minutes (if you have expensive carpets or flooring, you may want to do this outside). Tell him he can go to the potty anytime he wants to.
6. Over the course of a few days, leave the baby's diapers off longer and longer. Remind him every half hour or so to go to the bathroom. If he has an accident, don't make a big deal about it—it happens to everyone. Most daytime accidents are the result of the child being so caught up in another activity that he doesn't want to stop.
7. Don't worry about night training for a while—at least until the child is regularly dry after waking from his naps and occasionally dry in the morning. Overnight bladder control doesn't usually come for a year or so after daytime control.
8. Make sure your child knows how to wash his hands properly.

BOYS AND GIRLS DO IT DIFFERENTLY . . . AND SO DO THEIR PARENTS

Ninety percent of girls are bowel-trained by two years, seven months, while 90 percent of boys aren't bowel-trained until three years, one month—a difference of six months. Ninety percent of girls are bladder-trained by three years, six months, while 90 percent of boys take until four years, ten months—a difference of sixteen months. (These numbers are up over twelve months from the 1950s, largely because disposable diapers are so great at keeping babies dry and comfortable that they have less motivation to want to get out of them.)

Although boys lag behind in toilet training, there is no significant biological

Toilet Training Success Boosters

- Get the right equipment. Child's potty seats should be low enough that both feet can rest firmly on the floor. Skip the urine deflectors (shields that attach to the front of the seat to keep boys' urine inside the toilet). They seem like a great idea but can sometimes hurt boys who don't sit down exactly right, and the last thing you want is to have your child associate going to the bathroom with pain. Some seats have multiple stages: they start out as a child-sized seat that sits on the floor, then convert to an adapter that attaches to a regular toilet seat. Some even play music when there's butt-to-potty contact.
- Don't flush in front of the child. While some kids may be fascinated and want to flush over and over and over, others may be terrified, believing that a part of them is being sucked down the toilet (see pages 58–59 for more on fears).
- Minimize or eliminate liquids within an hour of bedtime. This will increase the chances that your child will wake up dry—something that will boost his confidence.
- Learn to recognize the signs. When you see that knees-together, bouncing-up-and-down dance, find a bathroom fast.
- Be positive, but not too positive. Too much excitement about the contents of a diaper can give a toddler the idea that what he's produced is somehow valuable—a twisted notion that may result in him wanting to keep it for himself (inside his body if necessary).
- Don't force it. Children who feel pressured sometimes try to regain control of the situation by not going to the bathroom at all. This can lead to constipation or other conditions that will need to be treated by your pediatrician. If you think your child is ready but just needs a little encouragement, try a few of the books on page 153.
- Be flexible. Some regression is perfectly normal, especially if you've moved, changed babysitters, or had a death in the family, or the child has been sick.
- Make it fun. Boys in the early stages of toilet training are notoriously bad at aiming. Putting some Cheerios or other targets in the water, or adding some blue food coloring (which turns green when the yellow urine hits it), can make urinating more fun for your son and less messy for you.

reason for the delay. The real reason girls are "trained" sooner may have more to do with the trainer than the trainee. Women have traditionally done the training, and girls have an easier time imitating their mothers than boys do. In fact, a lot of boys resist even trying.

It's completely normal for boys this age to start developing a male gender identity and rebel against their mothers (the same way girls this age start developing a female gender identity and rebel against their fathers). So a little boy may balk at sitting down when urinating (it's no fun to sit when you can stand), and may resist Mom's instructions on how to grasp his penis—after all, she doesn't even have one!

Besides being done with potty training earlier, girls also have a much shorter lapse between bowel and bladder training (eleven months) than boys (twenty-one months). This difference may be the result of girls' not being taught to differentiate between the two functions. (Girls can't see either their

THE TRADITIONAL MALE MODEL	THE TRADITIONAL FEMALE MODEL
♦ Urinary control is taught as a stand-up procedure with emphasis on skill, mastery, and fun.	♦ Sitting down for all elimination, wiping.
♦ Wiping only after bowel movements.	♦ Wiping after both kinds.
♦ Active participation and modeling by the father and/or other males.	♦ Use of the mother herself on the toilet as a model for imitation.
♦ Encouragement to touch and control the penis so as to aim the urinary stream.	♦ Discouragement from touching self.
♦ Greater tolerance for absence of bathroom privacy.	♦ Greater need for bathroom privacy.
♦ Control, function, and naming of urine is sharply differentiated from control, function, and naming of feces (boys tend to talk about "making pee pee" as opposed to "pooping").	♦ Minimal distinction between bladder and bowel training in vocabulary, timing, or technique (girls tend to talk about "going to the bathroom").

urination or defecation and wipe after both, while boys can see their urine—and are encouraged to aim it—and wipe only after moving their bowels.)

Men and women traditionally have very different ways of teaching toilet training. As you can see, "The female mode is compatible with and enhancing to the formation of a female gender identity," writes Moisy Shopper, a child psychologist who did an exhaustive study of toilet training (don't ask why). "The child is encouraged to be like mother; by seeing mother's eliminative functioning, they have an intimacy with each other's bodies that fosters the girl's gender and sexual identity." Using the female mode to train boys "in no way enhances the boy's potential for further body differentiation or supports the sexual differences between him and his mother," writes Shopper. "In fact, in many ways it is antithetical to the boy's maturation."

FOR BOYS ONLY

Basically, the primary role in toilet training boys should be yours. This, of course, does not mean that your partner isn't capable of training your son (except for not being able to provide a model for how to urinate standing up, there's no reason she can't) or that you can't train your daughter. Plenty of women support their sons' budding masculinity and encourage them to urinate standing up, holding on to their own penises.

A small number of mothers, however, won't allow their sons any autonomy, according to Dr. Shopper . And they feel "that they must hold their sons' penises as they pee. This is a rotten idea because your son may begin to question whether his penis belongs to him or to his mother, and that's just how serious sexual problems develop later in life."

When boys have a male model, they are much less conflicted about becoming toilet-trained, since training no longer carries the connotations of gaining their mother's love, submitting to her, and becoming like her.

Reading

CREATING A READING ENVIRONMENT

Having books and other reading materials readily available to your child will help him make books part of his daily life. And one of the best ways to do this is to be sure there are plenty of books on shelves or in racks that he can reach without having to ask for help.

The goal here is to have your child view reading as something he can do whenever he wants, without fear of being punished. So give him free and open access to board books and any other inexpensive or easily replaceable books you won't mind getting torn up or stuck together with drool. Keep the books you had as a child (and any others that you want to keep in one piece) far, far away and take them out only for special occasions.

SOME ADVANCED READING CONCEPTS

By now you've probably gotten into a nice, regular routine with your child, reading together in a quiet place at times when you won't be interrupted. As you're reading (or planning your reading), make a conscious effort to keep the experience as interesting as possible for both of you. Here are some things to keep in mind:

- **Tone**. It's better to read stories that are slightly too advanced for your child (and explain a word or concept now and then) than read ones that are too easy.
- **Variety**. Children's book illustrators use a huge variety of techniques: line drawings, photos, watercolors, charcoal, paint, collages, woodcut, needlepoint. Expose your child to as many approaches as possible and discuss what's unique about each of them.

"Surely there must be a video of this?"

- **Talk**. If your toddler interrupts the story to ask questions, follow his lead. You can interrupt the reading too. Questions like "How do you think he's feeling?" "Why did the bunny do that?" or "What's going to happen when she opens the closet door?" will help your child develop critical thinking skills and encourage him to be a more active participant.
- **Act out**. Instead of just reading *Little Red Riding Hood* for the 639th time, assign roles and switch off every once in a while—sometimes you're Little Red Riding Hood, sometimes you're the wolf.
- **Set an example**. Let him see you and your partner reading for pleasure.

Here are a few more books to check out from your local library or add to your collection:

Alfie Gets in First (and other Alfie books), Shirley Hughes and Bert Kitchen
Animals of the Night, Merry Banks
The Baby Blue Cat and the Smiley Worm Doll, Ainslie Pryor
Basket, Ella George Lyon
Bathwater's Hot (and others in the series), Shirley Hughes
Blue Hat, Green Hat (and others in the series), Sandra Boynton
Brown Bear, Brown Bear, What Do You See? (and others), Bill Martin Jr.
Carl (and the other Carl books), Alexandra Day
Corduroy (and others in the series), Don Freeman
Eat Up, Gemma, Sarah Hayes
Emma's Pet, David McPhail
Follow Me (and many others), Nancy Tafuri
General Store, Rachel Field
The Great Big Enormous Turnip, Alexei Tolstoy
In the Small, Small Pond, Denise Fleming
Kate's Car, Kay Chorao
Let's Make Rabbits, Leo Lionni
The Little Engine That Could, Watty Piper
Millions of Cats, Wanda Gag
The Mitten (and many others), Jan Brett
Miss Mary Mack (and others), Nadine Bernard Westcott
Moonlight (and many others), Jan Ormerod
Mr. Gumpy's Motor Car (and others in the series), John Burninghan
My World, Margaret Wise Brown
Peter Spier's Little Cats (and many others in the series), Peter Spier
Pretend You're a Cat, Jean Marzollo

Rosie's Walk, Pat Hutchins
The Runaway Bunny, Margaret Wise Brown
Shopping Trip (and others), Helen Oxenbury
Umbrella, Taor Yashima
A Very Busy Spider (and others), Eric Carle
A Very Special House, Ruth Krauss
Watching Foxes, Jim Arnosky
We're Going on a Bear Hunt, Michael Rosen
Where's My Teddy?, Jez Alborough
Who Said Red? Mary Serfozo
Yellow Ball, Molly Bang

ESPECIALLY FOR OLDER SIBLINGS

These books deal in a particularly sensitive way with the special concerns of kids who are suddenly (and usually against their will) displaced from the center of the universe by a baby sister or brother.

A Baby Sister for Frances, Russell Hoban
And to Think That We Thought We'd Never Be Friends, Mary Ann Hoberman
The Difference between Babies and Cookies, Mary Hanson
101 Things to Do with a Baby, Jan Ormerod
What Shall We Do With the Boo-Hoo Baby? Jonathan Allen

CONCEPTS

A You're Adorable, Martha Alexander
Alphabet under Construction, Denise Fleming
Anno's Counting House (and others), Mitsumasa Anno
Colors (and other concept books), Jan Pienkowski
Duck, David Lloyd
Of Colors and Things (and other photography books), Tana Hoban
26 Letters and 99 Cents, Tana Hoban

FOLK TALES

Fables, Arnold Lobel
Little Red Riding Hood, James Marshall
The Three Little Pigs, Joseph Jacobs

TRANSITIONS: GOING TO SCHOOL, BIG-KID BED, SLEEP, OR DAY CARE

Billy's Big-Boy Bed, Phyllis Limbacher Tildes
Going to Day Care, Fred Rogers
The Goodbye Book, Kay Chorao
Howard and the Sitter Surprise, Priscilla Paton
My New Bed, Stan and Jan Berenstain
My Nursery School, Harlow Rockwell
Time for Bed, Mem Fox

POETRY/RHYMES

Egg Thoughts and Other Frances Songs, Russel Hoban
Getting to Know You: Rogers and Hammerstein Favorites, Rosemary Wells
The Land of Nod and Other Poems for Children, Robert L. Stevenson
One Fish, Two Fish, Red Fish, Blue Fish (and anything else), Dr. Seuss
The Owl and the Pussycat, Jan Brett
Whiskers and Rhymes, Arnold Lobel

TOILET TRAINING

Everyone Poops, Taro Gomi
Koko Bear's New Potty, Vicki Lansky
Max's Potty, Harriet Ziefert
No More Diapers, J. G. Brooks
On Your Potty, Virginia Miller

Family Matters

Family Planning

For a lot of couples, whether to have another child isn't really a question; it's a given. For others, though, it's more complicated. Quite often one spouse wants a second (or third) child, while the other isn't nearly as excited about the prospect—for a variety of reasons. Although I wanted a second child quite a bit, my memories of the incredibly long and painful labor my wife endured delivering our first baby made it almost impossible for me to consider putting her through another similar experience.

Besides the pain aspect of pregnancy and childbirth, plenty of other factors may affect your decision (or at least how you vote when you and your partner get around to discussing the issue):

AGE DIFFERENCE BETWEEN CHILDREN: 9 to 18 months

ADVANTAGES

- Because they're close in age, there's a better chance the kids will be great playmates.
- Your first child will adjust to the change more easily than if he were older; he won't really know what's going on and won't feel quite as displaced.

DISADVANTAGES

- You may not like having two kids in diapers at the same time.
- Your older child is still really a baby. He has plenty of baby needs and is going to have a tough time waiting for you to meet them.
- "You can expect her to act very clingy at times, perhaps alternating with aggressive behavior towards you or others," says nurse practitioner Meg Zweiback.
- Because they're close in age, they may compete with each other more.
- Babies conceived less than six months after the birth of a previous child are 40 percent more likely to be born prematurely or underweight, according to a study in the *New England Journal of Medicine*.

- Do you really like being a parent? Is it as much fun as you thought it would be? Is it more—or less—work than you thought? Generally speaking, a second child is less stressful than the first; you'll feel like an old hand when the second baby does things that made you panic with the first one. As a result, you'll probably enjoy the second child's childhood more than the first one's.
- Can you afford it? And if you can't, does it really make a difference? My parents, who were both starving grad students when I was born, claim that I spent my first two years sleeping in a dresser drawer.
- How are you and your partner going to divide the labor around the house? Are you both satisfied with the way things got handled the first time around? Two kids are going to be more than twice the work of one: each requires a certain amount of care and feeding, plus there's the additional job of keeping the two of them from killing each other.

AGE DIFFERENCE BETWEEN CHILDREN: 18 to 36 months

ADVANTAGES

- This is the most common age difference in the country, so some of your friends will probably have kids similarly spaced.
- This spacing leads to a lower incidence of low birth weight.
- Your older child is now more capable of waiting a bit before having his needs satisfied.
- The older child is more articulate and can entertain himself for limited amounts of time.
- The older baby is mature enough to enjoy the new baby and also to enjoy time away from you without seeing it as a threat.

DISADVANTAGES

- The two kids are far enough apart to have very different schedules, activities, and interests. This means that if you're doing the driving you'll probably end up feeling like a taxi driver.
- The older child is more likely to see the younger one as an invader. As a result, there's going to be more friction between the two.

AGE DIFFERENCE BETWEEN CHILDREN: 36+ months

ADVANTAGES

- The older child is even more articulate, more able to satisfy his own needs, and less likely to try to hurt the new child.
- The older child can—and may very well want to—help out quite a bit.
- A child whose sibling is more than four years younger may feel less sibling rivalry.

DISADVANTAGES

- A child who has been an only child for so long may have a very difficult time sharing you and your partner with anyone else.

♦ Do you have brothers or sisters, or were you an only child? How did you like growing up that way? Do you think your child would be better or worse off with a younger sibling?

♦ Your age and your partner's age. If she's close to (or over) forty, getting pregnant won't be as easy as it was the first time, and there's a greater chance of conceiving a child with a birth defect. In addition, some research shows that children of older dads have a slightly higher chance of being schizophrenic than children of younger dads.

- Do you think you'll be able to love the second baby as much as the first? This is one of the most common concerns of prospective second-time (and beyond) parents. The simple answer is that your capacity to love your children is infinite.
- The pregnancy is going to be different, especially for your partner. First, because the physical changes are familiar, she might not be as fascinated by what's going on inside her body. Second, many of the physical changes may happen sooner than they did the first time: she'll probably "show" sooner, she may gain more weight this time, and she may be more tired (being a parent is exhausting enough; trying to do it while you're pregnant is something altogether different).
- Try not to let the first baby's temperament influence your decision—it has absolutely no influence on how your next baby will turn out.

FILLING THE GAP

Once you make your decision to have another child, you will probably need to decide on how far apart to space them (see chart on pages 154-155).

Looking for Preschools

During the first eighteen months of your child's life, he should be the focus of his caregiver's attention. "Without this confirmation of self-importance, the child may experience insecurity that, in turn, will encumber the emergence of creative behavior," says psychologist John Rosemond. But over the second eighteen months, your child's needs change, and he needs to be taught—gradually—that he isn't the center of the universe.

Most preschools begin taking kids at around thirty-three months (two years, nine months). But in many major metropolitan areas, good preschools fill up months, sometimes even years, before the start of the fall semester. So get your applications together now. (It may seem kind of absurd to have to apply to get into a preschool, but if author Robert Fulgum is right, and you really learn everything you'll ever need to know in kindergarten, maybe it's not so crazy after all.)

THE CHOICES

There are literally dozens of preschool opportunities in your community, most of which fall into one of the following categories:

- **Cooperative**. The parents help out a lot, volunteering in the classroom, organizing activities, creating the curriculum.
- **Play-based**. Exactly what it sounds like.
- **Orthodox**. The teachers are trained in a specific method or philosophy of educating young children. This may involve using certain equipment or teaching methods. Montessori is the most common.
- **Free-form**. The school may include the best (or the worst) of a variety of educational philosophies.
- **Academic**. Structured classes in traditional subjects (math, language). Many early childhood development experts think this may be too much, too soon.

As with anything to do with education, preschools have lately become the subject of much controversy. One side cites research that "proves" that preschools are mediocre at best and that too many hours in preschool can lead to behavior problems, jeopardize toddlers' attachment to their parents, and set them on a path toward a life of delinquency and crime. The other side cites research that reaches the opposite conclusion, that kids who enter preschool as toddlers are more self-reliant and confident and do better in school. The contradictions are enough to drive you nuts.

Having looked at dozens of studies on the short- and long-term effects of preschool, I've reached a few conclusions:

- Family problems such as stress and insufficient income cause at least as many problems as full-time day care does. In other words, if you and your partner really need to work full time, reducing your (or her) hours at work so one of you can take on more child care could cause financial strain and tension at home that in turn would have a negative impact on your child.
- Your child will do best in a preschool that is safe and stimulating, where child-adult ratios are low, and the staff is experienced and educated. Yes, some preschools out there are bad. But you don't have to send your child there. If you know what to look for and what questions to ask, you can ensure a loving, caring learning environment for your child.
- Compared to other child-care options, preschools have some distinct advantages and disadvantages. A few are listed on page 158.

WHAT TO CONSIDER WHEN CONSIDERING PRESCHOOLS

Perhaps the most important factor is your child's temperament and how it meshes with what the school has to offer (see the chart on pages 160–61). Another important factor is stability—particularly that of the children. "In

ADVANTAGES

- Most teachers have some experience in early childhood education and development.
- Children learn to socialize and get along with people who aren't in their family.
- State or local licensing ensures that the school will meet at least minimum health and safety standards.
- Usually less expensive than a nanny or other in-home care option.
- Schools probably have more equipment and a larger play area than you do. They also have a structured program that should expose your child to a wide variety of activities.
- You might meet some other parents who have similarly aged children.
- You don't have to worry about a nanny or sitter getting sick and leaving you without care.

DISADVANTAGES

- Your child may have to be potty-trained before being accepted.
- Your child may be sent home if he's sick.
- You may need to make a year-long commitment to a minimum number of days per week.
- The child-teacher ratio may be higher than you'd like. This may mean that your child could get less individual attention than with a nanny or other caregiver.
- Schools may be closed on holidays or for training day, which could leave you scrambling to find a caregiver.
- The school's scheduled operating hours may not work well for you, or there could be extra charges for early drop-off or late pickup.

child-care settings, the availability of a stable group of age-mates results in more complex, coordinated play," say the Newmans. "Children who have had many changes in their child-care arrangements are less likely to engage in complex social pretend play."

GENERAL GUIDELINES

Because finding the right preschool is the first big decision you'll have to make about your child's education, it will probably take a while, and you shouldn't give up until you've got exactly what you were looking for or have come as close as you possibly can. At a minimum, the day-care center you choose for your child should comply with your state's rules and regulations. But standards vary wildly from state to state, so licensing and accreditation are not necessarily the guarantees of quality that they ought to be. On the national level, however, the National Association for the Education of Young Children (NAEYC) accredits programs that meet their extremely high standards, and you can get referrals to accredited providers in your area at their Web site, www.naeyc.org. Another great source of high-quality referrals is Child Care Aware (www.childcareaware.org or 800-424-2246).

But accreditation and assurances of quality aren't all there is. You should also keep the following general guidelines in mind (some of which were suggested by the NAEYC, Child Care Aware, and the American Academy of Pediatrics):

RATIOS

The younger the kids allowed in the preschool, the lower the teacher-child ratio should be. In a typical preschool, kids' ages range from two and a half to five. Overall, there should be no more than seven kids to each adult caregiver, and the total size of the group (not including the teachers) shouldn't exceed twenty.

NUTRITION AND HEALTH

- No smoking on the premises.
- Proof of immunization required of each child.
- If the school provides meals and/or snacks, they should be varied, wholesome, and nutritious. Menus should be available in advance.
- Rest and nap times should be scheduled, and each child should have a clean, individual place to sleep. There should also be special quiet activities for kids who don't nap.
- Teachers wear disposable gloves and clean hands with soap and water or alcohol gel whenever changing diapers. They should also wash their hands after helping a child go to the bathroom and before touching food.
- Parents should be notified immediately of any accident or contagious illness, and there should be a clear policy for what to do (isolation, for starters) with kids who get sick while at school.
- Teachers should give medication to children only with a parent's written permission.

Temperament and Preschool

TRAIT	SPECIAL CONSIDERATIONS
ENERGY LEVEL	
• High	• Your child will need lots of room to run around, plenty of indoor activities for rainy days, lots of ways to burn off excess energy. He will, however, need some moderately structured activities. Look for a program that has many kids his age or older: he'll admire their skills and want to emulate them. And make sure the teachers' energy level is at least as high as your child's.
• Low	• This child needs a quieter, smaller setting, and small groups.
• Moderate (especially those who are also a bit slow-to-warm)	• Your child will probably stick to the sidelines for a few days, watching and learning. He'll jump in after about a week. He likes more structure and predictability, and doesn't do well in large preschools, especially if there are a lot of more active kids his age—they can be frightening.
SENSORY THRESHOLD	
• Low	• Look for a fairly calm, subdued, relaxed environment. Lots of noise, colors, and activity can frighten your child.

- Emergency numbers should be clearly posted near a phone.
- At least one teacher (but all would be better) should have up-to-date first aid and CPR certifications.

GENERAL CLEANLINESS

- Hot running water, soap, alcohol gel, and paper towels should be available—at kid level—and should be used after going to the bathroom and before all meals and snacks.
- The entire area—kitchen, tabletops, floors, sleep areas—should be clean. All garbage cans, diaper pails, and bathrooms should be cleaned thoroughly and regularly disinfected. So should toys that tend to end up in toddlers' mouths.

TRAIT	SPECIAL CONSIDERATIONS
ATTENTION SPAN	
• Short	• This child will need a constantly changing array of things to do and play with. Look for a staff that is large enough so that a teacher can spend extra time with your child to expose him to new things.
PREDICTABILITY	
• High	• This child will need a regular schedule, regular meal and nap times, and so forth.
• Low	• This child doesn't need much in the way of scheduling, but should have some anyway.
ADAPTABILITY	
• Slow	• Avoid schools with rigid schedules and highly structured activities. Also avoid unstructured schools. Look for teachers who will make a special effort to involve your child and introduce him to new materials slowly. Make sure you can stay with your child for a few minutes each morning (for at least the first week or so) to help ease his transition.
• Moderately slow-to-adapt, intense	• This child may occasionally bite or hit other children. This will fade as he becomes more articulate. He may be upset when you drop him off at school and just as upset when you come to pick him up.

SAFETY

- The facility should be licensed by your state.
- Outlets, heaters, and radiators should be covered.
- Equipment should be up-to-date and meet current safety codes.
- Cleaning fluids, medicines, and any other potentially dangerous substances should be kept in places inaccessible to the children.
- There should be an emergency plan, including regular fire drills. Fire extinguishers should be available as required.
- The school should have a plan for dealing with violent children. While some hitting, pushing, and biting is pretty normal for kids this age, anything more serious (stabbing, hitting with large objects, or repeated, unprovoked attacks) is not.

A Few Preschool Red Flags

As far as I'm concerned, any school that doesn't satisfy all the qualifications listed on these pages should be viewed with suspicion. Beyond that, though, here are a few things that should make you take a prospective preschool off your list completely and run the other way.

- Parents are not allowed to drop in unannounced. You need to call before visiting or coming to pick up your child.
- Your child is unhappy or scared after more than a few months.
- The staff seems to change every day.
- The staff ignores any of your concerns.
- You child reports being hit or mistreated, or you hear similar reports from other parents. Check this one out thoroughly, though. Kids have been known to fabricate stories.

- Children should not be allowed to ride in any moving vehicle without a properly installed car seat.
- Children should be adequately supervised on all field trips—even if it's only a nature walk around the block.
- Children should not be released to any adult whose name is not on a written list provided by you and your partner.
- Outdoor play areas should be carefully supervised.
- Outdoor areas should be safe from animal contamination (for example, the sandbox should be tightly covered).

PROGRAM

- The school's program and philosophy should be a good match to what you want and what your child needs. If you have a child with special needs that can't be accommodated at a mainstream preschool, contact the National Dissemination Center for Children with Disabilities at (800) 695-0285 or www.nichcy.org, a wonderful source of referrals and resources.
- To the extent possible, substitute teachers should be familiar to the kids.
- Children should have daily opportunities to participate in a variety of active and quiet activities, including free play, age-appropriate academics, art, music, and group and individual play.
- Children should have adequate time to play outside every day, weather permitting. There should be plenty of space for active, physical play, such as climbing, running, and jumping.

- Indoor areas must be large enough to accommodate all the kids at one time. The area should be well organized so kids know where things go and what happens where. There should be a wide variety of age-appropriate toys, books, and materials. And there should be more than one of each toy so that the kids don't have to wait in long lines to play.
- Parents should be welcome at any time, without advance notice. When you visit, pay attention to how the children behave. If they basically ignore you, that's good news: it means that they're involved and interested in what they're doing. If they come running over, that could mean that they're not being given activities that are stimulating enough.
- Overall, the preschool should be a place you wish you could have gone to when you were a kid.
- If you need child care but can't afford it, check out Head Start (www.headstartinfo.org) or Even Start (www.evenstart.org).

STAFF

- Should have completed some college level work in early childhood education and child development.
- Should seem to genuinely care for the children.
- Should be available to answer the children's questions and get down to their level when speaking with them.
- Should give you regular reports on how and what your child is doing.

EASING THE TRANSITION

Several months before our older daughter's first day of preschool, my wife and I started trying to get her ready. We'd visited the school a number of times; the principal had sent us a five-page handout on how tough this first big separation can be for kids; and my wife and I spent hours with our daughter reading books about other kids' first days, talking about who else would be at school, telling her about our own school experiences, and describing the fun things she would get to do. We bought her new clothes in her favorite colors and a Little Mermaid lunch box and reassured her over and over that we'd pick her up every day right after lunch and that, of course, we still loved her.

Even the school itself tried to help ease the transition. A few weeks before school started, one of the teachers came over to the house and spent hours playing with our daughter and getting to know her. She also brought along a Polaroid camera and left our daughter a snapshot of her with her new teacher. And on the morning of the fateful first day, we gave her honeycomb and cookies shaped like her favorite alphabet letters, to remind her that learning should

"Think of it as a brief interlude in, as opposed to a major disruption of, your life."

be a sweet experience. By the time we got in the car for the drive to school on the first day, I felt pretty confident that we had prepared her both psychologically and emotionally for this milestone.

As soon as we got inside the building, I knew I was right. My daughter caught sight of a few of her friends and the teacher who had come to our house, and promptly disappeared, laughing and giggling. I shouted a good-bye (which she barely acknowledged), reminded her when I'd be back to pick her up, and walked out to the car.

Some kids won't even notice when you've gone on the first day of school. Others will freak out completely. Either way, here are some absolute musts (and must-nots) for the first days:

- Prepare yourself. For more on this, see pages 234–36.
- No matter how well adjusted your child seems, never just drop him off on the first day. Go inside and get him settled.
- Never sneak out, even if he's deeply involved in some activity.
- Create a good-bye routine (kiss, do a quick drawing together, wave bye-bye through the window).

- Don't chastise your child for crying. Reassure him that you love him, and that you'll be back.
- Don't be upset if your child comes home covered with dirt, paint, glue, sparkles, or even an occasional bruise. It means he's interacting with other people and having fun.

PASSING THE BUCK

Coincidentally, the same week that my older daughter was admitted to preschool, a friend of mine was admitted to the University of San Francisco's medical school. My friend was griping about how much her tuition cost and was surprised when I wasn't more sympathetic. But when I told her that my daughter's preschool was more expensive than med school, she stopped. Naturally, not all preschools cost as much as medical schools, but it's not going to be cheap. If you have the money, great. But most of us could use (or wouldn't turn down) a little financial assistance. And asking your employer to help out a little may be your best bet. Here are a few alternatives:

- Direct financial assistance. Your employer pays for all or part of your expenses at the preschool of your choice.
- Negotiated discounts. Your employer—maybe in conjunction with other local employers—can negotiate group rates or discounts with a nearby preschool.
- Employee salary reductions or set-asides. You can have your employer put up to $5,000 of your pretax salary into a Dependent Care Assistance Plan (DCAP). These plans also go by other names, such as Flex. This will enable you to reduce your preschool expenses by paying for them with before-tax dollars instead of after-tax ones. Your employer will save money too, since he or she won't have to pay social security tax or unemployment insurance on your DCAP money.

Of course, asking your boss—or anyone else, for that matter—for help isn't easy. In fact, the reason employees most often give for not asking their bosses to get involved in employee day-care problems is fear of losing their jobs.

Nevertheless, it's worth a try. The first thing to do is to remind your boss that some assistance programs won't cost the company a cent (see above). Then read your employer this quote from the Child Care Action Campaign (CCAC): "Studies have shown that working parents' anxiety about their child care arrangements erodes their productivity—and directly affects employers' profit lines." And if you need a little more ammo, tell them about the recent study that found that employees of companies offering dependent-care services were more productive in at least one way: they were late to work less often because of family issues, they left work early less often, or they were able to concentrate better on their work.

If those approaches don't work, follow the CCAC's advice and:

- Talk to other employees. Do any of them have trouble finding or paying for a good preschool? How do their worries affect their productivity?
- Find out what other employers in your field are doing about preschool. Some prospective employees are making decisions on which companies to work for based on benefits, and if the competition offers a more family-friendly environment, your company will have to follow suit.
- If you're in a union, speak to your union rep. Have other employers bargained for family-friendly benefits? You may be able to include some in the next contract negotiation.
- Encourage other employees to let management know about child-care problems.

27–30 MONTHS

Time for a Financial Tune-up

What's Going On with the Baby

Physically

- You may have noticed that your child looks different lately—less like a baby and more like a little kid. Her arms and legs are growing much faster than the rest of her body, which makes her head seem less out of proportion. Her face is not as round, she's lost most of her baby potbelly, and those adorable little fat pads on the bottoms of her feet are almost gone.
- She's got a very busy schedule—lots of things to do and places to go. And you'll be busy too, chasing around after her to make sure she's safe.
- She can kick a ball in the direction she wants it to go and may be able to pedal a tricycle.
- She's getting much better at dressing herself and is especially interested in shoes (although she's still more than a year away from being able to lace them up). She can, however, manipulate Velcro fasteners, which she'll do over and over and over.
- Your child's emotions are more frequently expressed physically than verbally. When she's happy, she may jump up and down with glee; when angry, she may throw something down.

Intellectually

- "Self-control is still dependent upon factors outside himself, namely the approval or disapproval of his parents," writes child psychologist Selma Fraiberg. Your child is still a long way away from developing a conscience or a true ability to regulate her own negative impulses. But this is an important first step.

- Another by-product of her improving memory is her new ability to imitate you when you aren't there with her. Welcome to the true beginning of fantasy play.
- She continues to choose less physical and more intellectual ways of solving problems. She does a lot less by trial and error and a lot more by thinking things through. For example, rather than pull you over to the bookshelf and point to the book she wants you to get down, she may simply tell you, "Bring me book."
- Your toddler is able to focus on incredibly tiny details—ones you probably would never notice. In the middle of the 400th read-through of *Goldilocks and the Three Bears*, my older daughter suddenly stopped me and pointed out that the artist had made an error: in a picture of the bears' breakfast table, both the daddy bear's porridge (which is supposedly too hot) and the mommy bear's porridge (supposedly too cold) were steaming. What an outrage!
- She's now able to distinguish a group of two objects from a group of more than two. She may not, however, have a word for the larger group.

Verbally

- Your toddler is probably increasing her vocabulary by two to five words per day. She's so thrilled with the sound of her own voice that she'll repeat her new words over and over, including quite a few you had no idea she knew.
- She runs around naming every object she knows, and will accompany just about everything she does with a steady stream of chatter, which is directed mainly at herself. If she's looking for a conversation partner, she'll still choose you over another child almost every time.
- She's making some major advances in mastering the language. Her first two-word sentences probably consisted of one noun and one verb ("Kitty meow"), a noun and an adjective ("Pizza hot"), or a declarative statement ("All gone"). But over the next few months, she'll start creating possessives ("daddy's hat"), plurals ("daddy's fingers"), and using small but important words like "on," "in," and "the."
- She still makes a lot of really cute (but extremely logical) grammatical errors, though ("I went to he's house," "Give the cup to she"). And she's a little unclear on past and future tenses: "I go to store" can mean "I am going now," "I went," or "I will go."
- Perhaps the most interesting language-related development is that at this age, according to Fraiberg, "language makes it possible for a child to

incorporate his parents' verbal prohibitions, to make them part of himself." This isn't always 100 percent successful, though. You may find her sitting on the floor, eating sugar out of the box, and saying, "No, baby not eat sugar," between mouthfuls.

- In addition to "Whazzat?" your toddler now asks such questions as "Why?" and "Where is ____?" According to child development experts Louise Bates Ames and Frances Ilg, your child will master more space words (*in, out, up, down, in front of, behind,* and so on) in the six-month period from two to two and a half than in any other six-month period of her life.

Emotionally/Socially

- Your toddler shows incredible pride in the things she's able to do, and actively seeks your approval. She will implore you a hundred times a day, to "Look at me!!!" as she climbs up the stairs to the slide, fills up her bucket with sand, draws a straight line, or rides her trike.
- You might not be able to tell yet, but she's slowly becoming more interested in other kids. You'll realize it for yourself when, out of the blue, she starts making a strange noise or using a word she never used before—the same noise or word used a few days before by that two-year-old at the park, the one your child seemed to be ignoring completely.
- Another way she shows her interest in other kids is by physically exploring them. Unfortunately, this may involve some hitting, pushing, shoving, and hair-pulling. But remember, your child isn't intentionally being mean; she's still learning about the difference between animate and inanimate objects and is fascinated by cause and effect. As Ames and Ilg write, "A child may begin stroking another child's hair because he likes the way it looks, then may pull it to see how it feels."
- Marked by near-instant 180-degree mood swings and arbitrary mind changes, this can be an exceedingly demanding time for you and your child.

What You're Going Through

Taking a Long, Hard Look at . . . Yourself

I always feel proud when someone tells me how much my daughters look like me (although it embarrasses them to no end). And I feel tickled inside when my parents or other relatives tell me how much the girls act like I did as a kid. But I'm a little less enchanted when one of the girls spits out one of my "god-dammits" when she can't tie her shoes.

When this kind of thing happens to you (and if it hasn't yet, it will very soon), you may suddenly find yourself imagining your child imitating some of your less savory and less cute behaviors. And you'll be horrified. "The honest and direct response of children to some 'bad habits' forces men to confront these behaviors and consider the consequences, not only for themselves but also for their children," says parenting educator Glen Palm. If, for example, you eat a lot of candy bars and potato chips, you may find yourself questioning the kind of example you're setting and start cutting back on partially hydrogenated oils. Or if you're a smoker, seeing your child sitting in her high chair smoking her spoon could be just the incentive you need to quit.

Bottom line? Your child is looking at everything you do, and she'll be modeling her behavior on yours. She's still too young to care about whether you cheat on your taxes or under-tip a waitress. But I remember taking my two-and-a-half-year-old to a movie. When I got to the front of the ticket line, the clerk asked how old my baby was. Seeing a sign that read "Two and Under Free," I didn't miss a beat. "Almost two," I lied. Unfortunately, my excessively verbal daughter didn't miss a beat either, and yelled out, "No, Daddy, I'm two and half!" In that incredibly long moment of embarrassment, I wondered whether saving three or four dollars was worth teaching my daughter that lying is okay.

Your child will also be paying special attention to your relationship with your partner. If you have a son, he'll use you as an example of how to treat (or not treat) the women in his life. If you treat your partner with respect and love, share the workload at home, and take an interest in her and her life, he'll probably do the same with his own partner and children when he gets older. If you get stuck in the role of disciplinarian or leave all the parenting up to your partner, he'll do that instead.

If you have a daughter, she's learning how she should expect to be treated in her future relationships and how important it is to have an involved, loving dad around. If she sees you taking an active role, she'll expect her future partner to do the same. If she sees you on the periphery, that's where she'll expect the father of her children to be.

Throughout all of this, make sure your child sees you and your partner having some fun—as individuals and as a couple. There's no question that parenting is an incredibly demanding job. But it can be incredibly fun too. So laugh a little.

Emotional Changes

One of the most commonly heard complaints about men is that we are out of touch with our emotions or that we suppress them. A few years ago I think I might have agreed. But since becoming a father, I strongly disagree. Fathers—

especially those who are actively involved with their children—feel tremendous joy, anger, affection, fear, and anxiety. The problem is that men in our society don't have places where they can safely express their feelings. We're supposed to be the tough guy, the stoic provider-protector. It's hard for most men to talk about their deepest emotions with their male friends. And it's even harder to talk about them—especially the negative ones—with the women in our lives.

As a result, we learn to regulate our emotions. But please remember: regulating is not the same as suppressing. "The ability to control one's own impulses in the service of caring for one's children and emotionally supporting one's spouse would seem to be an important marker of maturity," write family researchers Phil and Carolyn Cowan. Nevertheless, don't forget that you provide a crucial model for how your child learns to express her own emotions—fear, anger, disappointment, sadness, happiness, and excitement.

Besides regulating our emotions, fathers undergo a variety of other changes in the way we experience and react to the world around us. Here are some of the many ways men say that being a dad has broadened their emotional range (see pages 118–21 for some of the other changes fatherhood brings). It's drawn from research done independently by Glen Palm, Barbara and Philip Newman, Phil and Carolyn Cowan, and me.

- **Empathy**. Learning to see the world from another person's perspective (in this case, your child's) is what empathy is all about. Toddlers aren't very good at disguising their emotions, and the more time you spend getting to know her, the more aware you'll be of her feelings and how she sees the world.
- **Expressiveness**. Seeing how emotionally expressive your child can be and helping her express and accept her feelings (from "I love you" to "I'm sad, because my feelings are hurt") may allow you to accept and express your own more readily.
- **Selflessness**. Another major marker of maturity is the ability to take pleasure in doing something for someone else—without any expectation of repayment.
- **Sensitivity**. Try to equate your child's bruised and unhappy feelings with physical bruises. This is exactly the approach taken by one father interviewed by parent-child communication experts Adele Faber and Elaine Mazlish. "Somehow the image of a cut or laceration helped him realize that his son required as prompt and serious attention for his hurt feelings as he would for a hurt knee," they write.
- **Outrage**. I know that before I was a father, I had seen plenty of parents hit

or even abuse their children, and I'm sure it bothered me. But not like it bothers me now (see pages 174–75 for more on this), and I'm more bothered by reading or watching reports of kidnapped or murdered children than I ever was before having children of my own.

- **Expansion**. Before becoming fathers, men are generally limited in the ways they express affection: kissing, hugging, holding hands, and having sex. But having children frequently allows men to expand their repertoire. Kissing, hugging, and holding hands are still appropriate affectionate gestures, but so are tickling, rocking, tumbling, snuggling, and stroking.
- **Emotional control**. Although being a dad will expand your emotional range, it also requires learning when and how it's appropriate to express emotions such as anger and frustration. You won't suppress them entirely, but you'll simply be more aware of how your emotions affect the people around you.

You and Your Baby

Deployed Dads: Staying Involved When You Can't Be There

For about half a million toddlers, Dad or Mom (sometimes both) is in the military. It used to be that most military families could stay together—on base or off—no matter where the soldier was stationed. But these days, there's a good chance that you could find yourself deployed overseas and away from your family for a year or longer.

Being separated from the people you love most in the world is never easy. But it's especially hard—on everyone—during times of war. For that reason, it's important that you prepare yourself and your family as far in advance as you can. If you think you're in any danger of getting deployed, start by making contact with your built-in support network. A number of organizations offer resources and services to military personnel. You can get help preparing a will, find checklists of things to take care of before you go, learn about how you and your family can stay in touch, get your partner plugged into a spouses' support group, and much more. Two great resources are the National Military Family Association and the *Personal and Family Readiness Guide* that's published by the Air National Guard. Contact and ordering information, as well as other resources for military families are on page 268.

Once you get your orders, here are a few tips that can make the incredibly stressful time before you ship out a little more bearable.

- Spend as much of time as you can with your child. Talk with her about your upcoming trip. She won't be able to understand many of the details, but tell her you're going away for a while and that you'll be thinking of her and that you'll send her kisses every night. If your child cries or seems sad, don't try to talk her out of her feelings. Encourage her to express as much as she can. Offer to draw a picture for her of what she's feeling. (For more on how to talk to your child, see pages 177–80.)
- Take care of business. If you're the one who's managed the family finances, paid the bills, or done all the online banking, start handing off those duties to your partner. Make sure she has access to all your accounts, has a schedule of which bills need to be paid and when, and knows where all your important papers are. Since you probably won't need much money while you're overseas, arrange to have most or all of your paycheck automatically deposited into an account your partner can access.
- Write a bunch of notes to your child and give them to your partner. Ask her to "find" one every few days and read it to your child.
- Take a picture of you with your child and get it framed so she can look at it whenever she wants to, and so your partner can show it to her to keep your image firmly implanted in her memory.
- Try not to change your routines before you go, and ask your partner to maintain them after you've left. Whether or not your child is fully aware of the consequences of your deployment, her life will be very different without you. Her routines will be something she can count on. If you don't have any routines or rituals, start some now.
- Make tapes or burn a CD of you reading books. Record some of her favorites and some brand-new ones she hasn't heard. Ask your partner to make "reading" a story with Daddy part of her nighttime routine. And don't forget to tell your child and your partner at the end of every recording that you love them.
- Make sure important people (day-care providers, grandparents, parents of playmates, and so on) in your child's life know what's going on and let them know that your child's behavior could change suddenly.
- When it's time for you to leave, say good-bye—don't just disappear.
- After you leave, communicate as frequently as possible. Depending on where you are, you may be able to send e-mail, snail mail, or possibly even audio- or videotapes. Tell your partner and your child everything you're allowed to—even the most mundane details. Include drawings or small keepsakes if possible. Ask your partner to send you as much as she can—tapes of your toddler saying, "Hi, Daddy!" finger paintings, and anything else that's practical for her to send and for you to receive.

- Take this book with you and read up on child development. Your toddler is going to look and sound very different when you get back. Knowing what to expect and where she is developmentally will help you stay up-to-date.
- Don't forget about your partner. She's going to miss you a lot too, and she's going to have a lot more responsibilities and stress in her life when you aren't there. And because she's the one who reads the papers and watches the news and knows the risks soldiers face, she's going to be worried and frightened. She needs plenty of reminders that you're okay and that you're thinking about—and missing—her.
- If your partner is the stepmother of one or more of your children, be sure to take advantage of the military's free legal services to draft documents that will give her the legal authority she'll need to make decisions that affect the children. (This is assuming the children's biological mother is out of the picture for some reason. If she isn't, try to draft an agreement that will allow your partner to have regular contact with the children while you're gone. She and they need to maintain their relationship.)

Technology for Toddlers, Part II

Before you let your child sit down at the computer or pick up a "smart toy," there are a few things you should do to prepare for the big event.

- Don't allow anyone (even you) to bring food anywhere near the computer. Don't even do it when you're alone—you'll leave a dish next to the keyboard one night, and your child will remind you about it every day for the next six months.
- Get a plastic keyboard protector. Even if you do follow the no-food rule, a plastic protector also keeps dirt and paper clips out of the keyboard and acts as a handy anti-slobber device.
- No fighting, kicking, running, or roughhousing near the computer. One good smack could destroy a lot of valuable stuff.
- Preview smart toys. A friend got my youngest daughter a toy oven that "talked" whenever certain buttons were pushed or doors were opened. It seemed like a fairly harmless toy at first, and my daughter loved it. But then I got to thinking about the mixed messages she was getting. On one hand, my wife and I tell her that our oven is hot and that she shouldn't open the doors or touch it at all. On the other hand, the talking oven encourages her to do exactly the opposite.
- Get a clock. Computers and computer games for young toddlers should be fun, with any educational component as icing on the cake. Your child probably won't be interested in spending any more than a few minutes at a

time playing, but those short sessions can really add up. So limit your child to an absolute max of an hour total per day.

- If possible, give your toddler her own computer. If you think you can get away with putting a twenty-first-century child in front of your old Mac or your Pentium II, think again. Your child may actually need a newer system than you do, one that uses the most advanced graphics, sound, and animation capabilities. So if you have an old clunker lying around, donate it to your favorite charity and get a tax deduction while you still can.
- If you *are* planning to share a computer with your child, you'll want to back up everything on your system first. Once you've done that, be sure to keep your personal files in an area of the computer your child won't be able to access. If you think you might be raising a future hacker, password-protect your adult applications and data. The last thing you want is for your baby to start playing around with your tax returns.

Get a separate keyboard for your child and put colored stickers on some of the more commonly used keys: Enter, Backspace, the letters of your child's first name, cursor keys. Use the stickers as a temporary crutch to help your child

"And always remember I'm here for you, son, at Dadman@connect.pop.net."

Picking Software

Basically, what you're looking for in a software package for your child are the following factors:

- ♦ ease of use (by the child)
- ♦ ease of installation (by you)
- ♦ age-appropriateness
- ♦ ability to challenge the child
- ♦ degree to which the program is childproof
- ♦ the program's ability to entertain (this should be the primary goal)
- ♦ the program's ability to educate (a secondary goal at best)
- ♦ flexibility (can be used for kids of varying ages)

As you might expect, the ad copy on any box of software will tell you that besides satisfying all the above criteria, the program will also make you rich and your child smarter and more beautiful.

You could buy the program and test it out, but it's nearly impossible to return software these days. And unless you're a specialist in early childhood education, you probably won't be able to make a very informed decision about the program's appropriateness.

Fortunately, as mentioned on page 34, you can get reliable reviews and recommendations from Childrenssoftware.com and Superkids.com.

remember where they are. Do not start saying, "Push the red key"—your child's next computer probably won't have stickers on the keyboard. A somewhat pricey alternative to doing all this work is to buy a large-key keyboard. And while you're at it, you might want to consider a kid-sized mouse. Some great places to get this and other kid-friendly computer equipment are listed on page 34.

ALL ABOUT SOFTWARE

All your hardware precautions and preparations will be entirely wasted if the software you're running is worthless.

According to researchers Susan Haugland and Daniel Shade, there are two basic types of software: *nondevelopmental* (also called "drill-and-practice"), which, according to Shade, is the "computer equivalent of flashcards and is not good for preschoolers"; and *developmental* (open-ended), which provides children with "the opportunity to explore an environment, make choices, and then find out the impact of these decisions."

Haugland recently tested four groups of children: the first used nondevelopmental software; the second used developmental; the third also used developmental, but supplemented it with additional activities; and the fourth group used no computers at all.

After eight months, the kids in the three computer groups all showed huge gains in self-esteem over the kids in the fourth group. However, children who used the drill-and-practice software experienced an amazing 50 percent drop-off in their creativity—a drop not experienced either by the kids who used open-ended software or by those who had no computer exposure. "Clearly," write Haugland and Shade, "nondevelopmental software may have a detrimental effect on children's creativity."

Kids who worked with the developmental (open-ended) software had "significant gains on measures of intelligence, nonverbal skills, structural knowledge, long-term memory, and complex manual dexterity."

Listening So Your Child Will Talk

Generally speaking, there's not a lot of sense in talking if no one's listening. And the only way your child will ever learn how to be a good listener is if you show her the way. Here's how to do it:

- **Pay attention**. When your child wants to talk, face her and look her in the eye. Turn off the TV or radio, don't answer the phone, and disregard any other distractions. You may not even need to speak; sometimes all your child wants is for you to look at her.
- **Allow your child to have her feelings**. Don't tell a kid who says she's sleepy (or hungry or sick or sad or angry) that she's not.
- **Keep things moving**. Asking yes-or-no questions is the quickest way to end a conversation. Instead, pick up on something your child said and ask a question that restates it or uses some of the same words your child used. Doing this has two purposes. First, you're sending a strong signal that she's important and that you value what she has to say. Second, by repeating some of her words, you're reinforcing her budding language skills.
- **Don't interrupt**. If you're having a discussion with your child, listen respectfully to her ideas—from beginning to end—before jumping in. You want her to do the same for you, right?
- **Be patient**. No matter how verbal she may be, your toddler still has a limited vocabulary, and there may be occasional delays between what she's

thinking and what actually comes out of her mouth. Let her struggle for a few seconds before you start filling in the missing words.

- **Get your child involved**. Asking your child for her vote on the dinner menu or weekend plans (and taking her advice once in a while), or asking for her opinion of a movie you saw together or on how to rearrange the furniture, shows her you respect her and that what she says is important.
- **Acknowledge your child's feelings**. According to Faber and Mazlish, short, simple phrases like, "Oh, I see," and "Hmmm," are much better for stimulating your child to talk than jumping in with advice.
- **Give your child's feelings a name**. If your child tells you she wants to smash a friend's face in, telling her, "I can see that you're really angry," is far better than telling her that she shouldn't talk that way about her friends. "Parents don't usually give this kind of response," say Faber and Mazlish, "because they fear that by giving a name to the feeling, they'll make it worse. Just the opposite is true. The child who hears the words for what he is experiencing is deeply comforted. Someone has acknowledged his inner experience." But watch out: children usually hate it when you repeat their exact words back to them ("Daddy, I hate Bobby!" "It sounds like you really hate Bobby." Duh.)
- **Help her fantasize**. Rather than give a logical, rational response to your child's irrational request ("No, we can't go to Grandma and Grandpa's house for dinner—they live in Paris, and it's too far to go right now"), jump in and fantasize ("I wish I could just snap my fingers and take us there right away").
- **Watch for nonverbal cues**. Your child's mood, tone of voice, and energy level may tell you more about what she's feeling than what she actually says. Encourage your child to talk about her feelings.
- **Don't ask why**. Kids don't always know why they feel a particular way (do you?). "It's easier to talk to a grown-up who accepts what you're feeling," say Faber and Mazlish, "rather than one who presses you for explanations."

Talking so Your Child Will Pay Attention to You

Once you and your child are able to communicate with each other verbally, you'll find that a lot of what you say to her is, in one form or another, an attempt to gain her cooperation. Here's how to improve the chances that your child will (a) hear what you say, and (b) respond the way you want her to:

- **Describe what you see, not what you think**. Instead of "You always take off your socks in the living room and dump sand on the rug. Do you have any idea how long it takes me to clean up after you every day?" try something like, "There's sand on the rug."

- **Give information.** Instead of "What on earth is the matter with you? I've told you seven hundred times to stop jumping on that couch!" try "Couches are not for jumping on."
- **Say it with a word.** Instead of "I've been telling you for the past hour and a half to put your crayons away, get your clothes off, and get ready for bed," you'll probably have better luck with, "Pajamas!" This approach, by the way, works equally well with teenagers, who also don't like long-winded sermons.
- **Talk about your feelings.** Rather than criticize the child in a personal way ("You're really annoying me with your constant shouting and screaming, you're such a pain"), keep the focus on you ("I get frustrated when you yell at me like that. I do much better when people speak to me in a nice way").
- **Make specific—not general—requests.** "I want you to help me put your cars back in the box" is much better than "Clean up your stuff."
- **Be consistent.** Don't mumble "No" a few times and then forget about it. That only encourages your child to ignore you.
- **Give choices.** "Do you want an apple or an orange?" is far more likely to get a response than "What do you want to eat?" Offering choices in this way is just about guaranteed to reduce the number of adult-toddler power struggles.
- **Don't ask questions if you don't want answers.** "Can you help clean up your room, please?" only gives the child the (incorrect) impression that she has a choice.
- **Don't repeat yourself.** If she didn't listen the first six times, why would you think she would the seventh?
- **Don't make idle threats.** Kids often take a threat as a challenge. Will you really carry through? If you don't, you've lost credibility. If you do, you might have to raise the ante every time you want your child to do something.
- **Admit your mistakes.** Your child will learn that it's okay to be wrong once in a while.
- **Keep your promises.** Your child may not have a very developed sense of time, but she'll never forget that trip to the zoo or that candy bar you promised her. And if *you* do, you've lost a ton of credibility.
- **Whisper.** Kids hate to miss anything that might have anything to do with them. Speaking softly has been known to stop even the loudest child in her tracks.
- **Do your scolding in private.** Take your child into a separate room—it'll be less embarrassing for both of you. It will also reduce your child's instinctive need to try to save face by flouting your authority in public.
- **Praise effectively.** Statements like "Great job" can become so automatic that they lose their meaning. Try to be more specific: "Wow! Did you ride

your trike all the way around the block?" Besides being more satisfying, this type of praise encourages conversation.

- **Make a big deal out of good behavior**. As we've discussed elsewhere, your child craves your attention—any way she can get it. And if the only time you pay attention to her is when she's misbehaving, she'll misbehave as often as she can, feeling that behaving well is a waste of time, since no one seems to notice.
- **Say "yes" more often and give your child lots of opportunities to succeed**. Children hear the word no (or "You can't" or "You shouldn't" or "Stop that" or "Don't") about ten times more often than yes. That explains why no is many children's first word. It also explains why kids frequently ignore the word. You can decrease the number of negatives your child hears by keeping your rules reasonable, keeping her out of situations (such as stores with lots of breakables on low shelves) where you'll likely need to stop her, and analyzing situations where your child repeatedly ignores you to find out why she's doing what she's doing.

Family Matters

Even More about Nutrition

Just a few months ago you may have been worried that your baby was eating only one food for days at a time. Well, at least she was eating. But now she may seem to be giving up food altogether.

And in a way, that's true. For the first two years of life your baby was storing body fat, and her weight was increasing by about 9 percent every month. But now that she doesn't need all that fat, she's slowed way down, gaining only about 1 percent a month.

The good news is that your child isn't starving to death. When it comes to eating, toddlers are notoriously unpredictable and picky. She may go a day or two without eating much, but then the next few days she'll put away more food than you would have thought possible. During those odd moments when your toddler does eat, she'll probably limit herself to only two or three foods. The solution? You decide what your child eats and when, she decides whether to eat it and how much.

I know, I know, that sounds like the nutritional equivalent of giving your toddler the keys to your car, but it really works. Expecting her to eat three balanced meals and two healthy snacks every day is completely unrealistic. But if you keep offering a wide variety of options, she'll balance things out on her

Dealing with Desserts

Promising your child a cookie if she stops crying may seem like a good idea at the time, but in the long run it's not. Using dessert as a bribe is sending the message that whatever it is you're offering (which will probably be packed with fat and sugar and empty calories) is extremely desirable. The same thinking happens when you tell your child that she can't have dessert until she eats everything on her plate. She interprets that as an admission on your part that the food she doesn't want to eat is disgusting, and the dessert that you're dangling in front of her is wonderful.

A nutritionist friend suggests that the way to avoid these problems is to put all the food you'd like your child to eat on the plate at the same time—including dessert. Her theory is that when dessert is no longer forbidden, it becomes less desirable, and your child won't be any more attracted to a brownie than to a carrot. (Of course, you can have fresh fruit or low-fat ice cream for dessert, and brownies don't have to be an option at all.)

own over the course of a week or so. Giving your child some control over her own food intake may have the additional side effect of making her braver and more willing to try new things.

MINIMIZING FOOD FIGHTS

Mealtimes are a great opportunity for the whole family to spend time together. They're also a great opportunity for your toddler to test some limits. Here are some suggestions that can make family meals a little more enjoyable for everyone:

- **Relax**. If your child doesn't want to try a new food, leave her alone; the bigger the deal you make of it, the more fights there will be. You may have to introduce a new food as many as twenty times before she takes her first bite. In the meantime, let her sniff it, play with it, and even spit it out a few times. And does she really have to eat in a high chair? Just put her someplace where she can't make a huge mess (or at least where her mess will be fairly easy to clean up).
- **Keep serving sizes reasonable**. A toddler's serving size is about one quarter of an adult's, so limit servings to one or two tablespoons—an amount roughly as big as your child's fist. Much more than that could intimidate her.

The Dream Diet

Just in case you were wondering what an ideal toddler diet would look like, your child should have the following every day:

- Four servings of cereal, bread, rice, pasta (one serving is one-half slice of bread or bagel, one-quarter of a cup of rice or cooked pasta, or one-half cup of dry cereal).
- Two servings of veggies, particularly broccoli, cauliflower, Brussels sprouts, cabbage, and beans (one serving is one-half cup of cooked vegetables or one-third cup of raw vegetables).
- Two or more servings of fruit, such as apricots, cantaloupe, carrots, spinach, yams, oranges, grapefruit, or tomatoes (one serving is one-quarter of a piece of fruit or one-half cup of 100 percent fruit juice).
- Three to four servings of dairy (one serving is three-quarters of a cup of milk, or one-half cup of low-fat yogurt or cheese).
- Two to three servings of poultry, fish, meat, or high-protein vegetarian equivalent (one serving is an ounce or two of lean meat or tofu, one tablespoon of peanut butter).
- Seven to eight grams of fiber (good sources include whole-grain breads and foods such as apples, bananas, figs, plums, pears, berries, peas, potatoes, spinach).
- Two healthy snacks, which can be fruit, cheese, or vegetables.

Sounds great, doesn't it? Unfortunately, getting a toddler to eat anything that remotely resembles the ideal diet is going to be a struggle. But here are a few things you can do to improve your chances:

- **Serve only 100 percent juice**. Anything that has the word *drink* in its name is probably more sugar than juice. A single can of Coke has the same effect on a toddler that drinking four cups of coffee does on you.

- **Be a good role model**. If your diet consists mostly of peanut butter and jelly sandwiches, you can't really expect your toddler to be very adventurous.
- **Spy**. When your child is at someone else's house—especially one in which there are older kids to imitate—find out what she ate. She may try something at a friend's that she wouldn't have touched if you had given it to her.
- **Keep foods far away from each other on the plate**. Kids this age like

- **Limit fast foods and caffeine.** Lunch meats, hot dogs, and many other processed fast foods contain sodium nitrates, which the American Cancer Society believes may cause cancer in children.
- **Limit candy and other junk food.** Kids between two and three consume about 1,300 calories a day, and a candy bar has about 200 calories—a pretty big chunk of the day's intake.
- **Limit fat.** Starting at about two years of age, no more than 30 percent of your child's calories should come from fat. You can reduce fat by using less butter, serving less meat and more fish and poultry, and using lower-fat cooking methods such as grilling and broiling rather than frying.
- **Limit dairy.** Unless your pediatrician says otherwise, your child should probably not have more than a quart of milk a day (which should be low- or nonfat). Any more than that could interfere with absorption of iron.
- **Set a good example.** If you stop at a convenience store for a candy bar, brush your teeth and don't leave the wrappers lying around. If your child doesn't smell the chocolate on your breath, she'll certainly recognize the empty packaging and know she's been left out.
- **Take things out of their original packages.** What's often most attractive about certain foods is the box they come in. Transferring cereals and other sugary things into a large jar or plastic container can make them a lot less attractive.
- **Eat in full color.** Naturally colorful foods tend to be high in vitamins and other important nutrients.
- **Talk to your pediatrician about vitamins and supplements.** If your child is getting a balanced diet, she probably won't need any. But if she's especially picky or absolutely refuses to eat, get the doctor's advice.

to keep everything in its own special place (just another way to exercise control), and mixing two foods—even if they're both favorites—could end up causing a tantrum. In a similar vein, kids like to have certain quantities of things and may ask for more milk in their glass even though there's already plenty there.

- **Peel foods with peels (apples, pears, plums).** Some kids are looking

"Relax. The important thing is that he drinks his milk, not how."

for any excuse not to eat something, and a tough-to-chew peel is a perfect pretext.

- **Grow a garden**. Even kids who don't like vegetables may be willing to eat something they planted, watered, and picked.
- **Get your child involved**. Have her set the table, decide on pizza toppings, make shopping decisions.
- **Have fun**. Even liver can look more appetizing if you cut it into the shape of a friendly animal or familiar cartoon character.
- **Encourage snacking**. Your child is burning tons of calories. Make sure she gets plenty to eat throughout the day, and if she wants some apple slices or a piece of cheese between meals, let her.

- **Encourage exercise**. Active children tend to be hungrier than less active ones.
- **Pay attention**. Your child isn't going to starve herself to death just to show you up. If you're truly worried about her eating habits, check with your pediatrician. Early signs of malnutrition include uncharacteristic constant crankiness, frequent illness, listless behavior, and little or no weight gain over a long period of time.

Food and Your Child's Temperament

Researcher Jim Cameron has found that your child's eating habits—like just about everything else in her life—are greatly influenced by her temperament:

- The slow-adapting toddler may consider your efforts to feed her intrusive and may try to get out of her high chair as if it were a straitjacket. She often rejects new foods, not because they taste bad but because they taste new. And old foods prepared in new ways may be rejected on principle.
- The intense toddler may seem to exist only on five or six foods. Don't bother introducing a new food when your toddler is really hungry—she's probably tired and not in the mood for new things. Her first reaction to new foods will be one of suspicion, so if you really want her to try something new, wait until she's a little hungry and not too tired. The more intense your child, the more problems you'll have trying to get her to stick to a strict eating schedule. The more you insist, the more likely your efforts will result in a tantrum.
- The energetic toddler wants to be in complete control of her meals. She may refuse to be fed by anyone but herself, and may not eat if she can't hold the food (or at least the utensil it's supposed to be on). It's impossible even to guess how much she'll eat or when. If she's tired, she won't eat much, but you might get her to try an old favorite. If she's well rested, she'll eat even less (she'll want to run around instead). Have lots of snacks available for quick refueling, and don't waste your time trying to get her into a high chair.
- The irregular, slow-to-warm toddler may be the toughest of all. You can expect her to sit at the dinner table for a while, but don't expect her to actually eat anything. Instead, she'll want to eat on her own schedule; again, have lots of healthy snacks around for her swings through the kitchen.

Giving Yourself a Financial Tune-up

Whether you're rich or poor, when it comes to money there are only three kinds of people:

- Those who spend less than they bring in and save the difference.
- Those who spend exactly what they earn and have nothing left over.
- Those who spend more than they earn and get deeper and deeper in debt.

If you're in the first category, congratulations! About 40 percent of Americans spend more than they earn. And a variety of surveys have found that most adults aren't saving enough for retirement and that over 40 percent aren't saving at all. According to one survey, over 60 percent of Americans haven't calculated how much they'll need for retirement. If you're in either of the other two categories (or if you're in the first and want to make your financial situation even better), you're going to have to get under your financial hood and do a little tinkering. It's a simple process, really, with only two steps:

- Reduce your expenses (and your debts)
- Increase your savings

"I'd like to give you more, but I can't. I'm restrained by an 'allowance cap.'"

When Things Get Really, Really Out of Control

Of course you want to pay what you owe. Just about everyone does. But sometimes, despite your best intentions, things just get to the point where they're no longer manageable. Fortunately, debtors' prisons went out with the nineteenth century. But that probably won't keep you from feeling helpless, humiliated, infuriated, frustrated, and, often, somehow less than a man. Men are supposed to know how to handle money, after all. If you've gotten to the point where you're feeling completely overwhelmed by your debts and you're being hounded by creditors and collection agencies, you have three basic options.

- Continue doing what you've been doing. But since that hasn't worked up to this point, why keep making yourself miserable?
- Get some professional help—a far more sensible approach. The Consumer Credit Counseling Service (www.cccsintl.org) is a nonprofit group that helps people avoid bankruptcy and restructure their debts. They also offer free online counseling. You might also want to contact your local chapter of Debtors' Anonymous. You can find local chapters or even attend an online meeting via their Web site, www.debtorsanonymous.org. But whatever you do, *do not* get involved with one of those companies that promises to cancel your credit card debts and restore your credit. As the old saying goes, if it sounds too good to be true, it probably is.
- File for bankruptcy—truly the option of last resort. Bankruptcy can essentially wipe out all debts from credit cards, auto loans, medical bills, utilities, and a few others. And you certainly won't be alone: In 2003 alone, about 1.5 million U.S. households filed for bankruptcy. On the downside, though, it'll screw up your credit report for at least seven years. And even after you're done, you'll still owe any debts related to alimony and child support, taxes (in most cases), and student loans. Bankruptcy isn't for everyone. So if you're even considering it, get some sound advice first. Nolo Press (www.nolo.com) is a good place to start.

REDUCING EXPENSES AND GETTING OUT OF DEBT ON THE WAY

Although starting a savings or investment plan sounds like a lot more fun than going on a financial diet, the truth is that you can't save money until you've got a good handle on your expenses. The first step is to take a hard look at your current spending. It may be a little scary, but trust me, it's important.

Picking a Financial Planner

Although you may be tempted to do your retirement planning and investing on your own, think long and hard before you make your final decision. Sure, it's fun to buy a stock you read about in the paper or that a friend tells you about. You might do fairly well for a while, but the long-term odds are against you. Even professional traders have trouble outperforming the market. These are people who do nothing all day long but follow individual stocks or sectors. If they can't beat the market with their armies of researchers and all sorts of fancy computer models, what makes you think you can? Still, your odds are better with a professional. So unless the financial markets are your passion or you've decided to quit your job and manage your money, have someone else handle things.

Many financial planners are paid on a commission basis, based on your insurance purchases, stock trades, and/or the total value of your portfolio. So whether or not your investments do well, the financial planner gets his commission. Commissions typically range from as low as 4 percent on some mutual funds to the entire first year's premium on a cash value life insurance policy. Other planners are paid on a fee basis and typically charge from $50 to $250 per hour, often depending on how much money they're helping you manage. In most cases, they make recommendations and have you execute the actual transactions yourself, usually through low-fee companies such as Waterhouse, Vanguard, or Fidelity.

This doesn't mean, of course, that fee-based planners are inherently better than their commission-based colleagues (although many experts believe that you'll be happier, and possibly richer, with someone who charges an hourly fee). Your goal is to find someone you like and who you believe will have your best interests at heart. Here are a few things you can do to help you weed out the losers:

- Get references from friends, business associates, and so forth. Alternatively, the Financial Planning Association, (800) 282-7526 or www.fpanet.org, can refer you to certified planners in your area, and the National Association of Personal Financial Advisors, (800) 366-2732 or www.napfa.org, makes referrals only to fee-based (as opposed to commission-based) planners.
- Select at least three potential candidates and set up initial consulta-

tions (which shouldn't cost you anything). Then conduct tough interviews. Here's what you want to know:

- ◊ Educational background. Not to be snobby here, but the more formal the education—especially in financial management—the better. Certified Financial Planners (CFPs) go through a rigorous training program, and the CFP certification can help you differentiate between someone who's really a planner from someone who just sells stocks and insurance.
- ◊ Licenses. Is it important to you that the planner be legally able to buy or sell financial products suck as stocks, bonds, mutual funds, and insurance?
- ◊ Level of experience. Unless you've got money to burn, let your niece break in her MBA on someone else. Stick to experienced professionals with at least three years in the business.
- ◊ Profile of the typical client. What you're looking for is a planner who has experience working with people whose income level and family situation are similar to yours.
- ◊ Compensation. If fee-based, how is the fee calculated (hourly or as a percentage of assets)? If commission, what are the percentages on each product offered? Any hesitation to show you a commission schedule is a red flag.
- ◊ Sample financial plan. You want to see what you're going to be getting for your money. Be careful, though: fancy graphics, incomprehensible boilerplate language, and expensive leather binders are often used to distract you from the report's lack of substance.
- ◊ References. How long have customers been with the planner? Are they happy? Better off? Any complaints or weaknesses?

♦ Check your prospective planner's record with state and federal regulators. The North American Securities Administration Association has a list of each state's security regulators at www.nasaa.org/nasaa/abtnasaa/find_regulator.html. On a national level, you can also contact NASD at www.nasd.org or (800) 289-9999 to check on disciplinary action and to see whether your candidates have ever been sued.

DRIP a Little Savings into This

If you're going the do-it-yourself route and you're thinking about investing in stocks, here's a way to save yourself some real money. Hundreds of companies now offer current shareholders dividend reinvestment plans (DRIPs) that allow them to buy stock directly from the company without having to pay a broker. Some make this service available to new investors as well. These plans almost always allow investors to reinvest dividends without commission. Many allow for automatic electronic purchases direct from your checking account, and several dozen actually allow DRIP participants to buy stock at a below-market rate. Finally, most plans will also let you sell your stock at rates far under what even a discount broker would charge.

So how can you find out about DRIPs? The hard way is to contact individual companies directly to find out whether they offer such programs. A much easier way is to check out one of the online companies that specialize in DRIPs. I've listed several Web sites in the Resources guide at the end of this book.

Gather together every money-related scrap of paper that's crossed your hands in the past four or five months. Categorize them by type of expense (housing, insurance, medical, food, and so forth). Using several months' worth of data will help you average variable expenses, such as gas and clothes, and include irregular expenses, such as auto repairs or major appliance purchases. Be sure to include the money—especially cash—you spend on lunch, dry cleaning, gifts, and the like.

Once you've got this done, go over each of the expense categories to see where you can do some cutting. Here are a few areas in which you can produce almost immediate, and often painless, returns:

- Food. Buy in bulk from Costco or other discount outlets, use coupons, and eat out less.
- Comparison-shop. Prices vary widely on everything from refrigerators to long-distance carriers, so check three or four places plus the Internet before you buy anything.
- Make a sensible tax plan.
- Carpool or try to telecommute a day or more per week. This can help you reduce many auto-related expenses, such as gas and oil, repairs, and insurance rates.

- Auto insurance. If your car is more than five years old, you can probably save some money by getting rid of your collision and comprehensive coverages. Check with your insurance agent.
- Health insurance. If you and your partner are both on employer-paid plans, your employer might be willing to refund some of the money they pay for you if you can prove that you're covered under your partner's plan. If you're self-employed and paying for your own plan, consider increasing your deductible or putting your child(ren) on a separate plan. Sometimes "family" coverage is much more than two separate policies—one for the adults, one for the kids.
- Use savings to pay off your debts. If you have $1,000 invested at 2 percent, you're earning $20 a year, which becomes $14.50 if you're in the 28 percent tax bracket. If you owe $1,000 on a 20 percent credit card, your interest payment is $200 a year, which, since you're using after-tax dollars, is really $278 if you're in the 28 percent tax bracket. Get the point? In this scenario, taking the money out of savings would save you about $264 a year. That may not sound like a lot, but it's enough to pay for most of the clothes your child will go through in a year, or a good chunk of your annual health club membership, or a few sessions with your therapist. You'd have to earn more than 30 percent (before taxes) on your investment to justify not using your savings to pay off your debt. And if some emergency comes up and you really, really need the money again, you can always get a cash advance on your credit card.
- Stop charging—especially for things that lose their value, such as gas, clothing, cars, furniture, and meals out. If you can't afford to pay cash for these things, maybe you can't afford them at all. (One study found that

The Best Investment

After paying off your credit cards, one of the most important—and safest—investments you can make is in yourself. If you never finished high school or college or grad school, get it done now. Someone with a bachelor's degree earns an average of about $15,000 more per year than someone with only a high-school diploma. Having a master's degree adds another $11,000 per year, and a doctorate kicks in $15,000 on top of that. Over the course of your life, the higher salary you'll command and your increased self-esteem, confidence, and general level of happiness will more than pay for the cost of the extra education.

people who use credit cards to charge fast food meals spend as much as 50 percent more than when they pay cash.) Making a 2 percent minimum payment on a $1,000 charge will take about 20 years to pay off and cost you a total of over $3,000. And if you keep buying stuff, you'll never get clean.

- If you still insist on charging, at least try to pay off your balance in full every month. 60 percent of Americans don't, and on average, every American family owes over $8,000 in credit card debt.
- Use a debit card instead. These cards look just like credit cards but take the money directly out of your checking account. Keeping that in mind might just scare you out of using the card altogether.
- Take charge of your credit cards. You probably get a few offers a week for credit cards that offer zero or low interest on balance transfers. The hitch is that most of the time those low rates are temporary. If you're extremely disciplined, you can keep rolling your balances from card to card and never pay interest. But if you're not, you could end up in worse trouble than when you started.
- Take out a consolidation loan or home equity line of credit. Chances are that your bank or credit union offers loans at lower interest rates than those you're paying now. In many cases the lender may want you to cancel your credit cards (or at least turn the cards over to them). The interest you pay on these loans may be tax deductible. Either way, you'll be able to pay off your bills faster and at far lower cost.

BOOSTING YOUR SAVINGS

Now that you've done everything you can to cut your expenses, you're ready for the fun stuff. For most people, the first big questions are: "How much should I try to save," and "When should I start?" The short answer is, "As much as you possibly can, and as soon as possible." A more accurate answer depends on a number of factors, including:

- How old you are now.
- How old you think you'll be when you retire, and how old your partner will be when she retires.
- How long you expect to live (people are generally retiring later and living longer).
- Where you'll live when you retire (for example, will you sell your house and move to a smaller place?).
- What you expect your expenses to be while you're retired (for example, will your house be paid off by then?).
- Whether you think you and/or your partner will work while you're retired.

- How much you and your partner have already invested for retirement, and how much income you expect those assets to generate for you.
- Your other assets.
- Your best guess about how much you'll be able to earn on your investments, and what the inflation rate will be from now until you retire.
- How big an estate you want to leave to your heirs.

Since the answers to these questions are different for everyone, it's impossible to tell you exactly how much you'll need to save. But working backward, the conventional wisdom is that most people will need about 70–75 percent of their current income to meet their retirement expenses.

Again, the most important things are to save as much as you can and to start as soon as you can. Here are a few points to keep in mind as you're getting started:

- **Put together a plan**. Your answers to the questions above will help you get a handle on how much you'll need to have on hand at retirement and how much you'll need to save between now and then to meet your goal.
- **Pay yourself first**. The theory is that if you force yourself to live on your after-retirement-savings income, you'll adjust your spending accordingly.
- **Start an emergency fund**. Ideally, you should have enough cash on hand to pay for three to six months of your current expenses, just in case you get laid off or the economy goes completely to pieces. In addition, it's a good idea to have some extra money to pay for big expenses you know are coming up, such as braces, boarding school, weddings, bar mitzvahs, down payment on a house, major renovations of your current home, the vacation of a lifetime, and so on.
- **Out of sight, out of mind**. This means having money taken out of your paycheck automatically—that way you'll miss it less than if you had to write a check out every month, and you'll be more inclined to do it regularly. Most employers have direct deposit, and most financial institutions are more than glad to help you set up regular electronic withdrawals to a savings account of some kind.
- **Regularity**. Make your savings plan a habit for life. Making investments of the same amount each month is called "dollar cost averaging" and has some great benefits: when prices are up, you're buying a smaller number of shares. When prices are down, you're buying more. On average, then, you'll be fine. This strategy also keeps you from falling into the trap of buying high (just to get on the bandwagon) and selling low (when the bottom has fallen out of the market).

- **Avoid temptation**. Don't put your long-term savings money in any kind of account that has check-writing privileges. Making your money hard to get may increase your chances of having it for a while.
- **Reinvest any interest and dividends**. It's free money, so why take it out? Leaving earnings in the account also helps your balance grow faster. Along the same lines, immediately invest any bonuses or raises. If you're able to live on what you're currently making, all that extra money can go directly into savings.
- **Get an ESOP**. No, it's not a fable, it's an Employee Stock Ownership Plan, and it's offered by more than 10,000 employers across the country. Basically, these plans allow employees to purchase stock in their company without paying commission. Sometimes you can make your purchases with pretax dollars, sometimes with after-tax dollars. Some employers let you buy at below-market prices, and some even match your contributions or contribute extra money to your account, which vests (becomes yours) over time, usually five to seven years.
- **Max out all of your retirement options**—especially the ones that your employer contributes to.
- **Think about Uncle Sam**. Before (or at least at the same time as) you make any real changes to any part of your financial picture, you should be sure to talk to someone knowledgeable about the tax consequences. Your financial planner may be able to offer some help, but a good accountant would be a lot better.

The next big question is, "So what do I do with all the money I'm going to be saving?" Again, there's no magic formula. Whether you put your money in government bonds or short the pork belly futures market will depend on your individual and family goals and how much risk you're willing to tolerate.

Correctly analyzing all of these factors is a process that's far too complicated to cover here in a way that would be at all helpful. So unless you're already sophisticated financially, get yourself some help. It is, of course, possible to do it yourself, and if you think you want to try, Eric Tyson's *Personal Finance for Dummies*, 4th edition (New York: John Wiley & Sons, 2003) will walk you through the whole process. If you want a more personal and professional touch, you'll need to get yourself a financial planner (see pages 188–189).

30–33 MONTHS

Hey, Who's In Charge Here?

What's Going On with the Baby

Physically

- There's almost nothing your two-and-a-half-year-old can't do on his feet. He walks short distances on tiptoe, broad-jumps with both feet, makes sudden starts and stops while running, turns sharp corners on the move, and even steps over obstacles. He'll charge up stairs, alternating feet, but he's not quite as confident on the way down and may put both feet on each step.
- His fine motor skills are coming along nicely too. He can now differentiate between the two sides of his body (in other words, when pointing with one finger, he doesn't extend the same finger on the other hand).
- He can draw an *X* on purpose and a circle if you draw one first, and can consistently catch a large ball.
- He uses a cup and spoon like a pro, can build incredibly high block towers, likes making shapes—especially snakes—with Play-Doh, and is able to button up his clothes.
- He loves puzzles and has graduated from the one-piece-per-hole kind to simple jigsaws. He'll have an easier time of it, though, if each piece has a handle.

Intellectually

- Kids this age are still quite egotistical and have trouble controlling their impulses. Your toddler may have to pull all the books off the bookshelf 275 times before he's able to forgo his own pleasure in favor of parental approval.

- Symmetry, order, and patterns are especially important to your two-and-a-half-year-old. Half an apple (or a cookie with a bite taken out of it) is completely unacceptable. He won't appreciate any deviations from his rituals, such as you being too tired to read him a bedtime story. And if you forget to fasten your seatbelt before starting the car, you're likely to get a stern talking-to.
- He's also beginning to recognize a double standard when he sees one, and might ask why you get to snack before dinner and he doesn't.
- Band-Aids are your child's best friend, so you'd better stock up. Every single bump, scrape, or bruise—whether you can actually see it or not—can be "cured" instantly with a Band-Aid. As child psychologist Selma Fraiberg put it, "It's as if a leak in the container, the body, is sealed up and his completeness as a personality is reestablished by this magic act."
- Although he's just as physically active as before, he seems to be a bit more focused. Instead of doing things and going places for the simple pleasure of doing or going, he now has a specific goal in mind for each action.
- He's getting more and more aware of the people around him. If you pay attention, you'll notice that he uses different words and intonation when he's talking to you than he does when talking to a playmate, an older sibling, or your dog.

Verbally

- Your toddler is not much of a conversationalist. He still initiates most verbal interactions but doesn't always respond when you speak to him. When you do, he understands just about everything you say. But he gets extremely frustrated if you don't understand what *he's* trying to say.
- He's the absolute master of the word *no*. And his negative reactions to you (or refusals to cooperate) are more likely to be verbal than physical.
- He still hasn't completely grasped the concept of large chunks of time (yesterday, today, tomorrow), but he can express small pieces and sequences: "I get dressed now, then I have my cereal."
- Feeling pretty confident about his budding language skills (and why not—he probably knows a thousand words and is adding a few more every day), your toddler is now starting to play with language, in almost the same way that he plays with objects. He knows what words are "supposed" to sound like and laughs hysterically when you replace a few words of a familiar nursery rhyme with nonsense syllables. Soon he'll begin to imitate these language games and will start giving silly-sounding names to objects he doesn't know.

Emotionally/Socially

- He's rebellious, defiant, negativistic, and exasperating; he doesn't always know what he wants, but he knows that he doesn't want to do most of the things you want him to do. Sound like a teenager? Could be, but it's also a description of the average child between the ages of two and three. It's no wonder that psychologist Fitzhugh Dodson calls this period "first adolescence."
- He may drive you nuts with his seeming inability to make a decision and stick to it. This can make something as simple as getting dressed frustrating. You: "Do you want the red pants or the blue?" Toddler: "Red." You: "Red it is." Toddler (screaming): "No, I want blue!" You: "Okay, let's put the blue ones on." Toddler: "No!" You get the point. If you're taking care of him, he'll demand his mother. If she is with him, he'll demand you. And if you're both with him, he may demand to do it "myself."
- Being contrary and disobedient is an exhausting job for so young a child, and your toddler is likely to be tired a lot. Unfortunately, tiredness usually makes tantrums worse.
- For most toddlers, this is a fairly aggressive time, and minor violence is common. Fortunately, most aggressive behavior is still experimental and not intended to cause real harm. Ames and Ilg have found that it's "as if the child wonders what kind of response he will get. Thus, a child may hit, grab at, or push another child, then look closely to see what is going to happen."
- Despite all these struggles, when he's in a good mood, he's delightful, cooperative, happy, and affectionate. Don't miss a second of it.

What You're Going Through

Power Struggles

Here are perhaps the three most important words you will ever hear as a parent: *choose your battles*. Basically, this means that you should think carefully about whether it really matters that your child wants to wear one blue sock and one orange instead of a matched pair. As your child gets older, he becomes more independent. And the more independent he becomes, the more he tends to resist the limits you set. It's all part of growing up: your child needs to know how serious the rules are and how you'll react when they're broken.

I used to spend huge amounts of time arguing with my middle daughter, trying to get her to put on her shoes before she got in the car. I'd threaten, cajole, plead, and bribe, and gradually I'd wear her down and she'd put them on. But the moment she was strapped into her car seat and I was behind the wheel,

Of Young Dads and Old Dads

It may seem obvious that at the same time we're developing as fathers, we're developing as men as well. What's a little less obvious, though, is that the two developmental paths aren't always parallel. This means that two fathers of three-year-olds—one in his twenties or thirties, the other in his forties or fifties—are probably going to parent very differently.

If you're in the young category, you may be just out of college, not yet solidly established in your career, and trying to carve out your place in the world. You may also still be doing some experimenting—trying lots of new things, taking risks, having a great time. You're also probably spending a lot of time rolling around on the floor with your child, or playing other physical games.

If you're in your forties or fifties, you're less likely to be wrestling with your child and more likely to be doing something intellectually stimulating. Overall, older dads tend to be more relaxed, caring, flexible, supportive, interested in parenting, involved in daily child care, and likely to have a positive experience as fathers, according to Ross Parke. They also feel more appreciated by their children than younger fathers.

she'd yank off her shoes and smirk at me in the rearview mirror. Finally, I gave up, and we're both a lot happier.

A friend who lives in Chicago told me that his son suddenly began refusing to get into the family car unless he was stark naked. My friend and his wife made themselves and their son miserable for a few days before shrugging their shoulders and giving up. The three of them enjoyed several peaceful months, and when winter came their son rather sheepishly asked for some clothes. Earlier we discussed the importance of setting firm, consistent limits for your child. But believe me, if you're prepared to go to the mat to enforce compliance with every request you make, you'll spend a lot of unnecessary time butting heads with your child. And you won't have the energy to enforce the rules that really matter, such as, "Don't go into the street unless you're holding hands with a grown-up." More importantly, you'll waste a lot of perfectly good quality time fighting.

Regaining Control

During your child's first year, you had to get used to the idea that your baby was pretty much running the show. It was the baby, not you or your partner, who de-

The Mouth That Roars

Has your child asked you (loudly, of course) whether that African-American woman in front of you is made of chocolate, or whether that obese man has eaten an elephant? Or has he let loose with a string of four-letter words that sounds eerily like what came out of your mouth when you stubbed your toe on a table leg? He will.

In 1977 Art Linkletter wrote a book called *Kids Say the Darndest Things*. And boy, was he right. Every parent has dozens of stories about the shocking, embarrassing, horrifying, and hilarious things their innocent toddlers have said. I remember taking two of my kids to a matinee a while back. The theater was crowded, so my older daughter had her own seat and the younger one, who had just turned two, sat on my lap. A few minutes into the movie, I felt something wet on my leg and instinctively put my hand on the baby's bottom to feel whether her diaper had leaked. Suddenly, at the top of her lungs, she screamed, "Get your hands out of my pants!" It was one of the more discomfiting (and funny) moments of my life.

Fortunately, not everything your child says will make you want to disappear down the nearest hole. But in many ways the unembarrassing statements and the ordinary "Why?" questions are harder to deal with than the embarrassing ones. They'll make you think about the world in a way you never have before, and jar you into realizing just how little thought most of us give to what's going on around us and how much basic information we just take for granted. How, for example, do you explain homelessness, terrorism, AIDS, natural disasters, and violent crime?

When faced with tough questions, the best thing to do is turn them into learning experiences (even questions about people being made of chocolate can lead to a discussion about what it means to have your feelings hurt). One of the greatest sources of these "teachable moments" is the newspaper (it's got enough pictures to spark the child's interest and is a lot easier to censor than the television). My two oldest "read" the paper with me over breakfast in the mornings and ask me to explain the articles that accompany interesting photos.

cided when to eat, when to sleep, when he wanted to be changed, and when he wanted to play. Everyone else around him simply adjusted to his desires. Not being in control is hard, especially for men. After all, we're bigger and

"My dad says my mom is a Pagan because she serves burnt offerings for dinner"

smarter and older, and we should be in charge, dammit. But it doesn't work that way.

Fortunately, as your child gets older, things will change. There's an old saying that we spend the first two years of our children's lives teaching them to walk and talk, and the next sixteen years trying to get them to sit down and shut up. All that walking and talking requires a shift in the balance of power from your child to you. You're setting basic boundaries for health and safety. And you're gradually establishing other rules—say, for how to speak to and behave with other people, how to treat animals, when to go to bed, and so on. You're also getting close to selecting your child's school and taking your first steps toward overbooking him: soccer, piano, chess club, polo lessons. . . .

Don't expect much cooperation from your child, for two reasons. First, while you're trying to be the boss, your child is continuing his never-ending quest for independence, which involves rejecting you and your rules. Second, intellectually, your child isn't quite ready to forget the idea that he's the center of the universe.

There are still plenty of times when you won't be in control at all, or at least not as much as you'd like to be. If your child is disabled or chronically ill, for example, his needs will still dictate your schedule. And ill or not, when he throws himself down next to the bananas in the grocery store and has a huge tantrum, you'll remember the incredible frustration of not being in control.

Stepping into a Prefab Family

About half of all marriages are remarriages for at least one of the partners, a lot of whom have children. It's quite possible, then, that you're starting your fatherhood experience with someone else's child. Or your new partner might be the incoming stepparent. We'll talk about stepmothers on pages 220–22. Either way, the most important thing to remember is to have reasonable expectations and be patient.

It's not easy being a stepfather, and there isn't a lot of social support out there. Fortunately, though, you're not alone. In fact, more than half of Americans have been, are now, or will be in one or more blended families during their lifetime. And there are over 2.5 million families (including more than 6.5 million kids) made up of a biological mother and a stepfather.

A lot of stepfathers erroneously think that they're going to ease into their new situation right away and that their new, blended family will behave just like a regular biological family would. In reality, this hardly ever happens. It's not always clear what the stepfather's role in the new family is and how he's going to fit into the new family structure. And it's not easy trying to mold relationships with children who already have a father somewhere else. Stepfathers also rarely have any kind of legally established authority—that stays with the biological father. Still, if their places were clearly prescribed and protected by law, most men, even if they're fathers themselves, don't have much practice or training in parenting other people's kids.

Many stepdads are also surprised when the love they expected to feel for and from their stepchildren doesn't materialize—either as soon as they'd hoped or at all. In one important study, fewer than half of stepfathers said that they felt "mutual love" between themselves and their children.

Marriages that include children are twice as likely to end in divorce as those without. So if you are already a stepfather or are about to become one, there are a number of important issues that you may find yourself dealing with. Ignored, they can get out of control and interfere with your new partner, her kids, and even your own kids, if you have any.

Tips for Successful Stepfathering

According to researcher Kay Pasley, three factors accurately predict whether a stepfather will be satisfied with his role:

1. The level of communication with his stepchildren—the more, the better.
2. The amount of time he spends with his stepchildren. Again, the more, the better.
3. The support he gets from his new partner for his involvement in the discipline of the stepchildren. What a surprise: the more, the better.

Besides communicating well, spending lots of time with your stepchildren, and getting plenty of support from their mother, here are some other very important steps you can take to make stepfathering a more enjoyable experience for everyone:

- **Have realistic expectations**. The idea that her children and you are going to fall instantly in love with one another is a fantasy. Relying on it too much will only set you up for failure. Taking a stepparenting class can help you keep your expectations reasonable.
- **Don't try to get attached too fast**. Doing so makes you vulnerable to rejection, which you're probably going to get a lot of for quite a while anyway.
- **Don't let the stepkids get to you**. Or at least don't let them see that they did. It will make them use the same hurtful tactics over and over.
- **Be a grown-up**. If they hurt your feelings, don't try to get even by rejecting them.
- **Establish some new family traditions**. Rituals and customs help families bond. You have some from your family; your partner has some from hers. Neither is better or worse, they're just different. Coming up with something new can make all of you feel that you're working together to create something special.
- **Devote a lot of time to keeping your relationship with your new partner healthy**. And be sure to discuss the role she expects you to take in her children's life, or that you expect her to take in your kids' life. Don't be naive and think that everything will work itself out—it won't. Over half of remarried women and about two-thirds of remarried men get divorced again. Major problems include conflicts over child-rearing, the children's behavior, and the relationship between the stepparent and the stepchildren. So don't be afraid to get some couples therapy if you need it.
- **If you and your new wife both have kids from previous relationships, pay special attention to how the kids react**. Moreover, don't underestimate the magnitude of the changes they're going to experience: new

Stepdad vs. Biological Dad

A lot of kids, regardless of their age, fantasize that their parents will get back together. Your marriage to a child's mother dashes that hope. Expect to hear a lot of "You're not my father, so I don't have to listen to you."

Don't be offended if your stepchildren want to spend a lot of time with their biological dad. There's going to be some natural competitiveness between the two of you, especially if your partner tells you he isn't a particularly nice guy. But you absolutely must support the kids' relationship with their father. (If the situation is reversed, try to help your new wife to understand that your kids are going to want to spend a lot of time with their mother and that she should try as hard as she can to support that relationship.)

One of the most important factors in a child's adjustment to a stepparent is trying to maintain the one-on-one relationships he had with his natural parents. Kids often feel that they're losing their biological parent to the new stepparent. And the truth is that in a way, they're right. Before, it was just them and their mother, but now they have to share her with some interloper—you. This brings up all sorts of loyalty issues for a lot of stepkids. They may feel that if they love you, they're somehow being disloyal to or betraying their father. As a result, they may lash out at you for what seems like no reason at all. Even stranger, these explosions often happen just when you think your relationship with your stepchild is getting better. If (when) they happen, try to take them as a compliment.

routines, a new house, new customs, new bedrooms—they may even have to share a room—and even a new birth order. A child who was once the oldest, with all the privileges that went along with that, might resent being bumped by an older child. The opposite might happen to a child who gets displaced as baby of the family. Don't make the mistake of expecting that everyone's going to live in one big, happy family. Give the kids plenty of time to get used to each other and to their new stepparents. It's not going to be easy on any of you.

"I don't want to see The Lion King *again, I want to read a book."*

You and Your Baby

Early Readers

According to reading expert Jim Trelease, studies of children who learned to read early have identified four characteristics of their homes. The first two are fairly obvious, and you're probably doing them already: the child is read to on a regular basis, and a wide variety of printed materials—books, magazines, newspapers, comics—is available in the home at all times.

The other two are a little less obvious but may be even easier to implement than the first two:

1. Paper and pencil are available to the child. Most kids are made curious about written language by watching their parents write things.
2. People in the home stimulate the child's interest in reading and writing by answering questions, praising the child's efforts at reading and writing, taking the child to the library frequently, buying books, writing down stories that the child dictates, and displaying the child's creations in a prominent place in the home.

At this point, your child is still at least a year away from reading—and there's no need to rush him. But if he seems to be taking an interest in letters and what they symbolize, don't hold him back. He may, for example, point to various words and ask you to tell him what they say. Or he may imitate you by "reading" a book to his stuffed animals. If he's got one of his favorite books memorized, he might even want to "read" it to you, turning the pages in all the right places.

This is a good age to subtly introduce letters. Sing the alphabet song a few times a day, just so he can get the sounds down. And point out the letters you see as you're out and about—stop signs, exit signs, on store awnings, and so on—especially the ones that are in your child's name. If your child is especially interested, you might want to point out "unintentional" letters—a bent straw making an L shape, for example, or an X pattern in a fence.

HOME LIBRARY UPDATE

Here are suggestions for the latest additions to your child's ever-growing library:

Blueberries for Sal (and others), Robert McCloskey
Bread and Jam for Frances (and the other Frances books), Russell Hoban
Carl Goes to Daycare (and others), Alexandra Day
The Cat in the Hat, Dr. Seuss
Curious George (and others), H. A. Rey
Frog and Toad Are Friends (and others), Arnold Lobel
Gossie, Olivier Dunrea
The Gingerbread Man, Paul Galdone
Happy Birthday, Moon, Frank Asch
Harry the Dirty Dog (and others), Gene Zion and Margaret B. Graham
How Do Dinosaurs Say Good Night? Jane Yolen
Louella Mae, She's Run Away! Karen Beaumont Alarcón
Madeline (and others), Ludwig Bemelmans
Mike Mulligan and His Steam Shovel (and others), Virginia Burton
Moo Who? Margie Palatini
Rollie Pollie Ollie (and others), William Joyce
The Snowman, Raymond Briggs
The Snowy Day, Ezra Jack Keats
The Story of Babar, Jean de Brunhoff
The Story of Ferdinand, Leaf Munro
Strega Nona (and others), Tomie dePaola
When I Am Old with You, Angela Johnson
Where the Wild Things Are, Maurice Sendak
Wibbly Pig Likes Bananas, Mick Inkpen

CONCEPTS

Cats (and many others in the series), Seymour Simon
How Many Snails, Paul Giganti
If You Look Around You, Testa Fulvio
Let's Eat! Beatrice Hollyer
Numbers (and others), John J. Reiss
Trucks You Can Count On, Doug Magee

FOLK TALES

Goldilocks and the Three Bears, Jan Brett
Jack and the Beanstalk, Joseph Jacobs
Stone Soup, Marcia Brown
Teeny Tiny, Jill Bennett
The Three Billygoats Gruff, Marcia Brown

POETRY

All Small, David McCord
Blackberry Ink, Eve Merrian
I'll Be You and You Be Me, Ruth Krauss
Miss Spider's Wedding (and others), David Kirk
Where the Sidewalk Ends, Shel Silverstein

GOING TO SCHOOL/DAYCARE

Molly, Ruth Shaw Radlauer
School, Emily McCully

GOING TO THE DENTIST

Curious George Goes to the Dentist, H. A. Rey
Doctor De Soto, William Steig
Just Going to the Dentist, Mercer Mayer

ESPECIALLY FOR OLDER SIBLINGS

Babies! Dorothy Hinshaw Patent
Baby's Catalog, Janet Ahlberg and Allan Ahlberg
Julius, the Baby of the World, Kevin Henkes
Let Me Tell You about My Baby, Roslyn Banish
Oonga Boonga, Frieda Wishinsky
Peter's Chair, Ezra Jack Keats
Shadow's Baby, Margery Cuyler

The Very Worst Monster, Pat Hutchins
When You Were a Baby, Ann Jonas

Screening Your Baby's Entertainment

Throughout this book I've talked about the fantastic benefits of reading to your child. But as your baby gets older, he'll get more and more of his information from other sources, in particular television and videos (we've discussed computers elsewhere in this book, so I'll leave them out of this discussion). In principle, there's nothing wrong with TV and videos. There are several great shows out there for very young children and some excellent videos as well, including the *Baby Einstein* series and the *All By Myself* series, both of which my youngest loved. But there are a number of problems:

- Children watch entirely too much television. A study done at the Children's Hospital Medical Center of Cincinnati in 2003 found that 40 percent of children under three watch at least three hours of television a day. Even worse, a third of children live in a home where the television is on *all the time*—even if no one's watching. And a quarter of children under two actually have a television in their own room.
- Most of the time babies are exposed to television, they're not watching age-appropriate programming. Instead, they're watching something selected by their parents or an older sibling. A significant amount of recent research has shown that even babies as young as ten to twelve months are influenced by the behavior of the characters they see on television.
- TV is passive and deprives the child of one of his most important ways of learning: questions. There's no one to ask, and no one to answer.
- TV discourages thinking. It's nearly impossible to show a character thinking through a problem on TV, and commercials tend to give the message that there is no problem that can't be solved by artificial means—by buying something.
- There's a link between watching television and obesity. A recent study done in England found that almost a quarter of children under four were overweight, and nearly 10 percent were obese. Only ten years earlier, those number were 15 percent and 5 percent, respectively. I don't mean to put all the blame on television—poor diet and lack of exercise are the main causes of obesity. But there's no question that watching TV contributes to the problem, largely because kids have a tendency to sit motionless in front of the tube, snacking.
- There's a link between watching television and developing behavior problems. The more toddlers watch, the more likely they are to be

diagnosed with attention deficit disorder later in life. Researchers are also exploring a link between TV and aggressive behavior.

- The messages kids get from TV are flawed. Most fathers, whether in commercials or in programming, are portrayed as clueless, incompetent boobs.

There are, of course, exceptions to the above-mentioned drawbacks, and you're probably not planning to toss your television out the window anytime soon. So if you're going to put your child in front of a screen, at least try to keep the following guidelines in mind:

- **If there's a television in your toddler's room, take it out.**
- **Set some basic rules.** For example, no watching during meals or in the middle of family time. And don't just leave the TV on as background noise; turn it off when your show is done.
- **Don't use television or movies as a babysitter.** From experience I can tell you that this is an incredibly easy trap to fall into, and one your child won't be in any hurry to get out of.
- **Make sure that whatever your child watches is made specifically for toddlers.** You may love sci-fi thrillers, but watch them after he's down for the night.
- **Watch together.** Little kids can't always tell the difference between reality and what's happening on the screen and may become frightened or confused. So use whatever you're watching as the topic for a discussion.
- **Monitor the media.** This does not mean turn it off. Watching television and movies with your child can be a great way to talk about issues of morality, right and wrong, politics, and more. And don't believe everything you hear about how video games, superheroes, comic books, and make-believe violence in the media lead to real-world violence. Media critic Gerard Jones did an exhaustive study and found that, contrary to what we've all come to accept as the truth, fantasy violence often gives kids important coping skills. "Instead of banning head-bonking TV shows and gory games like *Doom*, we should harness the tremendous power of fantasy to help our kids better navigate the world around them," he writes. It's an interesting argument, one that's worth investigating further. In the meantime, use your TV- and/or video-watching time to cuddle and talk about what's on the screen. If you need a few suggestions about what to watch, the Parents Television Council (www.parentstv.org) has extensive listings and reviews.

Play: Getting Physical

One of the biggest myths about play is that extremely active entertainment, especially roughhousing, teaches kids to be violent. The evidence, however, supports the exact opposite conclusion:

- Physical play is a model for socially acceptable assertion but not necessarily aggression, according to John Snarey, who has spent several decades studying fathers' impact on their children. "Children who roughhouse with their fathers, for instance, usually quickly learn that biting, kicking, and other forms of physical violence are not acceptable."
- Children who play with their fathers tend to be more helpful, cooperative, and likely to share. They also have better communication and leadership skills, according to pioneering fatherhood researcher Ross Parke.
- Parke and his colleagues have also found that for girls, high levels of physical play are associated with such desirable social attributes as positive emotional expressiveness and clarity of communication as well as originality, novelty, and creativity. Boys become more empathetic, more popular among their peers, and less likely to be hyperactive or sad.
- Physical play builds children's—especially girls'—confidence, assertiveness, and academic achievement. Several studies of successful women have shown that almost all of them had fathers who engaged in a lot of physical play with them.
- As we've discussed before, fathers and mothers generally play very differently with their boys and girls. And this serves to reinforce children's "socially acceptable" (that is, stereotyped) sex-typed behavior, especially for boys. So if you're interested in reducing the chances that your child will end up trapped in a set of gender-based behaviors, play with him or her actively and frequently.

Sounds like throwing your kids around just about guarantees that they'll grow up confident, strong, and smart, doesn't it? Well, lots of physical play may increase the chances, but there are three other important contributing factors:

- You've got to do more than wrestle with your child or turn yourself into a human jungle gym. Be sure to spend plenty of time talking, reading, teaching, changing diapers, and so on. See pages 210–11 for some additional suggestions.
- If you have a daughter, don't hold back. Dads tend to play more gently with their daughters than their sons. There's absolutely no reason to do that.

Girls are just as hardy as boys, and as the evidence I've cited in this chapter shows, they benefit enormously from having a close, physically playful relationship with Dad.

- Don't force your children to play with you if they don't want to; it can actually do more harm than good. Research consistently shows that children whose fathers are overly "directive" (meaning they give too many commands) may become socially withdrawn, have fewer friends, are more likely to watch activities than get involved, and have more behavior problems.

Other Kinds of Fun

LARGE MOTOR SKILLS

- Take a walk on a balance beam, along the curb, or even down a line on the sidewalk.
- Play catch (start with a large, slightly deflated ball).
- Jump over things (anything more than a few inches, though, will be too high for most kids this age).
- Throw, kick, roll, and toss balls of all sizes.
- Ride a tricycle.
- Spin around till you drop.
- Pound, push, pull, and kick.
- Make music using drums, xylophones, flutes, and anything else you have handy.
- Play Twister.

SMALL MOTOR SKILLS

- Puzzles (fewer than twenty pieces is probably best). You might even want to cut up a simple picture from a magazine and see whether your toddler can put it back together.
- Draw on paper or with chalk on the sidewalk.
- Sculpt with clay or other molding substance.
- Finger paint.
- Play with string and large beads.
- Pour water or sand or seeds from one container to another.
- Get a big box (from a dishwasher or refrigerator), then build, paint and decorate a house together.

THE BRAIN

- Matching games.

- Alphabet and number games (put colorful magnetic letters and numbers on the fridge and leave them low enough for the child to reach).
- Lots of dress-up clothes.
- Dolls of all kinds (including action figures).
- Pretending games with "real" things (phones, computer keyboards).
- Imaginary driving trips where you talk about all the things you see on the road. Be sure to let your toddler drive part of the way.
- Sorting games (put all the pennies, or all the triangles, or all the cups together).
- Arranging games (big, bigger, biggest).
- Smelling games. Blindfold your toddler and have him identify things by their scent.
- Pattern games (small-big/small-big).
- Counting games (How many pencils are there?).

A FEW FUN THINGS FOR RAINY DAYS (OR ANYTIME)

- Have pillow fights.
- Make a really, really messy art project.
- Cook something—kneading bread or pizza dough is especially good, as is roasting marshmallows on the stove (see pages 214–20 for more).
- Go baby bowling (gently toss your toddler onto your bed).
- Try other gymnastics (airplane rides: you're on your back, feet up in the air, baby's tummy on your feet, you and baby holding hands).
- Dance and/or sing.
- Play hide-and-seek.
- Stage a puppet show.
- If it's not too cold, go outside, strip down to your underwear, and paint each other top-to-bottom with nontoxic, water-based paints. Otherwise, get bundled up and go for a long, wet, sloppy, muddy stomp in the rain. If you don't feel like getting wet, get in the car and drive through puddles.

Group Activities

If you haven't already done so, it's a good idea to start getting your child involved in some regular group activities. Actually, it's a good idea for both of you: it'll give your child an opportunity to meet some new people and to practice his budding social skills. And while he's playing, you'll have a great opportunity to spend time with some adults who probably have many of the same questions and concerns that you do.

If you're interested in joining an ongoing group or an organized activity, you

It's All in Their Heads

In the movie *Harvey*, Jimmy Stewart (in the lead role) had an imaginary friend (all right, a six-foot-tall rabbit), and there's little doubt in our minds that he was more than just a bit nuts. But if your child has an imaginary playmate, there's nothing to worry about. Having imaginary playmates is a normal part of growing up—especially in the toddler years—and they serve several important functions:

- They can be wonderful companions for pretend play, which is an important way to stimulate creativity and imagination. Having an invisible friend can make those long trips to the moon or back in time a little less lonely.
- They can act as a child's trusted confidant when there's no one else to tell his secrets to. Even small children have issues that are too private to tell us.
- They can help kids figure out the difference between right and wrong. Kids sometimes have a tough time stopping themselves from doing things they know are wrong. Blaming the imaginary friend for eating cookies before dinner is often a sign that the child understands right-versus-wrong distinctions but isn't quite ready to assume complete responsibility for his actions.
- They can give you some valuable insights into your child's feelings.

can find a dozen options within a few miles of your house. Here are a few places to start looking:

- Your local YMCA has classes and get-togethers for toddlers and their parents, and there's probably a Gymboree or something similar not far from you.
- Your local parenting newspaper will have listings of activities.
- Zoos, museums, planetariums, science centers, and others often have activities geared for toddlers.
- Church or synagogue groups.
- Slowlane.com and rebedad.com have listings of dads' groups all over the country.

If you're adventurous and want to start a group of your own, here are some things to consider:

Listening to your child bravely comfort an invisible friend who's about to get a shot may be a clue that he is more afraid than he's letting on.

While it's generally perfectly fine to humor your child and go along with his claims about the existence of an imaginary friend, there are a few ground rules:

- Don't let the "friend" be your child's only companion. Kids need to socialize with others their own ages. If your child seems to have no human friends or has no interest in being with his peers, talk to your pediatrician.
- Don't let your child shift responsibility for everything bad to the friend. Saying that the friend is the one responsible for a nighttime accident is okay. Blaming the friend for a string of bank robberies isn't.
- Treat the friend with respect. This means remembering his name, greeting him when you meet, and apologizing when you sit on him.
- Don't use the friend to manipulate your child. That means no comments like, "Maggie finished her dinner, why don't you finish yours?"

Most kids lose their imaginary friends between their third and fifth birthdays. Sometimes the friends are forgotten, sometimes they're sent on a distant—and permanent—trip, and other times they're killed in a horrible accident.

- Find a place where you can easily keep an eye on the kids while you're talking to the grown-ups. A fenced park with benches can be great.
- Don't let the group get too large. Even if each adult keeps track of his or her own kids, any more than five or six is pushing it. And try to keep an even number so the little ones can pair off without excluding anyone.
- Meet regularly. As you well know, kids love routines.
- Bring some of your toddler's own toys. This should help reduce the amount of grabbing, shoving, and tears.
- Bring some food. Your child will probably prefer to eat someone else's, but some other kid will eat what you bring.
- Don't hover. Let the kids do what they want, as long as it's safe.
- Play with the other kids—but not too much. If the other little ones seem to be having too much fun with you, your child may get very jealous. Kids this age aren't too thrilled about sharing their daddies.

- Don't push togetherness. Kids may not want to play with each other all the time. They need plenty of time to play alone, too.
- Have a backup plan in case you get rained out of your regular place. Places like Chuck E. Cheese are hot foul-weather destinations. If your backup meeting place is your house, be prepared for a bit more friction than usual. Having to share his house and his toys may be more than your child bargained for.
- Keep your sick kid at home. Although chances are that whatever he's got has already been passed around, the other parents will be nervous anyway.

Music

During the last half of your child's third year, his language skills make a sudden, often dramatic spurt forward. You'll see this development in two distinct yet connected ways:

First, you'll notice that his imitation skills have become quite sharp: he can now repeat nearly any word or two-word phrase. He can also now tell when he's imitating something correctly and when he's not. Second, now that he's got a good grasp of the sounds that make up his native language, he'll begin using them as toys, amusing himself, and you, by making up his own "words." Musically, a similar development is taking place. "Once they've acquired a simple vocabulary of tonal patterns and rhythms, they can start creating their own songs," says music educator Edwin Gordon.

After a while he'll combine all these skills, and by his third birthday he may be able to sing all the words of a short song (like "Happy Birthday") or entire phrases of longer, familiar songs ("Baa, baa, black sheep, have you any wool? Yes, sir. Yes, sir. Three bags full," for example. But he won't be able to sing the whole song for another few months). He may also make deliberate changes to songs he already knows ("Baa, baa, blue sheep . . .") just for the fun of it.

Your child's sense of rhythm has also been developing nicely. Notice that now when he moves in response to the music he hears, he's moving in time with the beat (as opposed to making the seemingly random movements you saw just a few months ago).

This is a great time to try some imitation games with your child. Sing a note, then wait for him to repeat it. If he does that pretty well, try two notes, then three (a lot of kids can't do three-note patterns until well after they turn three, so don't get your hopes too high). Also try tapping out various rhythms and asking your child to repeat them.

Keep exposing your child to a wide variety of music and play it wherever you are. You can get children's CDs, but whatever you're listening to will work as well. Just keep a lid on the volume. Loud music can damage his hearing. If you play an instrument, let your child see you in action. If he wants to participate and your instrument isn't too fragile, let him.

Cooking with Kids

Although it seems like a lot of trouble, cooking with your toddler can be a wonderful experience for both of you. Your child, of course, gets to make a huge mess for you to clean up. But besides that, here are a few things that Mollie Katzen, cookbook writer extraordinaire, says that kids get out of cooking:

- Confidence, self-esteem, and a feeling of accomplishment
- Early math skills—measuring, counting, time sequences
- Fine motor skills
- A greater understanding of cause and effect
- An appreciation of the importance of following directions
- Practice working as a team

There's also the added benefit of seeing you involved in a nontraditional task, which will help your child keep an open mind when considering careers of his own.

You, of course, gain in very different ways. First of all, you get to use your time more efficiently—having fun and cooking dinner (or part of it) for the whole family simultaneously. It's not unlike taking a college course that satisfies a science requirement and a humanities requirement at the same time. Second, there's a good chance that your child will eat some of the food he makes, thereby expanding his food repertoire beyond plain pasta and white rice with soy sauce.

No matter what you're making, your child can participate in at least some part of the preparation. How long he'll actually stay in the kitchen with you depends on how much of a mess you'll let him make and whether or not what he's making is worth licking off a spoon. If you're willing to cooperate, just about any three-year-old can:

- Stir (my kids loved this)
- Tear up leaves for salad (they hated salad, but they loved destroying things, so this worked out nicely)
- Knead and roll out dough (my kids' absolute favorite kitchen activity)
- Break eggs (actually, this may be their favorite)

- Measure ingredients and dump them into bowls (if this isn't the favorite, it's certainly a close second, or third)
- Sprinkle toppings (hmmm . . . that's a lot of favorites)

Here are some fun, simple, quick recipes that you and your child can make together. In fact, he can probably handle most of the tasks by himself if you let him. But here are a few rules to keep in mind before you get started:

- Read the "Cooking Safety" section on page 219 very carefully.
- Don't force. If he doesn't want to do a particular step, let him alone.
- Have fun. Yes, he'll get flour all over the floor (and the walls and his clothes). And yes, he'll get broken eggshells into the batter. If you're not in the mood to deal with these things, save your cooking adventure for another day.

KIDSICLES

What you'll need:
1 cup fresh or frozen fruit
1 cup milk or yogurt
Popsicle molds (or ice cube trays and Popsicle sticks)
A blender

1. Blend fruit and milk or yogurt.
2. Pour into molds or tray.
3. Freeze for at least four hours. Overnight is best.

Let your toddler get as involved as possible, but keep him away from the blender itself. If you want him to help pour, transfer some liquid from the blender into a smaller, easily pourable container.

LIZ'S EGGS IN THE NEST

What you'll need:
1 egg
1 piece of toast
Cookie cutters (optional)

1. Cut a hole about the size of a golf ball in the middle of the piece of toast. If you've got some cookie cutters with simple shapes like animals or hearts, cut the hole with them instead.
2. Put the toast into a small skillet on low.

3. Crack the egg into the hole.
4. Cook until the egg is how your child likes it.

FRENCH TOAST

What you'll need:

4 eggs

1 cup milk

1 teaspoon vanilla extract (optional)

Pinch of cinnamon

6 to 8 slices of bread (Stale is fine; moldy is not. If you want to make this even more fun, cut the bread into animal shapes, cars, or faces before you start.)

1 tablespoon butter

Syrup, jam, sour cream, or any other kind of topping

1. Combine eggs, milk, vanilla, and cinnamon in a bowl.
2. Stir (or whisk, if you have one) until mixed thoroughly.
3. Pour the mixture into a pie pan or any bowl or dish that's large enough to hold a slice of bread.
4. Drop a slice of bread in the mixture, let it soak for a few seconds, flip it over, and do the same on the other side.
5. Heat a skillet and add some of the butter.
6. When the butter melts, spread it around and add a slice or two of the batter-soaked bread (as many as can fit on the surface of the skillet without overlapping).
7. Cook until light brown on the bottom. Be careful about this—most kids will refuse to eat anything that's anywhere close to being burned.
8. Flip over and cook until light brown on the other side (or somewhat less, if you happened to have overcooked the first side). Repeat until all slices are cooked.
9. Serve with your child's favorite topping.

QUESADILLAS

What you'll need:

Cooking spray or 1 tablespoon butter or margarine

Two 6-inch tortillas (Wheat are usually softer, but if your child is allergic to wheat, corn is fine.)

Nice-sized handful of your child's favorite cheese, grated

Several tablespoons of refried beans (optional)

Several tablespoons of steamed rice
Several tablespoons of cooked fresh or frozen vegetables (optional)

1. Put the cooking spray, butter, or margarine in a skillet and place over medium heat.
2. Drop a single tortilla on the skillet and sprinkle some of the grated cheese all over it.
3. If you think your child will eat them, add the refried beans, rice, and/or vegetables.
4. Cover the first tortilla with a second one.
5. Cook for 30 to 45 seconds, or until the cheese has melted enough to keep the two tortillas stuck together.
6. Flip over and cook for another 30 to 45 seconds. If you can flip the tortilla sandwich in the skillet, your child and all her friends will consider you the absolute coolest guy in the neighborhood. If you can't, practice.

MILKSHAKES

What you'll need:
1 cup milk
Large piece of your child's favorite fruit
Several ice cubes
1 to 2 drops vanilla extract (optional)
1 to 2 teaspoons chocolate syrup (optional)

1. Put all the ingredients in a blender.
2. Cover and blend until smooth.

PRETZELS

What you'll need:
1 package yeast
1½ cups warm water
1 tablespoon sugar
1 tablespoon salt
4 cups flour
1 egg, beaten

1. Preheat the oven to 425° F.
2. Mix the yeast, water, sugar, and salt until everything is completely dissolved.

3. Stir in the flour.
4. Knead into a soft dough.
5. Roll into long ropes about the thickness of your finger.
6. Shape into pretzel shapes, numbers, letters, or anything your child feels like making.
7. Brush the beaten egg on the shaped dough.
8. Bake for 12 to 15 minutes.
9. Take out and let cool before eating.

PANCAKE ART

What you'll need:
1 box of Bisquick
All the additional ingredients listed on the box
Cookie cutters (optional)

Cooking Safety

Cooking with kids can be a huge amount of fun. But because it involves dealing with knives and flames, there's also the potential for getting hurt. Following these safety rules should help you get through the process with a minimum of bloodshed.

- Wash your hands before you start. No explanation necessary, right?
- Work at your child's level—either at the kitchen table or, better yet, at your child's very own table. This reduces the chances that he'll slip off the stool he's been standing on or that he'll pull a heavy bowl off the counter and onto his head.
- Use back burners and keep pot and pan handles pointed toward the back of the stove. Again, this reduces the chances that hot dishes will get pulled off the stovetop.
- Remind your child to be careful about touching anything that used to be hot. Electric stove coils stay hot even after they're turned off, and so do pots and pans. Repeat the reminder every ten minutes, as necessary.
- Opening ovens, closing them, putting things into them, and taking things out are adult-only jobs. Don't even think about letting an almost three-year-old try any of these jobs.
- Dress appropriately. Long sleeves can get dragged through batter or yanked into blenders. Short sleeves are better. Topless is better still, and the most fun.

1. Make the pancake batter following the recipe on the box.
2. If you've got a steady hand, drizzle the batter into the heated pan and make whatever shapes or letters your child wants.
3. Alternatively, put a cookie cutter (metal only) into the pan and pour batter into the cutter.
4. When bubbles appear in the batter, remove the cookie cutter and turn the pancake over. Be very careful when touching the cutter, since it will be extremely hot.

POPCORN BALLS

What you'll need:

10 to 12 cups popped popcorn

1 cup corn syrup, OR one 10-ounce package of marshmallows

¼ cup butter or margarine (only if you use the marshmallows instead of the syrup)

1 or 2 packages of gelatin, any flavor(s) you like

1. Half fill several large bowls with the popcorn.
2. Put the corn syrup, or the marshmallows and margarine, in a pan and melt over low heat.
3. Add the gelatin. Stir until it's completely dissolved.
4. Remove the mixture from the heat and pour it over the popcorn. Stir quickly so that the popcorn gets covered evenly.
5. Shape the popcorn into baseball-sized balls.
6. Place the balls on a sheet of waxed paper and refrigerate until firm.

EVE'S CHOCOLATE LEAVES

What you'll need:

16-ounce package chocolate chips

New ¼-inch paintbrush

Cookie sheet covered with waxed paper

Some thick leaves with stems, gently washed and completely dry (Check with your local garden shop to make absolutely sure they're not toxic; camellia and magnolia leaves are pretty widely available and are fine.)

1. Melt the chocolate chips over low to medium heat or in the top of a double boiler.
2. Paint the surface of the leaves with a thick coat of the melted chocolate.
3. Put the painted leaves on the waxed-paper-covered cookie sheet.

4. When you've painted as many leaves as your child thinks is fun, put the cookie sheet into the refrigerator until the chocolate has hardened.
5. Hold the leaf chocolate-side down, and with your other hand gently pull up the stem and carefully remove the leaf from the chocolate.
6. Show your child the way the stem and vein pattern of the real leaf has been replicated in the chocolate.

You and Your Partner

Helping Her Cope with Being a Stepmom

On pages 201–3 we talked about you becoming a stepfather. But what if the situation is reversed, and you're married to a brand-new stepmother? Most of what I said earlier applies here—just reverse the genders.

In short, you are the single most important factor in determining how the new woman in your life will deal with her new role. You're the one who has to welcome her into your family, and you're the one who has to make sure your children understand her role. Like just about anyone stepping into a preexisting family unit, she's going to feel a little insecure. Here are some ways you can help her through this tough transition:

- **Let her know that she doesn't have to be your child's mother.** In fact, she probably *can't* be—your child already has a mother. What she can and should do, however, is treat your child with love and respect. After a while she'll get the same back.
- **Give her plenty of time to develop her own relationship with your child.** This means letting things happen at their own pace and not forcing her to take on more responsibility than she's able to.
- **Give her some feedback.** She may not say so, but she really wants to know that the kids like her and that she's doing a good job. So if they say something nice to you about her, pass it on. Compliment her when she does something great with the kids, and give her some gentle pointers if she does something wrong (but not while she's doing it—wait until the two of you are alone). Hovering over her shoulder puts way too much pressure on her. Instead, let her discover how to do most things for herself the same way you did: by making mistakes.
- **Talk to your kids.** Make sure they know what her authority is, and that they know what's expected of them in relation to her.
- **Encourage her to tell you how she's feeling.** She may be having the time of her life, or she may be frustrated, exasperated, and annoyed. Help

her celebrate the joys and be supportive when she needs to cry on your shoulder.

- **Help her deal with your ex**. Your new partner and your ex probably won't have all that much to do with each other. But they might bump into each other at family, school, or other events. You can help minimize potential conflicts by being balanced in the way you talk about your ex. If you've been saying nothing but bad things, your new partner is probably going to be somewhat hostile. But if you've been nothing but complimentary, she may be jealous.
- **Set up some ground rules**. It's critical that you and your new partner reach a clear understanding about the following issues:
  - Discipline. Who's going to do it, and how? This can be especially important if she has kids of her own and an established way of handling them. Generally speaking, you should handle disciplining your children for at least a few years.
  - Other involvement. To make her feel part of the family, you have to give her some authority over the kids and back her up when she uses it. At the same time, you don't want her stepping in and telling you how to run your (and your kids') life. Also, will she be expected to help the kids with their homework? Drive the carpool? Attend parent-teacher conferences?
  - Money. How will you handle household finances? Will any of her income be used to pay child support for your children or, even worse, alimony? If she has children of her own, will any of your income be used to pay for them?

Family Matters

Preparing the Older Sibling

BEFORE THE BIRTH

- Don't start too early. Wait until your child asks some questions about his mother's physical changes, about why you're moving furniture around, and so forth.
- Don't make too big a deal about how great it's going to be to become a big brother or sister, and don't try to force your child to get excited about the prospect.
- Take your toddler to the prenatal doctor visits. If he's interested, have him hold the Doppler to hear the baby's heartbeat; take him to see the ultrasound pictures. If he's not interested, leave him alone.

- Some hospitals offer older-sibling prep classes. In them kids learn the basics of what their mothers are going to go through during the birth; the kinds of things they can and can't do with their new sibling; and that Dad and Mom still love them very much, even though they aren't going to be the center of the universe anymore.
- Expose him to other babies you know. If you don't know any, the nursery at the hospital should have plenty of extras. (Although with many hospitals tightening nursery security, it may be harder to visit babies that aren't your own.)
- If you're moving the older child out of a crib, moving to a new house, or making any other major changes, do it long before the baby arrives. Otherwise, the older child will think he's being moved out to make room for the new baby.

AFTER THE BIRTH

Handling your older children's reactions to their new baby brother or sister requires an extra touch of gentleness and sensitivity. Although kids are usually wildly excited (initially, at least) at their new status as big brother or big sister, when it hits them that the baby is going to be a permanent visitor, things change. Psychologist Henry Biller found that most kids show some negative reactions, such as being more disobedient and demanding. A lot of brand-new older siblings also exhibit some regressive behavior.

For example, older children who are already toilet-trained may start wetting themselves again (my older daughter did this). They may become clingy, start using "baby talk," crawl or demand to be carried instead of walking, or have crying jags for no reason at all. It's as if your older child is saying, "If all you wanted was a crying baby, why didn't you say so? I can do that."

These behavioral changes are perfectly normal and are really the result of the older child's feeling that the baby has stolen something that was exclusively his: your love and affection. Interestingly, Biller also found that children who have close relationships with their father adjust much better to the birth of a new sibling and have fewer ongoing problems.

Here are a few things you can do to ease the transition for your older kid:

- As soon as the new baby is born, call the older child and tell him first. Let him make the announcement that he is a big brother to the other members of the family.
- Have the older child come to the hospital right away (even if it's past his bedtime). Take a few pictures of him holding the baby.
- Don't expect your older child to love the baby instantly. It can take a long,

long time. Really. A friend of mine told me that for years, every time he drove by the hospital the baby had been born in, his oldest son would ask, "So can we take her back yet?"

- Don't make a big fuss about the new baby or smother her with gifts in front of the older child—it will only make your toddler feel left out, jealous, and resentful. It could also result in the older child trying to hurt the baby. Have everyone who comes to visit the baby spend a few private minutes with the older child first, hopefully talking about something other than what he thinks of being a big brother.
- Make sure you and your partner each spend some time alone with your toddler doing special activities, going to special places, reading his favorite books, or whatever he wants. He's going to need constant reminders that he's as important to you as the new baby. Just saying so won't do the trick.
- Don't blame yourself. Friction between your older and younger kids is normal. Saying, "If only I'd done . . . he'd love the baby," is a waste of time.
- Get some special gifts for your toddler.
- Read some of the books listed on pages 152 and 206.
- Go through your photo albums, reminding your toddler what a wonderful baby he was.
- Encourage your toddler to get involved. Let him help as much as possible with "his" baby—holding, feeding, diapering, clothing, singing or talking, and running errands around the house. And be sure to be extra appreciative.
- Teach your toddler how to play with the baby. It might be fun to show him how to elicit reflex actions from the baby (I've got a big section on this in *The New Father: A Dad's Guide to the First Year*, pages 60–65). But never leave the baby alone with your older child, not even for a second (unless, of course, your older one is over twelve). Your primary consideration is, of course, to keep the new baby alive and uninjured. And you'll need to remind the older child (dozens of times) that hurting the baby is simply not allowed. Make it clear that doing so will result not only in not being allowed to play with the baby for a while, but also in the loss of some special big-kid privileges.
- Give your toddler some space of his own that's completely off-limits to the baby.
- Allow him to have things he doesn't have to share at all. With toys that must be shared, be meticulous about giving each child equal time—set a timer with a loud beep.
- Give your toddler plenty of opportunity to be out of the home regularly—sleepovers at friends' and grandparents', off with the babysitter, and so on.

Otherwise, he'll feel like he's competing with the baby all day. Be careful, though, not to do too much of this—you don't want to give the child the impression that you're booting him out.

- Give your toddler a few privileges—a later bedtime, perhaps.
- Encourage your toddler to express his emotions. Ask a lot of questions about how he feels. Keep the questions focused on him —not on the baby.
- Treat every vocal expression of pain or rage as positive, Biller recommends. You can't force a child to feel love if he doesn't feel it. And it's far better for him to say something hurtful than to express the idea physically. If he needs to burn off some hostility, make sure he gets plenty of exercise.
- Empathize. Vicky Lansky suggests letting your child see you expressing your own occasional annoyance with the baby's demands, but not so often that he gets the idea that the new sibling is a permanent nuisance. Express your joy, too. And talk about your own experience as an older child (if you were one).
- Look at the world from the older child's perspective. Imagine how it feels to your toddler when he sees his younger sister wearing something that used to be his—even if he outgrew it long ago. To him it can seem like there's nothing left of him.
- For a child, the expression "It's not fair" really means "It's not the same." So get two of everything, and make sure your toddler gets first pick.
- Be prepared. When older children are forced not to hit younger siblings (life is tough, isn't it?), their aggression doesn't just disappear. It has to come out somewhere, and frequently it is reborn as a temper tantrum.

33–36 MONTHS

Learning to Let Go

What's Going On with the Baby

Physically

- Over the course of this last year, your toddler has put on only a few pounds. But she's getting longer and longer, especially in the legs and torso. She throws, catches, pedals her trike, and loves to jump off things.
- If it wasn't already, it should be fairly clear by now whether your child is left- or right-handed.
- Her hand coordination is constantly improving. She tries to imitate your writing and can draw a pretty passable circle (or at least a swirl).
- She very neatly lays out her clothes for the next day the night before and has no trouble putting on her own pants, socks, T-shirt, and jacket. Buttons, snaps, and zippers may still give her some trouble.

Intellectually

- As she approaches her third birthday, your toddler will be quite comfortable with many short-term time concepts. She regularly uses "soon," "in a minute," and the endearing "this day" (instead of "today").
- She's also deepening her understanding of spatial relationships—she's mastered "in" and "out," but the more abstract "near" has eluded her until now.
- She's very concerned that every object has its own special place, and she may get quite upset if things aren't where they're supposed to be.
- Her attention span continues to grow, and she can now focus on an activity

for as long as five to eight minutes. This means she's ready for longer-lasting games such as hide-and-seek.

- Her sorting skills are very well developed, and she loves to help you by separating the laundry into whites and colors, matching up pairs of socks, or putting away the silverware (with supervision, of course).
- She can now count up to three. (She may be able to say her numbers up to ten, but she doesn't really know what they mean.)

Verbally

- By her third birthday your child will understand the majority of the conversational language she'll use for the rest of her life. And about 80 percent of what she says can be understood, even by strangers.
- Boys' verbal skills and vocabularies are still lagging a bit behind girls'. Boys generally tell shorter stories whose main characters are usually

"Excuse me for sounding like a Jewish mother, but may I point out that your kid is getting wet."

themselves. Girls' stories are longer, and their main characters are more likely to be adults.

- Your toddler is finally able to use tenses (although not always completely accurately). My mother fell down and tore a ligament in her knee, and we told my younger daughter about it the next day. For months afterward, she would look up and announce, "Grandma fell down boom and hurt her leg yesterday."
- Kids acquire most of their understanding of time words in the six months between ages two and a half and three.

Emotionally/Socially

- Like their teenage counterparts, "first adolescents" are incredible know-it-alls. But the veneer of confidence is pretty thin. "It helps to remember that the child is bossy not because he is sure, but actually because he is unsure," write child development experts Louise Bates Ames and Frances Ilg. "The world still seems big and dangerous to him. If he can command even a small part of it (his parents), it helps him to feel secure." As your toddler's language skills improve, thus enabling her to gain some control over her impulses, the world will become (in her eyes) much less dangerous.
- Your "first adolescent" may still be quite negative and contrary. But it's critical to keep in mind that her negativity is part of an important developmental stage. "The first step toward a positive self-identity and sense of selfhood is a negative self-identity, a negation of the values and desires of his parents," writes psychologist Fitzhugh Dodson. "A negative self-identity must precede positive self-identity."
- It's taken a while, but your toddler is finally beginning to interact regularly with her playmates. She loves the act of sharing but will often grab back whatever she's given someone. And she still spends a lot of time protecting her toys and her territory from intruders.
- Although her sense of humor is getting more sophisticated, it's still the incongruous that gets the biggest laughs: try to put on her shoes or wear her pants on your head, and you're likely to reduce your toddler to hysterical laughter. Other things that are usually good for a laugh: accidents (unless someone is injured), silly questions ("Where are your wings?"), and adults imitating baby talk or pretending to throw a tantrum.

What You're Going Through

Speaking Up

I was second in line to buy stamps at the post office when a young woman came into the lobby, dragging a three-year-old boy behind her. "Now just sit down over there and shut up," she snapped, pointing the boy to an empty seat on a nearby bench. But instead of sitting, the boy began to run around the lobby. And that's when his mother grabbed him. "I'm sick and tired of you," she said as she slapped his face, hard. "And you better quit that crying, or I'll—" He didn't. She did, this time knocking him to the floor.

I was stunned. Whatever that little boy had done, it certainly didn't warrant the treatment he was getting. At first I wanted to say something to the woman, but I couldn't bring myself to do it. Then I looked around the post office, hoping that maybe someone else would say something. But everyone seemed to be concentrating on the return addresses on the envelopes they'd brought. The woman was still chastising her child when my turn came. I bought my stamps, exchanged helpless looks and shoulder shrugs with the clerk, and quickly left. I sat outside in my car for a while, furious—not only at that woman for hitting her child, but also at myself and at everyone else in that post office. How could a bunch of responsible adults have stood by so silently?

Certainly, seeing an adult abuse a child is something that bothers just about everyone. But to parents concerned about the safety and welfare of their own children, it's especially disturbing. Unfortunately, though, it happens all the time. And since we're spending time in places where there are other families around, we're likely to see more than our share.

WHY WE DON'T SPEAK UP

Most of us know what we'd do (or at least what we think we'd do) if someone tried to hurt our children. So why are we so hesitant to speak up when someone else's kids are being abused? Are we just uncaring and insensitive? "Not at all," says psychology professor Mark Barnett. "Historically, children have been regarded as personal property. And we still tend to believe that parents have the right to deal with them however they see fit."

Another reason we don't speak up when we see someone treating a child inappropriately is that most of us try to blend into our surroundings, hoping that someone else will take the lead. But when no one does, "We downplay our own reactions and convince ourselves that what we initially thought was abusive behavior really wasn't that bad after all," claims Dr. Ervin Staub. Staub refers to this extremely common phenomenon as "pluralistic ignorance."

But hesitating to "butt in" and taking one's cues from others are definitely not the only factors that keep us silent. Imagine this scenario: you're walking home alone at night when you see a large man coming out the door of a house, carrying a screaming child. He quickly stuffs her into the back seat and gets ready to drive away. He sees you staring suspiciously at him and glares back.

Are you face to face with a violent kidnapper, or just with a frantic father taking a sick child to the hospital? If you play it safe and say nothing, you may experience one or both of the other feelings most likely to keep people from speaking up: fear of putting oneself in physical danger, or fear of making things worse for the child.

WHEN TO GET INVOLVED . . .

For better or worse, passersby almost never have a legal obligation to do anything. (Doctors, dentists, teachers, social workers, and, in some states, the people who develop film at the local drugstore, however, are required to report suspected abuse to the proper authority.) But there are clearly times when all of us have a moral obligation to do something. Looking for some guidance about when, exactly, to jump in, I spoke with Suzanne Barnard, a spokesperson for the Children's Division of the American Humane Society (www.americanhumane.org). Suzanne suggested the following guidelines:

- If an adult is causing a child serious or life-threatening injury (hitting hard enough to leave a mark or actually drawing blood), do something.
- If a child has been abandoned or negligently left in a dangerous situation (locked in a car in hot weather with the windows closed), do something.
- If the child's actions make it reasonably clear that he or she is scared, or that the person doing the suspected abuse is a stranger to her, do something.

. . . AND HOW TO DO IT

Okay, so now we know when we're supposed to do something. But what does "something" mean? For some of us, confronting others is no problem. "I'd rather risk embarrassing myself to save a child," a friend of mine once told me, "than have to live with myself knowing that I could have done something but didn't." Of course, "confronting" doesn't have to mean "attacking."

Here are a few approaches that might help defuse a potentially dangerous situation:

- **Make eye contact in the kindest way possible**. Looking disapproving or threatening could produce an effect exactly opposite to the one you're hoping for.
- **Strike up a conversation**. Perhaps talk about something completely out

of the blue, like "What an incredibly beautiful child." Your interruption could be enough to break the rhythm and give the adult time to regain his senses.

- **Be sympathetic**. Offering to help, or saying something like, "Kids can really push your buttons, can't they?" or "I know just how you feel. My daughter did exactly the same thing last week," makes you the angry adult's ally and increases the chances that she'll stop what she's doing.
- **Keep it positive**. Negative remarks or looks are likely to increase the parent's anger and could make matters worse.
- **Make a loud noise or knock something over**. Again, sometimes all it takes to diffuse a hot situation is a momentary diversion.
- **Divert the child's attention**. Talk to her or point out something of interest.

For many of us, however, approaching a stranger—even to do something as simple as ask directions—is simply too embarrassing or daunting. So if you can't, don't feel guilty—you're not a wimp. You still can make an anonymous report to the appropriate authorities, who will check it out for you.

If you're in a store, contact the manager immediately and have him or her call the police (if the manager refuses, call the police yourself). If you're outside, try to get the adult's license plate number and then call 911. If you're concerned about a neighbor, call your county child protective services and give them the address.

THE FEAR OF MAKING A MISTAKE

Sometimes it's obvious there's a problem: a child is getting beaten right in front of you, or you're driving down the highway and see the woman driving the car next to you is breast-feeding a baby (don't laugh—this actually happens). But what should you do when the situation is not so clear-cut, or when you're seeing something that might be a flash of temper rather than a case of prolonged abuse? After all, as parents we've all come close to "losing it" on a particularly bad day. And what about that kid you know who's always covered with bruises?

Before calling the police, take a good, long look at the situation and make sure your suspicions are reasonable. As you well know, children are always having accidents, and a few bruises and cuts are usually not an indication of abuse. If you need help evaluating what you've seen, or if you want to know how to make a report in your area, get in touch with Childhelp USA at 800-4-A-CHILD (422-4453) or www. childhelpusa.org. They can either take a report from you directly or refer you to the appropriate agency in your area. They're also the place to call if you're feeling out of control yourself and need someone to talk to. You'll find more child-abuse and/or parental stress resources in the Resources guide.

You and Your Baby

More on Sex Identity

A DIFFERENT KIND OF PLAYTIME

As you know by now, the toddler years are the age of exploration, a time when your child investigates her world and learns about all the great things she can do with her body. Giving your child as much freedom as possible to explore is critical to her developing sense of autonomy and self-confidence. And most parents are perfectly willing to let their children explore whatever they want to, as long as they keep their hands out of their pants.

Like it or not, almost all toddlers go through a genital self-exploration phase, and it's especially common right around the time when they start making the transition from diapers to big-kid underwear. After all, when they were wearing their diapers all the time, their genitals were pretty hard to grab hold of. But now that they're accessible nearly all the time . . . (Reminds me a little of the old joke: Why do dogs lick their crotches? Because they can.)

Still, it's a little discomfiting to watch a child play with his or her own genitals, and it's hard to resist pulling the child's hand away or shouting, "Stop that!" Maybe it's all those stories we heard about how masturbation causes blindness or hairy palms, or turns kids into perverts.

Whatever the reason, it's important that you resist the urge to step between your child and her genitals. Making a big deal out of it can give your child the message that that part of her body is dirty or that touching it is somehow wrong. For a little boy, "His penis is no more interesting than any other part of him," says Fitzhugh Dodson. "It is only when we react as though there is something bad or naughty about it that we teach him to become morbidly interested." The same obviously goes for little girls. The truth, of course, is that "our toddlers will only develop sex hang-ups if we teach them to," says Dodson.

At home, the best plan of action is neither to encourage nor discourage genital exploration. In public places, however, gently redirect your child to another activity, telling her that private touching should be done in a private place, such as her own room in her own home. Here are a few more things you can do:

- Teach your child the correct names for human body parts—including penis, vagina, and rectum—just as you did for belly button, nose, and elbow. Being able to name something makes it a lot less mysterious.

- Explain physical differences between adults and children. Adults' pubic hair (and the hair on your chest, legs, back, and elsewhere) and adult-size genitals are of special concern to kids. The simple answer (one that's perfectly adequate for kids this age) is that as you get bigger, everything gets bigger, and that when you get to be a grown-up, you get hairier.
- Talk about touching. It's simply not okay for anyone (adult or child) to touch anyone else in his or her private area—except if the adult is a doctor or a parent bathing a child or changing a diaper. Bathroom privacy (closing the door, knocking) is also a good topic to bring up now.
- Stay away from intimate touching or sex in front of your child. But be warned: your child will walk in on you one day. And scrambling around trying to cover up may make your child think there's something wrong with your (and, by extension, her) body.

MODESTY VS. SHAME: WHY IT MAY BE TIME TO KEEP YOUR PANTS ON

At about the same time as your child develops an interest in her own body, she may also suddenly become conscious of yours—and of the differences between yours and your partner's and between yours and hers (or his, if you've got a boy). This is most likely to come up if you have a habit of not wearing much clothing around the house.

Generally speaking, there's nothing wrong with your child's seeing you or your partner naked. But how do you know when a little more modesty is in order? The answer, of course, depends on many factors—your attitudes and comfort levels about nudity (do you think the human body is something to be proud of or something that should be kept completely private?), your child's awareness of the physical differences between you, and much more.

In my case, my daughters basically told me when to get dressed. I used to take baths with them, until one day, when the older one was about three, she decided to grab my penis in the bathtub—a pretty serious hint that either I should wear a swimsuit or she should bathe alone.

With my middle daughter the hint came a little earlier: one afternoon just after she'd turned two, she and I spent about half an hour talking about all the different kinds of tails animals have and why people don't have them at all. The next morning she strolled into the bathroom just as I was stepping out of the shower. We chatted for a second, but suddenly she gave me a stunned, betrayed look and pointed at my crotch. "Daddy has a tail," she announced.

Hyperactivity Alert

One of the most common behavioral diagnoses these days is attention deficit disorder (ADD), sometimes also called ADHD (attention deficit/hyperactivity disorder). Only about 5 percent of American children have ADD/ADHD, with boys being four to six times more likely to have it than girls. No one's quite sure what causes it, although some neurologists suspect that it's the result of deficits of two brain chemicals, dopamine and acetylcholine, which help the brain focus on one thing at a time.

Children with ADD/ADHD often have a short attention span, are easily distracted, behave impulsively, and seem to be in constant motion. Coincidentally, almost all toddlers have one or more of those symptoms, at least some of the time. For that reason, ADD/ADHD is overdiagnosed—often by day-care workers and teachers who don't have the training or experience to make an accurate diagnosis, but who naturally prefer children who obey and sit still to those who don't.

The natural consequence of this overdiagnosis is that it's becoming more and more common for kids—especially boys—to be drugged into submission. So if your babysitter, day-care provider, or preschool teacher tells you your child is hyperactive or suffers from ADD/ADHD, don't panic. Instead:

- Be skeptical. In some ways, diagnosing ADD/ADHD is like Supreme Court Justice Potter Stewart's famous definition of pornography: "I shall not today attempt further to define . . . but I know it when I see it." Over the course of a few days, compare your child's behavior with that of others her age. Is she significantly more active and less focused, and does she behave the same way every day? A lot of what is "diagnosed" as ADHD is nothing more than normal toddler behavior.
- Think about your child's temperament. Is she naturally active?
- If you're still worried, take your child to the pediatrician. Describe the symptoms carefully. If your pediatrician suggests it, have your child tested by a qualified child psychiatrist.
- If the child psychiatrist suggests drugs, get a second opinion.

"Soon you will be entering a phase son, in which you will no longer pay attention to anything I have to say. Please let me know when that changeover occurs."

More Adult Separation Problems

I don't think I'll ever forget the time I drove my older daughter a few blocks away from my house and abandoned her. Okay, I didn't really abandon her, I just took her to preschool. But it was my first time, and somehow I felt I'd done something wrong.

When our first child was born, my wife and I both cut our work loads to three days a week so we could spend as much time with her as possible. And for the first two and a half years of her life, at least one of us was with her almost all the time. But as I sat in my car after dropping her off for her first day of preschool, I began to wonder what kind of parent I was, leaving her all alone with people I hardly knew. Would they read to her? Could anyone possibly teach her as well as my wife and I had? Who would encourage her? And who would love her? I was nearly overcome by the need to run back to the school, grab her, and take her home where she belonged. After a few minutes of this sort of thinking, it became painfully clear that my wife and I had spent months preparing the wrong person for our daughter's first day of school.

Fighting the urge to go back to the school, I drove home and sat down in front of my computer. I tried to remind myself that up until then I had actually been looking forward to having my child in school, knowing I'd have a lot more time to write. But as I stared dumbly at the screen saver, I kept thinking that maybe my priorities were out of order. After all, what was more important, writing a few articles or making sure my child got the best possible education? Eventually, though, I had to admit that school was clearly the best place for my daughter, especially a school taught by teachers all our friends agree were gifted.

What it really comes down to, I guess, is that I knew I was going to miss my daughter while she was at school. I'd miss the wonderful times we had—the rainy-day matinees and museums and the sunny-day outings, the hours spent cuddling on the couch reading the same book ten times in a row, the time sitting at her table drawing. And most of all, I'd miss the long talks we had and the feeling of overflowing joy and pride I got from watching her learn new things and seeing how bright and articulate she'd become.

But missing her wasn't all there was. I was jealous, too. It just didn't seem fair that my daughter's teachers—people who hardly knew her—were going to be the beneficiaries of so much of her company. Oh, sure, the two of us would still have plenty of afternoons together in the park, and we'd still make pizza dough, and soak each other with the hose while watering the garden, and hide under the covers in my bed, ready to scare my wife when she came home from work. But no matter how much time we'd spend together now, I knew it would never seem like enough because I'd always remember the time when I didn't have to share her with anyone.

She was still so small and helpless, but at the same time already off on her own. It really seemed like the end of an era. I remembered then (and still do now) going into her room at night when she was a baby and marveling at her angelic, smiling face and her small, perfect body. It was always a struggle not to wake her up to play. Thinking about it now, I realize that I was jealous even of her dreams.

I guess I should have known what I was going to feel as I dropped her off on her first day of school. I remember going to pick her up at the park a few months before. I stood outside for a few minutes, watching her chat and play with her friends. She seemed so mature, so grown up, so independent. Until that moment, I'd felt that I knew her completely. I knew the characters she pretended to be, I knew what she liked and didn't like, and we told each other everything. But watching her interact with other people—sharing secrets I'd never hear—I realized that the process of separating from our parents doesn't begin by our moving out of their house at seventeen or joining the Marines. It really begins at three, in a park, digging tunnels in the sand with a friend.

You and Your Partner

More Communication Issues

As we've discussed throughout this book, you and your partner became parents at the same time, but not in the same way. As a result, the two of you have very different needs and expectations. Here's how this plays out:

YOU NEED YOUR PARTNER TO:

- Truly understand how hard it is to be an involved father today. She should also appreciate the commitment you've made to your family and the things you do for them—even if they aren't exactly what she wants.
- Understand that you and she will probably disagree on how you assess your level of support and involvement. Women tend to compare what their husbands do to what they do, and the men usually come up short. But men measure what they do against what their fathers did or what the guy down the street is doing, and they look pretty good in comparison.
- Be patient. She needs to know that adults develop at different rates, just as children do. In many families the mother acquires her skills faster; in others it's the father.
- Understand—and try to accommodate whenever possible—your desires for her attention and affection, your own space, time to see your friends, and a social life.
- Give you the freedom to do things your own way. "Many mothers, considering themselves the primary parent, have a difficult time watching their husbands parent differently from themselves, and take over to 'do it right,' " writes psychotherapist Jerrold Shapiro. Men and women parent differently and make different—but equally important—contributions to their children's development. If you give in and do everything her way, your child will end up with Mommy and Mommy's little helper, not Mommy and Daddy, which is what she needs. In my opinion, your partner has the right to determine exactly how the children are to be mothered. She has no right to determine how they are to be fathered.
- Support you in your efforts to balance work and family.
- Be your biggest fan. The more your partner supports you and your efforts to be a good dad, the more involved you'll be.

- Know you love her and the baby, even if you don't show it the way she wants you to. Men and women have very different ways of expressing love. Men tend to do, while women tend to speak. So make an effort to say the words a little more often. Hopefully she'll meet you halfway and accept that sometimes a wink, a smile, or a pat on the shoulder or the butt is just as effective a way of saying "I love you" as actually saying the words.

YOUR PARTNER NEEDS YOU TO:

- Be a full participant in your home, not just mother's little helper. This means taking responsibility for things (housework, meal planning, shopping) without having to be asked and assuming a major role in child care (including caregiving, arranging play dates, and doing clothes shopping).

DAD, THE VENTRILOQUIST

- Understand that although she may occasionally neglect your emotional and physical needs in favor of the baby's, she doesn't mean to hurt you.
- Listen to her carefully when she wants to talk about her doubts and anxieties. It's "more important to have our needs heard than it is to have them met," says psychotherapist Brad Sachs. "Though the specific needs may not be met, the more general and overarching one—the need for support and connectedness—will be."
- Not make her feel guilty when she makes mistakes. She wasn't born knowing how to parent any more than you were.
- Support her in her efforts to regain her prebaby body.
- Support her in her efforts to balance work and family.
- Understand that she may be feeling tremendous guilt at not being able to live up to society's expectations of her (as a good wife, mother, executive).
- Be sympathetic to her daytime loneliness and desire for adult company, if she's a stay-at-home mom.

PUTTING IT TOGETHER

Clearly, while there's some overlap between your needs and your partner's, there are also plenty of places where you're far apart. Those differences need to be reconciled, and the best way to do so is to learn to focus on the things you have in common rather than on your differences (although being aware of your differences is critical). "Couples who are able to focus their attention on what unites them and produces mutual joy usually end up at the end of the transition with a better, happier marriage," says researcher Jay Belsky.

Here, according to Belsky, are the things that can make a couple's transition to parenthood easier:

- Surrender individual goals and needs and work together as a team.
- Resolve differences about divisions of labor and work in a mutually satisfactory manner.
- Handle stresses in a way that does not overstress one partner or the entire marriage.
- Fight constructively and maintain a pool of common interests despite diverging priorities.
- Realize that however good a marriage becomes postbaby, it will not be good in the same way as it was prebaby.
- Maintain the ability to communicate in a way that continues to nurture the marriage. All couples have arguments. But the big issue is not who wins or whether you reach a compromise, it's that you keep talking to each other in a respectful, understanding, nonjudgmental way.

It's a tall order, but one that, if you're willing to put in the time and effort, will change for the better the lives of everyone around you.

What to Do if Communication Breaks Down

If you and your partner are communicating well and your marriage is strong, feel free to skip this section. Sadly, though, not all couples are able to communicate effectively, and not every relationship is meant to last. If you and your partner have tried everything to save your relationship—talking with each other, talking with a therapist, trial separations—divorce may be the only remaining option. This, of course, is a topic I'd rather not be writing about at all, but given that about half of all marriages in this country end in divorce, and that most of those divorces involve children under five, it's truly necessary to understand what to do if you find yourself contemplating yet another change in identity: from "father" to "single father." It's also necessary to understand the devastating way divorce affects everyone—you, your partner, and especially your children.

With any luck, you and your soon-to-be-ex will be able to remain civil enough to reach some kind of equitable agreement on child custody—without expensive lawyers and court costs. In fact, this is the case in about 80 percent of divorces nationwide. But whether your breakup is civil or acrimonious, there are a few things you should know before you make any major decisions:

- **Your defenses are down.** You're under stress; there are a thousand intense and scary feelings running through your head, and a million details

A Good Alternative to Litigation

There's no question that divorces can be expensive—especially if you and your wife can't communicate any other way than through your lawyers and in front of a judge. But if the two of you are getting along okay (not well enough to be married, just civil to each other), and you think you can continue to do so for a while, I strongly suggest that you consider mediation. This means that the two of you would split the expense of hiring one person (instead of two) to help you arrange custody and divide up your property. In the overwhelming majority of cases, mediation is cheaper, takes less time, and is much less psychologically damaging for everyone, including the kids, than a knock-down, drag-out court battle. (In some states you actually won't have a choice: mediation is mandatory for parents who can't agree on a custody arrangement.)

you have to take care of. You want to avoid more conflict. That's natural. But a lot of men facing divorce tend to lose track of what's good for them and make decisions they end up regretting forever.

- **You need a strategy**. Make the right moves now, and you can save yourself not only a lot of grief but a lot of money as well. And most important, you can minimize the damage the breakup of your marriage will have on your child(ren).

Some of what I suggest below may seem a little aggressive, but it really isn't. It's all about looking out for your own best interests instead of abandoning them. And far more important than that, it's about looking out for the best interests of your children. Please keep in mind that what you're going to read here is not an exhaustive treatment of the subject—you can find that in my book, *The Single Father: A Dad's Guide to Parenting without a Partner*. Remember that every case is different, and there are no easy solutions.

GET A LAWYER—NOW

The minute you suspect there's going to be a divorce, get yourself a lawyer. "Don't even consider representing yourself unless you have no possessions, no income, and no interest in the outcome of your case," says Timothy J. Horgan, author of *Winning Your Divorce*. Get the point? One recent study found that fathers who were awarded sole custody had been represented by lawyers 92 percent of the time, and those who won joint custody had lawyers 90 percent of the time. In contrast, among fathers who failed to win any type of custody, only 60 percent had hired lawyers.

And don't share a lawyer with your ex, either. He or she can't possibly represent your interests and your wife's at the same time. It's a conflict of interest waiting to happen.

If a friend of yours was recently divorced and ended up with what he wanted, get a reference. Or check with local men's or fathers' rights groups. But beware: while support groups can be a valuable source of contacts and comfort, they also can be a gathering place for extremely bitter and angry people, and a hunting ground for unscrupulous lawyers who prey on men who are at their most vulnerable.

Two excellent (and safe) resources are the American Coalition of Families and Children (www.acfc.org) and the Children's Rights Council (www.gocrc.org). Both these organizations are nonprofit and have chapters around the country. Whatever you do, don't let recommendations substitute for face-to-face interviews with the top prospects. Although it may cost you a little up front, finding the right lawyer can make the difference between feeling helpless and being in control.

Hiring a lawyer does *not* mean that you're heading for the courtroom—if you're lucky, you'll never even meet a judge. Nor does hiring a lawyer mean that you're expecting a confrontation with your soon-to-be-ex. What it does mean, though, is that you're getting someone involved who, without any unpleasant emotional attachments, will protect your interests and make sure that your concerns are properly addressed. Most divorce lawyers have seen dozens of cases just like yours and know exactly what to look out for. Do you? And finally, your lawyer can also help you draft fair property settlements and custody arrangements that will hopefully avoid conflict in the future. Here are a few points to keep in mind when interviewing attorneys:

- During the interview, ask a lot of questions and be completely honest about your situation—financial and emotional. If you aren't, you're just going to complicate your own case. And don't worry: any conversation you have while interviewing an attorney—even if you don't ultimately hire her—is completely confidential.
- Be prepared to answer a lot of personal questions about yourself and your partner. The more your attorney knows about your partner's character, the better he will be able to protect you.
- Ask the attorney about the strengths and weaknesses of your case, and find out what approach she would take to getting you what you really want.
- Be sure to find out how well the attorney knows local judges and other divorce attorneys. Each judge has his own prejudices, and having a lawyer who can maneuver within the system may be critical to your case. But stay far away from anyone who promises that he can "get you anything you want," or that she can "get the judge to see things your way."

Gender Strategy

Despite what you may have heard ("Judges are more sympathetic to women lawyers" or "Men are tougher"), the gender of your attorney probably won't affect your case in any way. But it is important to pay attention to his or her views on how much time fathers should be able to have with their children. Many lawyers of both genders believe that mothers should get full, or at least primary custody of the children. Get the best person you can afford who shares your views and who you think will put the best interests of your child first.

Here are a few ways to cut down on how much you'll be paying for your initial consultation:

- Before your first appointment, sit down and make a detailed list of all your assets and debts (including account numbers), real estate, full names and social security numbers of everyone in the family (kids, too), and your wife's and your birthdays, driver's license numbers, and dates of marriage and separation. Also bring along your tax returns for the last four or five years. You're going to need all this information soon anyway, and there's no point in paying someone $200 or $300 per hour to sift through your wallet, tax records, and other documents.
- Don't confuse your attorney's interest in your case with friendship. Sure, she'll interrupt her day to let you stop by and cry on her shoulder. She'll also charge you for it. And with many attorneys billing in quarters of an hour, that thirty-second plea for sympathy could set you back nearly $100.

DON'T MOVE OUT

In the old days, men facing a divorce would move out of the house—it was considered the chivalrous thing to do. Today, however, moving out may be the dumbest thing you could possibly do. Depending on where you live, moving out could end—or at least sharply curtail—your relationship with your child. In some states, your wife's attorney may be able to argue that since you left your children with your wife, you aren't interested in having a relationship with them, and your custodial rights should be severely limited.

Unfortunately, the judge is likely to agree. Most divorce attorneys find that the courts are generally quite reluctant to make any changes to the status quo in custody cases. That means that the one who's living in the marital home has a great advantage.

If there's no other alternative to moving out—for example, the judge orders you to—keep these things in mind:

- Work out a schedule—in writing—with your ex that has the children spend half their time with you and half with their mother.
- Get a place as close as possible to your former home so you'll be able to see the kids every day.
- Explain the situation to the children yourself, stressing that it's not their fault. (You may want to check with a mental health professional about the best way to broach this topic.)
- Be alert to what your wife is saying about you to the children. If she's badmouthing you, you'll need to make doubly sure that the children

Community Property

In some states everything acquired from the day you got married until the day you get separated is considered "community property." Even if you have a bank or stock account in your name alone, your wife is still entitled to half and vice versa. Just about the only exception to the community property rules is money or assets you or your wife owned *prior* to the marriage or inheritances left solely to either one of you even during the marriage. This is pretty complicated stuff, so if you live in one of the nine community-property states (Arizona, California, Idaho, Louisiana, Nevada, New Mexico, Texas, Washington, and Wisconsin), check with your lawyer.

understand what your leaving does—and doesn't—mean. One important warning: never respond to anything your ex is saying about you in front of the children. You never want to put your kids in the middle.

- Consider taking your valuables with you. If not, you might not see them again. Alternatively, make a written inventory of every item of value you're leaving behind. A videotape would be even better.

A word of caution: try not to let your refusal to move out escalate into a huge confrontation between you and your wife (She: "Get out!" You: "Screw you!"). Your anger may later be used as the basis for your wife getting a court order to evict you.

GET CONTROL OF YOUR FINANCES

In most states, assets and other property that have both your names on them (particularly things like checking accounts and money-market accounts) are assumed to be owned equally by you and your wife. But since it's tough to tell whose half is whose, there's nothing to stop your wife from completely cleaning out the entire checking account, leaving you penniless. Every divorce lawyer I've ever spoken with had literally dozens of stories about divorcing men who came home one day to houses that had been stripped bare and to checking accounts that were in much the same condition.

To protect yourself (and to make sure you've got enough to live on and to pay your attorney with), do the following immediately:

- Get half the money and any liquid assets you can put your hands on out of the joint accounts and into a separate one—in your name only. If you don't already know which accounts are liquid, have your accountant or your lawyer help you figure it out.

- But be sure to check with your lawyer before making withdrawals from any joint accounts. In some states, doing so without the permission of your wife can get you in serious hot water. And beware: taking more than half can put you in the uncomfortable position of having to explain to a judge why you cut your wife off without enough money to live on.
- Switch your automatic payroll deposits and put any other new deposits into your new account; any money that comes into the old, joint account may be lost forever.
- Get all your important financial records out of the house as soon as possible. Before doing this, however, make a complete copy of these records for your wife; she's entitled to one, and making her (or her lawyer) ask for it later will cost you. Documents such as bank and credit card statements, tax returns, and life insurance policies can be stored in a safety deposit box or at your lawyer's office. And don't forget to change the account address, so future statements don't go to your wife.
- Keep an extremely accurate accounting of all deposits into and withdrawals from the new account—you don't want anyone accusing you of blowing half the marital assets in Vegas.

Besides sharing ownership of all assets with your wife, you each also "own" half of all debts—mortgages, credit card balances, and so forth. So the next thing to do is close all your joint credit card accounts and credit lines, even the ones from department stores and gas stations. Do this in writing and mention the fact that you're getting a divorce—that usually speeds things up. Until you close these accounts, you'll be responsible for half of any debts your wife incurs until the divorce is final. Actually, according to the law, after the date of your legal separation you are responsible only for anything you charge (your partner is responsible only for what she charges). Unfortunately, most creditors don't really care about the law; all they want is their money, and they're perfectly willing to trash your credit rating if that's what it takes to get it.

KNOW THE DETAILS OF YOUR KIDS' LIVES

If you didn't want to be an active, involved father, you probably wouldn't be reading this book. So I'm assuming that at the very least you're going to want to get shared physical custody of your child(ren). If so, be aware that you've got at least two major obstacles to overcome:

- The strong societal assumption that women are biologically better parents than men
- The old stereotype that fathers are less important to children than mothers

Psychologist Richard Warshak, author of *The Custody Revolution*, calls these two ideas (which many men who don't know any better also buy into) the "motherhood mystique" and feels that they are responsible for the fact that mothers get primary physical custody more than 80 percent of the time.

So how do you overcome the motherhood mystique? Perhaps the best way is to demonstrate that you have exceptional parenting skills. And the best way to do that is to make sure you're up-to-date on everything that's going on in your kids' lives. The bottom line is that very few things can destroy your custody case more quickly than showing the judge that you lack knowledge about your child. Here are a few important things you should be doing (if you aren't doing them already):

- Get up early and make the kids' breakfast and lunch. Take them to day care.
- Get to know your children's day-care provider, doctors, playmates (and their parents)—and make sure they know you. They will be crucial ammunition if your wife's attorney tries to demonstrate what an uninvolved father you are.
- Get involved in arranging birthday parties, arranging play dates, and so on.
- Schedule some quality time with the kids every day, no matter how long your workdays are. Get up early if you have to, but you've got to demonstrate a deep and continuing interest in, and commitment to, the kids.

Whatever you do, be predictable. As mentioned above, judges don't like to make changes in children's schedules and living arrangements. Maintain a written log of everything you do with your children, and keep receipts (with your signature on them) of doctor visits, clothing purchases, and so forth. And pay attention to the details: know their clothing sizes, favorite foods, and all the other telling details that can demonstrate that your role in your kids' upbringing is critical. Remember, whether or not your wife knows the answers to these questions is irrelevant. The judge will assume she does, but you'll have to prove it.

Finally, keep your wife completely up-to-date on anything pertinent that happens while you've got the kids: if you bought clothes, tell her; if your child was injured and you took her to the doctor, tell her. Besides being the right thing to do, keeping your wife informed shows that you're trying to keep open the lines of communication.

WATCH OUT FOR ALLEGATIONS OF ABUSE

An accusation of child abuse is the atomic bomb of any divorce case. If you are accused, you will be presumed guilty—unless you can disprove the charges. And that's not easy. By the time you first hear that you're accused, your child has probably been seen by a therapist or a child protective services caseworker many of whom believe that their role is to "validate" the accusation. And things move pretty quickly from there. The instant you're accused of having molested your child, all your contact with the child will be cut off until the question gets heard in court, and that could be anywhere from a few days to a few months later.

Assuming you're innocent (if you're not, please close this book immediately and turn yourself in), you'll probably feel like strangling your ex and her lawyer. Needless to say, this won't help. Most attorneys agree that aggressive behavior will just make the judge more suspicious and negatively inclined toward you. It's critical, then, to be as cooperative as possible.

And as hard as it might be for you, try to give your ex the benefit of the doubt—she may have seen something she genuinely thought was a symptom of abuse. Try to imagine how you'd behave if you'd seen something suspicious. And remember, your goal should be to get the truth out, not to get revenge.

An accusation of domestic violence may have nearly the same effect as an accusation of sex abuse: no access to your child until a judge rules on the charge. But keep in mind that, as strange as it sounds, men are the victims of domestic violence at least as often as women. The problem is that men rarely see their wives' shoves, slaps, or thrown dishes as violence. Now's the time to change your thinking. If your wife has been violent toward you or the kids, file charges immediately.

This does two things: it helps protect the kids from further abuse, and it helps protect you if she attempts to bring charges against you. If you think your wife is the type who might use this kind of weapon, there are a few steps you can take to protect yourself in advance:

- Don't let yourself get suckered into a fight, particularly on the phone. Your wife and her lawyer are just looking for evidence that you're violent and unstable. Don't answer questions like, "Why did you touch Sally down there?" Categorically deny her accusations, and end the conversation immediately.
- Tape your conversations with her. But before you turn on your recorder, check with your lawyer to make sure doing so is legal in your state. It's a tricky area of the law, so be careful.
- Stay squeaky clean during the entire divorce process: don't drink, don't drive too fast, don't even stiff a waitress on her tip. A sharp lawyer

(employed by your wife) can make something as innocuous as a speeding ticket into just another example of what an irresponsible brute you are.

KEEP A LOG

Again, because men are at a disadvantage when it comes to custody battles, it's important to keep detailed notes about everything that happens. Be sure to include:

- Details of visits with the kids.
- Conversations with your ex, especially if she's threatening or baiting you.
- Phone calls with your kids.
- Details about what the kids are up to when you're not with them. This will demonstrate not only that you are actively involved when you're with your kids but that you are concerned about them all the time. Be extremely careful, though, not to grill the kids about what they're doing with Mom. This can put them in a very uncomfortable position.

A few warnings: first, do not show your log to anyone except your lawyer—not your friends, not your coworkers, and especially not anyone remotely connected with your wife. It's the kind of thing that could be twisted into yet another example of your controlling, obsessive nature. Second, remember that everything—good and bad—that's in your log may become part of the record. So if you've been having particularly violent or bitter thoughts about your wife, keep them to yourself.

GET SOME COUNSELING

Regardless of how well (or badly) you and your ex get along, the simple truth is that the two of you will be coparenting your child until the day you die. For this reason, it is to everyone's advantage—especially the child's—that the two of you get to a point where you can communicate civilly and reasonably, and that you do so as soon as possible.

One of the best ways to accomplish this is to go to joint counseling, which comes in two basic flavors: pre-divorce counseling and coparent counseling. As you can probably guess, pre-divorce counseling takes place in the early stages of the divorce process, most likely before any kind of custody or separation arrangements have been finalized. Pre-divorce counseling is designed to help you and your wife dissipate some of the anger and hostility between you, and to help you build a better base of communication. Then, hopefully, you'll be able to make mature, informed, and rational decisions and not get tripped up by your own vindictiveness. This is especially important, because the biggest predictor of how well children adjust to their parents' divorce is how well their parents get along.

Coparent counseling is similar to pre-divorce counseling, except that it happens after initial custody and separation arrangements are in place. You and your wife may find that your counselor's office is a safe, neutral place to have discussions about the kids.

WHAT TO DO IF YOU DON'T GET THE CUSTODY ARRANGEMENT YOU WANT

Although most states now have some kind of "gender-blind" legislation specifically barring judges from granting custodial preference based solely on gender, our family law system still favors women by a huge margin. As mentioned earlier, mothers are awarded sole custody over 80 percent of the time. Only 11 percent of men get sole custody of their children, and just 7 percent have joint custody. Women are presumed to be "fit" parents. Men have to prove it.

Worse yet, nearly 40 percent of noncustodial fathers have no legal access or custody rights at all. And the men who do have court-ordered access (as well as many of those who have joint legal custody) are traditionally limited to visits every other weekend, one or two weekday afternoons, alternate holidays, and possibly a week or two in the summer.

The bottom line is that your chances of getting the kind of custody arrangement you really want are not great (they can, however, be greatly improved by following the suggestions on pages 244–45).

If you end up with limited access to your children, it's hard not to get depressed. The constant good-byes are going to be incredibly painful, and in some cases, seeing the kids may be a stinging reminder of the loss of your mar-

The Language of Separation

Before agreeing to any kind of custody arrangement, it's critical that you understand the terms. The parent with legal custody is the one who is legally responsible for making decisions about anything that affects the health, education, and welfare of the children. Ideally you should have joint legal custody (this is already the law in several states). Physical custody simply refers to the child's primary residence. Again, you should seek nothing less than joint physical custody. But watch out: it's possible to have joint physical custody and still have the child's primary residence be at one or the other parent's home.

There's No Such Thing as Winning Custody

In case you were thinking that you could "win" a custody battle, think again. The fact is that everyone loses, especially the kids. If your wife gets sole or primary custody, your relationship with your children will suffer greatly, and your children will bear the many negative consequences associated with long-term father absence (poorer academic performance, poorer social skills, increased chance of abusing drugs or alcohol or of getting in trouble with the law, and a greater likelihood of starting sexual experimentation early). But if you get sole or primary custody, your ex will miss out on having a relationship with the kids. And while this may sound like the perfect way to hurt her, keep in mind that the negative consequences of mother absence are just as significant as those of father absence. The bottom line is that the best parent is both parents.

riage. According to several studies, these two factors are among the major reasons some divorced fathers taper off contact with their kids. So, as in most things, try to think of your kids before deciding you can't deal with seeing them. Seeing them may be painful to you, but not seeing you will be much more painful to them.

Right now the most important thing you can do is try to make the transition from one family to two as smooth as possible. And the place to start is by trying to keep communication with your ex as civil as possible. You may not have been terribly successful before, but it's more crucial now than ever: the children who suffer the least when their parents split up are those whose parents have the lowest levels of conflict (or at least those whose parents keep their conflicts to themselves). This doesn't mean that you and your ex have to be best friends or even that you have to speak to each other very often. What it does mean, however, is that you both have to agree to keep your eyes on what's really most important: your child(ren).

Next to the death of an immediate family member, getting a divorce is one of the most painful experiences you'll ever go through. And you certainly won't be alone; it will be hard on your ex and hard on your children as well. Rest assured, though, you will pull through. The breakup of a family is almost always a tragedy in the short term. But in the long term it sometimes turns out to be the best thing for everyone involved.

DO SOME READING WITH YOUR KIDS . . .

There are plenty of good children's books that deal with divorce and how it affects kids. Here are a few you might want to take a look at:

As the Crow Flies, Elizabeth Winthrop
Dinosaurs Divorce, Marc Brown
I Don't Want to Talk about It, Jeanie Franz Ranson
Let's Talk about It: Divorce, Fred Rogers

. . . AND FOR YOURSELF

Here are just a few excellent books on divorce and custody issues that can help you remember the priorities: kids first, everything else last.

Braver, Sanford. *Divorced Dads: Shattering the Myths*. New York: Putnam, 1998.

Brott, Armin. *The Single Father: A Dad's Guide to Parenting without a Partner*. New York: Abbeville Press, 1999.

Hickey, Elizabeth, and Elizabeth Dalton. *Healing Hearts: Helping Children and Adults Recover from Divorce*. Carson City, Nev.: Gold Leaf Press, 1994.

Margulies, Sam. *Man's Guide to a Civilized Divorce: How to Divorce with Grace, a Little Class, and a Lot of Common Sense*. Emmaus, Penn.: Rodale, 2004.

Ricci, Isolina. *Mom's House, Dad's House: Making Two Homes for Your Child*. New York: Fireside, 1997.

Family Matters

Teaching the Kids about Money

For most parents, the thought of teaching our preschoolers about money is almost as scary as imagining having to teach them about sex. We know we're going to have to do it sometime, but we hope we can put it off for a while.

But think about it: there's really nothing in our lives that we use as frequently as money—from paying the rent and the electric bill to giving charity to a homeless family—and there's nothing that causes us so many problems. Money issues, for example, are a leading cause of divorce.

The point of this section, then, is to get you to start teaching your child about money—what it does and doesn't do—while she's still young. Unfortunately, your child already knows a few more things about money than you think she does. For example, she knows in a general sort of way that one needs money to get things, and she knows (or thinks, anyway) that you always have some. But most toddlers (and some adults) aren't able to grasp the idea that you actually have to work to get money, and they'll absolutely refuse to accept "I don't have any money with me" as an excuse for not buying them whatever they want whenever they want it. After all, everyone knows that if Daddy and Mommy want money, all they have to do is take some out of one of those machines.

It's going to be a while before you can explain the mysteries of the banking system to your child, but if you start talking about money now, in a very matter-of-fact way, you'll be able to keep it from seeming too magical and alluring. Here are a few ways to do just that:

- **Go to the store**. Stores provide a great opportunity to talk about lots of money-related things: how much things cost, how you know the prices, paying for things by check or credit card, the mechanics of making change. All these themes introduce the idea that things cost money.
- **Awareness**. Let your child look at the check in restaurants. Show her that the numbers on the check are (or should be) the same as the ones on the menu.
- **Identification**. Get four jars, and label each with the name of a coin: penny, nickel, dime, quarter. Put a few of the appropriate coins in each jar. Then take a coin out of your pocket, tell the child what it is, and put it (or have her put it) in the correct jar.
- **Participation**. Let your child hand the money to the clerk and collect the change.
- **Counting games**. Have your child count out the forks and spoons when you're setting the table. Have her help you make recipes, scooping out the right number of spoonfuls of ingredients.
- **Equivalence games**. Using real coins, show your child that a nickel is the same as a stack of five pennies, that five nickels are the same as a quarter, or that two nickels are the same as a dime, even though a nickel is bigger than a dime. Two dimes and a nickel for a quarter is too complex at this age.
- **Categorizing games**. As you're going up and down the aisles of the supermarket, have your child help you spot round things, red things, boxed things, and so forth. Being able to organize items into groups is a critical math and money-handling skill.
- **Comparisons**. Which products are better bargains? If the store you're in sells three oranges for a dollar, and the other store you go to has two oranges for a dollar, which is a better deal? Why do you go to the other store at all?

The Family Payroll

There are four things you can do with money: get it, spend it, save it, and give it away. And since you need to do the first one before any of the others, you'll have to give your toddler some money of her own. When she's older, you want to tie her allowance to the performance of certain household chores. But for now, make it unconditional.

As soon as each of my children turned three, I started paying them their age in dollars every week—a veritable fortune to those of us who had to make do on an extremely sporadic fifty cents a week. But don't worry, it doesn't all go straight into their pockets. Here's how it works:

You pay out the three dollars as ten quarters and ten nickels, and the first thing your child does is take 10 percent of her money (one nickel and one quarter) and put it into a jar marked "Charity." She gets to decide what to do with this money (either give it directly to a homeless person or combine it with some of your money and send it by check to a deserving organization). She then divides the remaining coins into six neat piles—three with three quarters, three with three nickels. Next she takes a stack of both (ninety cents) and drops each one into three different jars:

- Instant gratification. Bite your tongue. It's her money, so let her spend it however she wants—even if it's on candy. She'll learn awfully quickly that once it's gone, it's gone.
- Medium-term. This one gets saved up for a few weeks or a month (anything longer than that and she'll forget what she was saving for) and can then be cashed in for a larger toy or expense.
- Long-term. Basically, she won't be seeing this money for a few years. Let it accumulate in the jar for a while, then take it (and your child) down to the bank and open up a savings account.

As wacky as this whole allowance scheme sounds, the opportunities for learning are amazing: counting, percentages, division, categorizing, the importance of helping others, the value of patience, the benefits of saving, and so much more.

- **Prioritizing**. Talk about which products your family needs and which ones you want. Having a firm grasp of the difference will help your child throughout her life.
- **Be patient**. It will take years for all these ideas to sink in.

Completing the Puzzle: Putting Together the Pieces of You

Before I became a dad, I worked as a commodities trader, a labor negotiator, and a trade consultant—the kind of jobs you get with an MBA, which I have buried someplace deep in my attic. But before my first child was even born, I'd already reached the conclusion that having an executive job and being an involved dad—at least the way I wanted to do it—weren't entirely compatible. I'd published a few articles, and in a moment of feverish optimism, I quit my job to write full time, which gave me the flexibility to spend plenty of time with my daughter.

I'm certainly not the only father to make a kid-related career move, and mine was certainly not the most dramatic. Actor Mandy Patinkin gave up the work he loved—and the money that went with it—to spend more time with his family. "I will not lose my family to this job," he said. Actor Ewan McGregor cut his schedule way back because of his daughter. And former secretary of labor Robert Reich gave up "the best job I've ever had and probably ever will" to spend more time with his family.

Okay, I realize that fatherhood isn't going have as big an impact on everyone's career as it did on mine (and Patinkin's and McGregor's and Reich's). In fact, making that kind of career transition isn't practical, or even desirable, for most dads. For some, the changes are more subtle. Here's how a U.S. postal worker, for example, reacted when he was told he'd have to work nights: "I told them I could not work nights because I had a ten-year old son and I am a single parent. . . . Being with my son two days a week is not a good way to be a parent."

Not everyone responds to fatherhood by making changes at work. But of the hundreds of men I've interviewed, I've never met one who didn't change his life in at least some ways after becoming a father, ways he never would have considered if he hadn't had kids. Here are a few of the changes dads have made:

- Moving to a larger (and usually more expensive) house. When you've got a child, suddenly having a backyard or a playroom or an extra bedroom or two becomes very important.
- Job choice. More and more people these days are making decisions about where to work based at least partly on whether a prospective job offers enough flexibility to allow for a healthy work-family mix.
- Moving to a different neighborhood, city, or even state so the kids can have access to better schools. Sometimes this is a change the whole family is okay with. But often this kind of change involves moving farther away from friends, family, movies, theater, museums, and other things that the parents enjoy.
- Becoming the sole breadwinner. A lot of women decide not to go back to work for a few years after having their babies. While it's great for the kids

to have a parent around so much of the time, it puts a lot of financial pressure on Dad, including paying for that bigger house and its bigger mortgage.

- Insurance and finances. Parents have to worry about paying for college, they're probably a little more conservative in their investments in general, and they tend to take out more life insurance. Music lessons and private school tuition bump that up even further.
- Non-house purchasing decisions. Besides the new house, a lot of dads buy a lot of other things they never would have considered: a station wagon or minivan, backyard swing sets, Nintendo play stations, and on and on.

Because your roles as worker and father are such important parts of who you are, there's no way to keep them from spilling over onto each other. Whether that spillover is positive or negative depends on a lot of factors, including:

AT WORK

- Your schedule. People who work more than forty-five hours a week report more work-family problems, while those who work fewer than twenty say their work schedule improves their family relationships.
- Other job-related factors. How much time you clock isn't all there is to it. Dads who put in long hours, have no control over their schedule, don't like or aren't challenged by their job, or have to work weekends or nights are more likely to suffer from what you might call "kick-the-cat syndrome." On the other hand, dads who have more control over their schedule and enjoy their jobs have children who are healthier and exhibit fewer behavior problems, according to researchers Jeffrey Greenhaus and Stewart Friedman. Other studies show that workers who have a lot of decision-making authority at work actually have longer life spans than those who don't.
- Money. Having a salary makes it possible to put shoes on everyone's feet, drive a car, and perhaps finance a vacation or some other luxuries now and then. That certainly makes life at home easier. But working too hard for that money could have the opposite effect.
- Your age. Younger dads, especially those who are trying to make a name for themselves in the business world, sometimes find that the hours and energy they spend at work lead to increased stress at home.
- Social support. Dads who enjoy the people they work with and feel respected and appreciated are less likely to report that their family life interferes with work and have children who do better in school.

AT HOME

- Family. The more people you're responsible for, the more likely you are to have some negative spillover from family to work. Worrying about small children and/or caring for an elderly parent or in-law increases problems at work even more and leads to what you might call "stare-at-the-screensaver-when-you're-supposed-to-be-working syndrome." However, having positive relationships at home keeps men from feeling the kind of psychological distress they ordinarily would feel when unhappy at work, according to researcher Rosalind Barnett. Barnett also found that the more involved a dad is in child care, the better his psychological well-being and the happier his wife will be.
- Social life. Having friends and spending time with them makes it less likely that you'll have stresses at home that will carry over to work. On the other hand, cutting back on time spent with friends in order to have more family time increases negative family-work spillover.
- Your partner's schedule. The more flexible it is, the less worried you'll be about things at home and the less your family concerns will cause you trouble at work. Your schedule will have the same effect on her.
- Boundaries. Keeping work and family separate naturally reduces the spillover between the two. But checking your work voice mail or e-mail from home, or dealing with personal issues while at work, can create problems in both places.

Trying to keep your work and family lives in balance is a feat of acrobatics you'll be working on for the rest of your life.

Conclusion

Throughout this book we've talked about the amazing ways your toddler has grown and developed. And we've also talked about the amazing ways you've grown and developed right along with her. It's probably hard to remember the way life was just two short years ago. But when you have a calm moment, spend a few minutes thinking about it. Better yet, dust off some of those photo albums and refresh your memory. It's amazing how far you've both come, isn't it?

Over the past two years your child has gone from a little baby who was just learning to walk and talk, to an independent person charging around your house, supremely confident in her own abilities. And you've made a similar journey, from a relatively new dad with lots to learn, to the guy who can handle almost anything.

But your job isn't done, and it never will be. As you move from the toddler years to preschool, adolescence, and beyond, you and your child will continue to grow—individually and in relation to each other. There'll be ups and downs along the way, but a few years down the road you'll look back—just as you have now—and you'll be amazed at how far you've come and at how much more lies ahead.

Selected Bibliography

Books

Acredolo, Linda, and Susan Goodwyn. *Baby Signs: How to Talk with Your Baby before Your Baby Can Talk*. New York: McGraw Hill, 2002.

Alliance for Childhood. *Fool's Gold: A Critical Look at Computers in Childhood*. College Park, Md.: Alliance for Childhood, 2000. Online at www.allianceforchildhood.net.

Ames, Louise Bates, and Carol Chase Haber. *Your One-Year-Old: The Fun-Loving, Fussy 12- to 24-Month-Old*. New York: Delta, 1982.

Ames, Louise Bates, and Frances L. Ilg. *Your Two-Year-Old: Terrible or Tender*. New York: Delta, 1980.

Austrian, Sonia G., ed. *Developmental Theories through the Life Cycle*. New York: Columbia University Press, 2002.

Baylies, Peter. *The Stay-at-Home Dad Handbook*. Chicago: Chicago Review Press, 2004.

Belsky, Jay, and John Kelly. *The Transition to Parenthood: How a First Child Changes a Marriage: Why Some Couples Grow Closer and Others Apart*. New York: Delacorte, 1994.

Berman, Phyllis W., and Frank A. Pedersen. *Men's Transitions to Parenthood: Longitudinal Studies of Early Family Experience*. Hillsdale, N.J.: Erlbaum, 1987.

Bettelheim, Bruno. *A Good Enough Parent: A Book on Child-Rearing*. New York: Vintage, 1987.

Biller, Henry B., and Robert J. Trotter. *The Father Factor: What You Need to Know to Make a Difference*. New York: Pocket Books, 1994.

Bluestine, Eric. *The Ways Children Learn Music: An Introduction and Practical Guide to Music Learning Theory*. Chicago: GIA Publications, 1995.

Bowman, Barbara, Suzanne Donovan, et al., eds. *Eager to Learn: Educating Our Preschoolers*. Washington, D.C.: National Research Council, National Academies Press, 2000.

Brazelton, T. Berry, and Bertrand Cramer. *The Earliest Relationship: Parents, Infants, and the Drama of Early Attachment*. Reading, Mass.: Addison-Wesley, 1990.

Brenner, Mark. *Pacifiers, Blankets, Bottles, and Thumbs: What Every Parent Should Know about Starting and Stopping*. New York: Fireside, 2004.

Britton, James. *Language and Learning: The Importance of Speech in Children's Development*. New York: Penguin, 1970.

Bronstein, Phyllis, and Carolyn Pape Cowan, eds. *Fatherhood Today: Men's Changing Role in the Family*. New York: John Wiley & Sons, 1988.

Brott, Armin. *Father for Life: A Journey of Joy, Challenge, and Change*. New York, Abbeville Press, 2003.

———. *The New Father: A Dad's Guide to the First Year*. New York: Abbeville Press, 2004.

Brown, R. *A First Language: The Early Stages*. London: George Allen & Unwin, 1973.

Cantor, Ruth F., and Jeffrey A. Cantor. *Parents' Guide to Special Needs Schooling: Early Intervention Years*. Westport, Conn.: Auburn House, 1995.

Caplan, Frank, and Theresa Caplan. *The Second Twelve Months of Life*. New York: Bantam, 1982.

Carnoy, Martin, and David Carnoy. *Fathers of a Certain Age: The Joys and Problems of Middle-aged Fatherhood*. Minneapolis: Fairview Press, 1997.

Cath, Stanley H., ed. *Father and Child: Developmental and Clinical Perspectives*. Hillsdale, N.J.: Analytic Press, 1994.

Chen, Milton. *The Smart Parent's Guide to Kids' TV*. San Francisco: KQED Books, 1994.

Cohen, Lawrence. *Playful Parenting*. New York: Random House, 2002.

Connors, Abigail Flesch. *101 Rhythm Instrument Activities for Young Children*. Beltsville: Gryphon House, 2004.

Cowan, Carolyn Pape, and Philip A. Cowan. *When Partners Become Parents: The Big Life Change for Couples*. New York: HarperCollins, 2000.

Cowan, Philip A., et al. "Mothers, Fathers, Sons, and Daughters: Gender Differences in Family Formation and Parenting Style." In *Family, Self, and Society: Toward a New Agenda for Family Research*, edited by Philip A. Cowan, Dorothy Field, and Donald A. Hansen. Hillsdale, N.J.: Erlbaum, 1993.

Dodson, Fitzhugh. *How to Father*. New York: Signet, 1974.

Faber, Adele, et al. *How to Talk So Kids Will Learn*. New York: Scribner's, 1995.

Flint Public Library. *Ring a Ring O'Roses: Finger Plays for Pre-School Children*. Flint, Mich.: Flint Public Library, 2000.

Fox, Mem. *Reading Magic: Why Reading Aloud to Our Children Will Change Their Lives Forever*. New York: Harcourt, 2001.

Fraiberg, Selma H. *The Magic Years: Understanding and Handling the Problems of Early Childhood*. New York: Scribner's, 1959.

Friedman, Stewart, and Jeffrey H. Greenhaus. *Work and Family: Allies or Enemies?* London: Oxford University Press, 2000.

Galinsky, Ellen. *Between Generations: The Six Stages of Parenthood*. New York: Times Books, 1981.

Garcia, Joseph. *Sign with Your Baby: How to Communicate with Infants before They Can Speak*. Seattle, Wash.: Northlight Communications, 2002.

Gordon, Edwin E. *A Music Learning Theory for Newborn and Young Children.* Chicago: GIA Publications, 1990.

Greenspan, Stanley, and Nancy Thorndike Greenspan. *First Feelings: Milestones in the Emotional Development of Your Baby and Child*. New York: Penguin, 1985.

Halle, Tamara, *Charting Parenthood: A Statistical Portrait of Fathers and Mothers in America*, Washington, D.C.: Child Trends, 2002. Online at fatherhood.hhs.gov/charting02.

Hass, Aaron. *The Gift of Fatherhood: How Men's Lives are Transformed by Their Children.* New York: Fireside, 1994.

Healy, Jane M. *Failure to Connect: How Computers Affect Our Children's Minds for Better and Worse*. New York: Simon & Schuster, 1998.

Heddle, Rebecca. *Science in the Kitchen.* London: Usborne, 1992.

Hetherington, E. Mavis, and John Kelly. *For Better or for Worse: Divorce Reconsidered.* New York: W. W. Norton, 2002.

Holtzman, Debra. *The Safe Baby: A Do-It-Yourself Guide to Home Safety*. Boulder, Colo.: Sentient Publications, 2004.

Hoppenhauer, Denise Harris. *Adopting a Toddler*. Lincoln, Neb.: iUniverse, 2004.

Katzen, Mollie, and Ann Henderson. *Pretend Soup and Other Real Recipes: A Cookbook for Preschoolers and Up*. Berkeley, Calif.: Tricycle Press, 1994.

Kellog, Rhoda. *The Psychology of Children's Art*. New York: Random House, 1967.

Kohl, MaryAnn F. *First Art: Art Experiences for Toddlers and Twos*. Beltsville, Md.: Gryphon House, 2002.

Kohl, MaryAnn F., and Jean Potter. *Cooking Art: Easy Edible Art for Young Children.* Beltsville, Md.: Gryphon House, 1997.

Kutner, Lawrence. *Toddlers and Preschoolers*. New York: William Morrow, 1994.

Lamb, Michael E., ed. *The Role of the Father in Child Development*. New York: John Wiley & Sons, 1997.

Linn, Susan. *Consuming Kids*: *The Hostile Takeover of Childhood*, New York: New Press, 2004.

McCoy, Bill. *Father's Day: Notes from a New Dad in the Real World*. New York: Times Books, 1995.

Minnesota Fathering Alliance. *Working with Fathers: Methods and Perspectives*. Stillwater, Minn.: Nu Ink, 1992.

Newman, Barbara M., and Philip R. Newman. *Development through Life: A Psychosocial Approach.* 6th ed. Pacific Grove, Calif.: Brooks/Cole, 1994.

O'Brien, Maureen. *Watch Me Grow: I'm One-Two-Three*. New York: Quill, 2002.

Odean, Kathleen. *Great Books for Babies and Toddlers*. New York: Ballantine, 2003.

Owens, Robert Jr. *Help Your Baby Talk: Introducing the New Shared Communication Method to Jump-Start Language and Have a Smarter and Happier Baby*. New York: Perigee, 2004.

Palkovitz, Rob. *Involved Fathering and Men's Adult Development: Provisional Balances*. Mahwah, N.J.: Lawrence Erlbaum, 2002.

Parke, Ross. *Fathers*. Rev. ed. Cambridge, Mass.: Harvard University Press, 1996.

———. "Fathers and Families." In *Handbook of Parenting*, edited by M. H. Bornstein. Hillsdale, N.J.: Erlbaum, 1995.

Patton O. Tabors. *One Child, Two Languages*. Baltimore, Md.: Paul H. Brookes, 1997.

Pruett, Kyle. *Fatherneed: Why Father Care Is as Essential as Mother Care for Your Child*. New York: Free Press, 2000.

Roehlkepartain, Eugene. *Building Strong Families: An In-Depth Report on a Preliminary Survey on What Parents Need to Succeed*. Chicago: YMCA of the USA; Minneapolis: The Search Institute, 2002. Available online at www.abundantassets.org/building.cfm.

Ross, John Munder. *What Men Want: Mothers, Fathers, and Manhood*. Cambridge, Mass.: Harvard University Press, 1994.

Sachs, Brad E. *Things Just Haven't Been the Same: Making the Transition from Marriage to Parenthood*. New York: William Morrow, 1992.

Schatz, William. *Healing a Father's Grief*. Richmond, Wash.: Medic Publishing, 1984.

Sheldon, S. H. "Sleep in Infants and Children." In *Sleep Medicine*, edited by T. L. Lee-Chiong, M. J. Sateia, and M. A. Carskadon. Philadelphia: Hanley & Belfus, 2002.

Shopper, Moisy. "Toiletry Revisited: An Integration of Developing Concepts and the Father's Role in Toilet Training." In *Fathers and Their Families*, edited by Stanley H. Cath, et al. Hillsdale, N.J.: Analytic Press, 1989.

Silvey, Anita. *100 Best Books for Children*. Boston: Houghton-Mifflin, 2004.

Snarey, John. *How Fathers Care for the Next Generation: A Four-Decade Study*. Cambridge, Mass.: Harvard University Press, 1993.

Spangler, Doug. *Fatherhood: An Owner's Manual*. Richmond, Calif.: Fabus, 1994.

Striker, Susan. *Young at Art: Teaching Toddlers Self-Expression, Problem-Solving Skills, and an Appreciation of Art*. New York: Owl Books, 2001.

Trelease, Jim. *The Read-Aloud Handbook*. 5th ed. New York: Penguin, 2001.

Tyson, Eric. *Personal Finance for Dummies*. 4th ed. New York: John Wiley & Sons, 2003.

Warshak, Richard. *The Custody Revolution: The Father Factor and the Motherhood Mystique*. New York: Poseidon, 1992.

White, Burton L. *The New First Three Years of Life*. New York: Prentice Hall, 1995.

Winnicott, D. W. *Playing and Reality*. New York: Basic Books, 1971.

Zweiback, Meg. *Keys to Preparing and Caring for Your Second Child*. New York: Barron's Educational, 1991.

Journals

Abkarian, G. G., et al. "Fathers' Speech to Their Children: Perfect Pitch or Tin Ear?" *Fathering*, February 2003.

Agras, Stewart, et al. "Risk Factors for Childhood Overweight: A Prospective Study from Birth to 9.5 Years." *Journal of Pediatrics* 145, no. 1 (2004): 20–25.

Bailey, William J. "A Longitudinal Study of Fathers' Involvement with Young Children: Infancy to Age Five Years." *Journal of Genetic Psychology* 155, no. 3 (1994): 331–39.

———. "Psychological Development in Men: Generativity and Involvement with Young Children." *Psychological Reports* 71 (1992): 929–30.

Barnett, Rosalind Chait, and Janet Shibley Hyde. "Women, Men, Work, and Family: An Expansionist Theory." *American Psychologist* 56 (2001): 781–96.

Baumrind, Diana. "Current Patterns of Parental Authority." *Developmental Psychology Monograph* 4, pt. 1 (January 1971): 1–101.

Bornehag, C. "The Association between Asthma and Allergic Symptoms in Children and Phthalates in House Dust: A Nested Case-Control Study." *Environmental Health Perspectives* 112 (October 2004): 1393–97.

Burke, Catherine. "Simple Technology Encourages Independence in Play and Communication for Infants and Toddlers with Disabilities." Birmingham, Ala.: University of Alabama at Birmingham, Civitan International Research center. No date. Online at www. circ.uab.edu/spages/cburk.htm.

Bus, Adriana, et al. "Attachment and Bookreading Patterns: A Study of Mothers, Fathers, and Their Toddlers." *Early Childhood Research Quarterly* 12 (1997): 81–98.

Cantor, Patricia. "Computers and the Very Young." *Focus on Infants and Toddlers* 13, no. 4 (2001): 1–2, 4, 6.

Cohn, Deborah A., et al. "Mothers' and Fathers' Working Models of Childhood Attachment Relationships, Parenting Styles, and Child Behavior." Typescript, 1997.

Cooney, Teresa M., et al. "Timing of Fatherhood: Is 'On-Time' Optional?" *Journal of Marriage and the Family* 55 (February 1993): 205–15.

Dahl, R. E. "The Development and Disorders of Sleep." *Advances in Pediatrics* 45 (1998): 73–90.

DeLoache, J. S., D. H. Uttal, and K. S. Rosengren. "Scale Errors Offer Evidence for a Perception-Action Dissociation Early in Life." *Science* 304 (May 2004): 1027–29.

DeLuccie, Mary F. "Mothers as Gatekeepers: A Model of Maternal Mediators of Father Involvement." *Journal of Genetic Psychology* 156, no. 1 (1994): 115–31.

Eaton, M. and B. S. Fees. "Perceptions of Influence on Child's Competence among Fathers in the Military Context." *Psychological Reports*, 90, no. 3 pt. 1 (December 2002): 703–10.

Elkind, Daniel. "Computers for Infants and Young Children." *Child Care Information Exchange*, 123 (September 1998): 44–46.

Fagot, Beverly I. "Sex Differences in Toddlers' Behavior and Parental Reaction." *Developmental Psychology* 10, no. 4 (1974): 554–58.

Fagot, Beverly, and Richard Hagan. "Aggression in Toddlers: Responses to the Assertive Acts of Boys and Girls." *Sex Roles* 12, nos. 3–4 (1985): 341–51.

Green, Frances L., John H. Flavell, and Eleanor R. Flavell. "Development of Children's Awareness of Their Own Thoughts." *Journal of Cognitive Development* 1 (2000): 97–112.

Hadaway, Nancy, et al. "Poetry for Language Development of English Language Learners." *Dragon Lode* (IRA Children's Literature and Reading Special Interest Group) 20, no. 2 (2002): Online at fatherhood.hhs.gov/charting02.

Haugland, Susan W. "What Role Should Technology Play in Young Children's Learning?" Pt. 1. *Young Children* 54, no. 6 (1999): 26–31.

Heath, D. Terri. "The Impact of Delayed Fatherhood on the Father-Child Relationship." *Journal of Genetic Psychology* 155, no. 4 (1994): 511–30.

Huttenlocher, Janellen, M. Vasilyeva, E. Cymerman, and S. Levine. "Language Input and Child Syntax." *Cognitive Psychology* 45, no. 3 (2002): 337–45.

Huttenlocher, Janellen, W. Haight, A. Bryk, M. Seltzer, and T. Lyons. "Early Vocabulary Growth: Relation to Language Input and Gender." *Developmental Psychology* 27, no. 2 (1991): 236–48.

Jeng, S. F., et al. "Prognostic Factors for Walking Attainment in Very Low-Birthweight Preterm Infants." *Early Human Development* 59, no. 3 (2000): 159–73.

Jewett, Don L., et al. "A Double-Blind Study of Symptom Provocation to Determine Food Sensitivity." *New England Journal of Medicine* 323 (August 1990): 429–33.

Katzev, Aphra R., "Girls or Boys: Relationship of Child Gender to Marital Instability." *Journal of Marriage and the Family* 56 (February 1994): 89–100.

Kazdin, Alan, and Corina Benjet. "Spanking Children: Evidence and Issues." *Current Directions in Psychological Science* 12, no. 3 (2003): 99.

Keogh, Barbara K., et al. "Children with Developmental Delays Twenty Years Later: Where Are They? How Are They?" *American Journal on Mental Retardation* 109, no. 3 (May 2004): 219–30.

Kutiper, Karen, and P. Wilson. "Updating Poetry Preferences: A Look at the Poetry Children Really Like." *Reading Teacher* 47, no. 1 (1993): 28–34.

Li, Jiong, "Mortality in Parents after Death of a Child in Denmark: A Nationwide Follow-Up Study." *Lancet* 361, no. 9355 (2003): 363–67.

McBride, B. A., and G. Mills. "A Comparison of Mother and Father Involvement with Their Preschool-Age Children." *Early Childhood Research Quarterly* 8 (1993): 457–77.

MacDonald, Kevin, and Ross D. Parke. "Bridging the Gap: Parent-Child Play Interaction and Peer Interactive Competence." *Child Development* 55 (1984): 1265–77.

———. "Parent-Child Physical Play: The Effects of Sex and Age of Children and Parents." *Sex Roles* 15, nos. 7–8 (1986): 367–78.

Marsiglio, William. "Contemporary Scholarship on Fatherhood: Culture, Identity, and Conduct." *Journal of Family Issues* 14 (December 1993): 484–509.

National Institute of Child Health and Human Development (NICHD). "Characteristics and Quality of Child Care for Toddlers and Preschoolers." *Applied Developmental Science* 4, no. 3 (2000): 116–35.

Newman, Philip R., and Barbara Newman. "Parenthood and Adult Development." *Marriage and Family Review* 12, nos. 3–4 (1988): 313–37.

Palkovitz, Rob, Marcella A. Copes, and Tara N. Woolfolk. "'It's Like . . . You Discover a New Sense of Being': Involved Fathering as an Evoker of Adult Development." *Men and Masculinities* 1 (July 2001): 49–69.

Palm, G. "Involved Fatherhood: A Second Chance." *Journal of Men's Studies* 2 (1993): 139–54.

Power, Thomas G. "Compliance and Self-Assertion: Young Children's Responses to Mothers versus Fathers." *Developmental Psychology* 30, no. 6 (1994): 980–89.

Rauscher, Frances, et al. "Music Training Causes Long-term Enhancement of Preschool Children's Spatial-temporal Reasoning." *Neurological Research* 19 (February 1997): 2–8.

Reis, Myrna, and Dolores Gold. "Relationship of Paternal Availability to Problem Solving and Sex-Role Orientation in Young Boys." *Psychological Reports* 40 (1977): 823–29.

Rescorla, Leslie. "Language and Reading Outcomes to Age Nine in Late-Talking Toddlers." *Journal of Speech, Language, and Hearing Research* 45 (April 2002): 360–71.

Rohner, Ronald P., and Robert A. Veneziano. "The Importance of Father Love: History and Contemporary Evidence." *Review of General Psychology* 54 (December 2001): 382–405.

Samuels, Andrew. "The Good Enough Father of Whatever Sex." Typescript, n.d.

Sorce, James F., et al. "Maternal Emotional Signaling: Its Effect on the Visual Cliff Behavior of One-Year-Olds." *Developmental Psychology* 21, no. 1 (1985): 195–200.

Straus, Murray A., and Carolyn J. Field. "Psychological Aggression by American Parents: National Data on Prevalence, Chronicity, and Severity." *Journal of Marriage and Family* 65 (November 2003): 795–808.

Vaish, Amrisha, and Tricia Striano. "Is Visual Reference Necessary? Contributions of Facial versus Vocal Cues in Twelve-Month-Olds' Social Referencing Behavior." *Developmental Science* 7, no. 3 (2004): 261–69.

Whaley, Kimberlee K. "The Emergence of Social Play in Infancy: A Proposed Developmental Sequence of Infant-Adult Social Play." *Early Childhood Research Quarterly* 5 (1990): 347–58.

Whitehurst, G. J., et al. "Accelerating Language Development through Picture Book Reading." *Developmental Psychology* 24, no. 4 (1988): 552–59.

Resources

This list of resources is by no means a comprehensive guide. Rather, it is designed to offer some immediate answers to your questions and needs and to steer you in the right direction.

Adoption

NATIONAL ADOPTION CENTER offers a great list of questions to ask adoption agencies; addresses tax issues, single-parent issues, and legal issues; and provides photos of kids waiting to be adopted, book reviews, lists of state and local contacts, and links to other adoption-related organizations.

(800) TO ADOPT
e-mail: nac@adopt.org
www.adopt.org

Advice, General

There are literally dozens of parenting resources out there for new parents. Among my favorites are:

BABYCENTER
www.babycenter.com

PARENTSPLACE.COM.
www.parentsplace.com

iPARENTING.COM
www.iparenting.com

PREGNANCY AND BABY
www.pregnancyandbaby.com

At-Home Dads

WWW.ATHOMEDAD.COM

WWW.DADDYSHOME.COM

WWW.SLOWLANE.COM is one of the most comprehensive resources for stay-at-home dads and primary caregiving dads. They have news, articles, advice, and a fantastic listing of dads' groups across the country.

CINCINNATI AT-HOME-DADS is an active group of stay-at-home dads. Besides being a great resource for dads in the Cincinnati area, they have a nice listing of other groups in states east of the Mississippi.

for the group itself: www.cincinnatidads.com
for the listings: www.cincinnatidads.com/otherdadgroups.htm

Child Abuse Reporting

THE AMERICAN HUMANE ASSOCIATION CHILDREN'S DIVISION
(800) 227-4645
www.americanhumane.org

CHILD HELP USA has a state-by-state list of phone numbers.
(800) 4-A-CHILD (422-4453)
www.childhelpusa.org

Childcare

CHILD CARE AWARE is a nationwide campaign created to help parents identify quality child care in their communities.
(800) 424-2246
www.childcareaware.org

THE NATIONAL RESOURCE CENTER FOR HEALTH AND SAFETY IN CHILD CARE is a wonderful general resource. Plus, it has listings of child-care regulations for all fifty states.
(800) 598-KIDS
nrc.uchsc.edu

Computers, Equipment

www.lilhands.ca/products.html
www.kid-computers.com
www.rjcooper.com/bigkeys-sf
www.fentek-ind.com/bigkey.htm

Computers, Recommended Games

LEARN THROUGH MUSIC (ages 1.5 to 4)
Fisher-Price, Inc.
(800) 432-5437
www.fisher-price.com

LEAPSTER SOFTWARE: LETTER FACTORY VIDEO (ages 3 to 6)
LeapFrog
(800) 701-5327
www.leapfrog.com

POWERTOUCH BABY (6 months to 3 years)
Fisher-Price, Inc.

Cooking and Other Messy Things

Blakey, Nancy. *Lotions, Potions, and Slime: Mudpies and More!* Berkeley, Calif.: Tricycle Press, 1996.

Heddle, Rebecca. *Science in the Kitchen.* London: Usborne, 1992.

Katzen, Mollie, and Ann Henderson. *Pretend Soup and Other Real Recipes: A Cookbook for Preschoolers and Up.* Berkeley, Calif.: Tricycle Press, 1994.

Kohl, MaryAnn F., and Jean Potter. *Cooking Art: Easy Edible Art for Young Children.* Beltsville, Md.: Gryphon House, 1997.

Fathers, Divorced or Single

AMERICAN COALITION OF FATHERS AND CHILDREN, with chapters nationwide, is dedicated to creating and promoting equal rights for all parties affected by divorce or the breakup of a family.
(800) 978-3237
e-mail: info@acfc.org
www.acfc.org

CHILDREN'S RIGHTS COUNCIL, with chapters in most states, has a well-stocked catalog of resources, including a listing of great books on the subject for kids and their parents.
(301) 559-3120
www.childrens-rights.org

MAKING LEMONADE is an online resource community for single parents of all kinds. Find support, information, referrals to experts, and a good laugh.
www.makinglemonade.com

Fathers, Military

MILITARY ONE SOURCE offers a full range of services 24/7/365
(800) 342-9647 from the U.S.
(800) 3429-6477 from outside the U.S.
www.militaryonesource.com

NATIONAL MILITARY FAMILY ASSOCIATION has many resources for military families
www.nmfa.org

Personal and Family Readiness Guide is a fantastic booklet filled with advice for military families about how to prepare for and cope with separation and deployment. Online at: www.nysuff.ang.af.mil/ANG_Readiness_Guide%5B1%5D%20%2004-03-03.pdf

Fathers, Older

THE OLDER FATHERS WEB RING is made up of a number of sites created by and for older dads.

www.geocities.com/olderdads

BABY CENTER'S BULLETIN BOARD FOR OLDER FATHERS is a great place to get—and give—advice.

bbs.babycenter.com/board/baby/dadsbaby/6694

Fathers, Step

CYBERPARENT.COM is a good source of information and referrals. www.cyberparent.com

STEPFAMILY ASSOCIATION OF AMERICA is a national, nonprofit membership organization dedicated to successful stepfamily living.

saafamilies.org

LeBey, Barbara. *Remarried with Children: Ten Secrets for Successfully Blending and Extending Your Family.* New York: Bantam, 2004.

Pickhardt, Carl. *Keys to Successful Stepfathering*. New York: Barron's, 1997.

Fatherhood, General

DADS AND DAUGHTERS is a nonprofit membership organization for fathers with daughters.

www.dadsanddaughters.org

FAMILIES AND WORK INSTITUTE is a nonprofit research organization focusing on work-family issues.

www.familiesandwork.org

FAMILY MAN ONLINE has a great newsletter with advice and commentary on all things father-related.

www.familymanonline.com

FATHERSWORLD.COM offers a huge listing of resources on many aspects of fatherhood.

www.fathersworld.com/resources/index.html

FATHERVILLE.COM has lots of articles by dads for dads about fatherhood.

www.fatherville.com

NATIONAL CENTER FOR FATHERING has resources designed to help men become more aware of their own fathering style and then work toward improving their skills.

(913) 384-4661
e-mail: ncf@aol.com
www.fathers.com

NATIONAL CENTER ON FATHERS AND FAMILIES is a great source of research and data on fathers, father involvement, and so forth.

(215) 686-3910
www.ncoff.gse.upenn.edu
links page: fatherfamilylink.gse.upenn.edu/

NATIONAL FATHERHOOD INITIATIVE offers membership that includes the quarterly newsletter *Fatherhood Today;* updates on family issues and political/legislative developments; the Fatherhood Resource Catalog of books, videos, and audiotapes, offering a discount on all items; and updates on activities and events.

600 Eden Road, Building E
Lancaster, PA 17601
(800) 790-DADS or (717) 581-8860
Fax: (717) 581-8862
www.fatherhood.org

Health Issues

AMERICAN ACADEMY OF PEDIATRICS has one of the biggest collections of resources for parents who need basic information fast on everything from colic and treating diaper rash to sleep problems and introducing solid foods.

www.aap.org

KIDS HEALTH has a full range of doctor-approved information.

www.kidshealth.org

Health Issues, Children with Special Needs

ASSISTIVE TECHNOLOGY INDUSTRY ASSOCIATION is a great resource if you're looking for equipment and other assistive tools.

401 North Michigan Avenue
MC: 2200-1
Chicago, Illinois 60611-4267
(877) OUR-ATIA (687-2842)
Info@ATIA.org

THE ASSOCIATION FOR CHILDREN WITH DOWN SYNDROME trains and educates children with Down syndrome.

www.acds.org

NATIONAL DISSEMINATION CENTER FOR CHILDREN AND YOUTH WITH DISABILITIES

P.O. Box 1492
Washington, DC 20013-1492
(800) 695-0285

e-mail: nichcy@aed.org
www.nichcy.org

NATIONAL FATHERS' NETWORK is devoted to supporting fathers (and families) who are raising children with special health-care needs and developmental disabilities.
(206) 747-4004
www.fathersnetwork.org

PACER CENTER, INC.
8161 Normandale Blvd.,
Minneapolis, MN 55437
(888) 248-0822
e-mail: fape@pacer.org
www.fape.org

SEE ALSO ADVICE, GENERAL

Most of the Web sites listed there also have experts who can answer questions on any topic you can think of.

Healthy Living

GREENHOME offers a full range of healthy, eco-friendly products for home and nursery, from paints that don't give off toxic gases to nontoxic insecticides and cleaning products.
www.greenhome.com

THE GREEN GUIDE is a wonderful newsletter (and Web site) filled with tips for healthy, organic living.
www.thegreenguide.com

Men, General

THE MEN'S HEALTH NETWORK is a national education organization that recognizes men's health as a specific social concern. They have a fantastic database of articles, resources, and links on every conceivable fatherhood issue.
www.menshealthnetwork.org

MENSTUFF is a huge collection of resources on men, men's health, fatherhood, parenting, relationships, and more.
www.menstuff.org

Music

KINDERMUSIK
www.kindermusik.com

MUSIC TOGETHER
www.musictogether.com

Both companies offer music and movement programs for infants and their parents. CDs and song books are available. Classes in each method are offered throughout the United States. Listings are available on the Web sites.

Parental Stress

CHILD HELP USA
(800) 4-A-CHILD (422-4453)

PARENTS' STRESS HOTLINE
(800) 632-8188

Reading

AMERICAN LIBRARY ASSOCIATION has reviews of children's books and lists of award winners.
www.ala.org

CHILDREN'S LITERATURE provides a searchable database of reviews of the latest kids' books.
www.childrenslit.com

CHILDREN'S LITERATURE WEB GUIDE has a wealth of information on children's books, recommendations, and links to other good sites.
www.ucalgary.ca/~dkbrown

THE HORN BOOK has lists of children's classics, medal winners, and other resources for parents.
www.hbook.com

INFANT LEARNING COMPANY produces a set of videos (and DVD) and books designed to help children of all ages learn to read.
www.infantlearning.com

Codell, Esme. *How to Get Your Child to Love Reading.* Chapel Hill, N.C.: Algonquin, 2003.

Coon, Cheryl. *Books to Grow With: A Guide to Using the Best Children's Fiction for Everyday Issues and Tough Challenges.* Portland, Ore.: Lutra Press, 2004.

Lewis, Valerie, and Walter Mayes. *Valerie and Walter's Best Books for Children.* New York: Quill, 2004.

Silvey, Anita. *100 Best Books for Children.* Boston: Houghton Mifflin, 2004.

Sign Language

BABYSIGNS offers videos and books based on the work of Linda Acredolo and Susan Goodwyn.
www.babysigns.com

MY BABY CAN TALK is a system designed to be used with children starting at about 10 months.

www.mybabycantalk.com

SIGN2ME offers videos and books based on the work of Joseph Garcia.

www.sign2me.com

Toys and Games

DR. TOY provides information, articles, reviews, and recommendations of educational and noneducational (just plain fun) toys. She also has tips on buying toys and top-ten lists for various themes (holidays, travel, and so on).

www.drtoy.com

NATURAL PLAY.COM sells toys and games made from all-natural materials.

www.naturalplay.com

See also Computers, Equipment, and Computers, Recommended Games

Twins and More

TOBUYTWO.COM is an auction Web site that features new and used equipment and supplies, with sections for twins, triplets, and more.

www.tobuytwo.com

TWINS FOUNDATION is a great source for research on twins.

www.twinsfoundation.com

TWINS MAGAZINE has print and online versions. Both offer advice, anecdotes, facts, support, and resources for parents of twins.

www.twinsmagazine.com

TWINSTUFF.COM is a Web portal for parents of twins and more.

www.twinstuff.com

We're constantly revising and updating this book and are always looking for ways to improve it. So if you have any comments or suggestions, please e-mail them to: armin@mrdad.com

Index

A

abstract thinking, 99
abuse. *See* child abuse
Acredolo, Linda, 70
activities. *See* games and activities
activity level, 109, 110, 113; ADD/ADHD diagnosis and, 234; discipline and, 126–27; eating habits and, 185; preschools and, 160
adaptability level, 109, 110, 112; discipline and, 126, 127; eating habits and, 185; preschools and, 161
adoption, resources for, 265
adoptive fathers, 95
age difference between children, 154–55
aggressive behavior, 88, 138, 169, 197, 208; physical play and, 209; at preschools, 161
alcoholism, 130
allergies to foods, 75–76
Alliance for Childhood, 31
allowances, 253
alone, toddler's capacity to be, 96–97
alphabet, 205, 211
ambivalence, father's feelings of, 121–22
American Coalition of Families, 241
Ames, Louise Bates, 137, 138, 169, 197, 228
anger, 52, 167; emotional control and, 172; at partner, 84–85; tantrums and, 52, 103, 107
animals: fear of, 18, 58, 59, 62–63, 65; safety concerns and, 44–45
animate vs. inanimate objects, 59, 88, 117, 169
antiques, 29
anxiety disorders, 130
approach/withdrawal level, 109, 110, 112, 130
approval seeking, 169
art, 37–41, 120; displaying of, 41; drawing and, 15, 37–38, 40, 86, 116, 195, 210, 226; painting and, 38–39, 40, 138, 210, 211; parents' role and, 39; and precautions against mess, 38–39; supplies for, 40
assertiveness, 126
assistive technological (AT) options, 32
at-home fathers, 21, 93; resources for, 265–66
attachment, 20, 42
attention, toddler's desire for, 18, 103, 180
attention deficit disorder (ADD), 207–8, 234
attention deficit/hyperactivity disorder (ADHD), 234
attention span, 39, 51, 139, 226–27; preschools and, 161; reading and, 35, 101
audiation, 100
audio tapes, 29–30
augmentative communication devices, 33
authoritarian parenting style, 123, 128
authoritative parenting style, 123, 129
auto insurance, 191
Ayas, Najib T., 19
Azzara, Christopher, 100

B

baby, new. *See* new baby
babysitters. *See* sitters
baby talk, 70, 228
bachelor's degree, salary and, 191

bad habits, of parents, 169–70
balance, toddler's sense of, 50, 86, 137, 210
balanced meals, 71–72
balloons, 29
ball play: catching, 195, 210, 226; kicking, 27, 51, 86, 116, 167, 210; throwing, 15, 26, 51, 86, 116, 210, 226
Band-Aids, 196
bankruptcy, 187
Barnard, Suzanne, 230
Barnett, Mark, 229
Barnett, Rosalind, 256
basement safety, 48
bath, fear of, 18, 58, 59, 60
bathroom privacy, 233
Baumrind, Diana, 123
bedtime, 126, 138; restricting liquids before, 147; routines and rituals for, 51, 66, 144, 196
bedtime stories, 27, 66, 196
behavior problems: television and, 207. *See also* discipline
Belsky, Jay, 80, 239
beverages, 182–83
bilingual toddlers, 69
Biller, Henry, 223, 225
birth defects, 156
birth order, of disabled child, 77
blaming imaginary companion, 212, 213
blanket sledding, 26
block building, 86, 137, 195
blowing bubbles, 26, 27
body: genital self-exploration and, 88, 139, 232–33; identifying parts of, 28, 232–33; of parents, toddler's interest in, 233; taking pleasure in, 97
books, 52; concept, 37, 102, 152, 206; about divorce, 251; lift-the-flap and pop-up, 36; for older siblings, 152, 206–7; suggested (lists), 36–37, 101–2, 151–53, 205–7; turning pages of, 14–15, 36, 51, 87, 137. *See also* reading
bookshelves, baby-accessible, 35–36
boredom: indications of, 39; reading same book and, 100–101, 138
bossiness, 118, 228
bottles, weaning from, 73
bowel movements, 139–40, 145
brain activity, during sleep, 144
breast, weaning from, 73
breath-holding, in tantrums, 106–7
bribes, 125–26, 130, 181
Britton, James, 88
Brody, Michael, 30
brushing teeth, 73–74, 86
buckets, drownings in, 45
Buckleitner, Warren, 31
Burke, Catherine, 32–33
Burton, Tim, 120

C

caffeine, 183
Cameron, Jim, 106–7, 126, 127, 185
cancer, 142, 183
candy, 183
capital gains tax, 132
Caplan, Frank, 52
carpooling, 190
car-seat safety, 44
catching, 195, 210, 226
categorizing games, 252
cause and effect, 27, 34, 68, 138, 169
Center for Human Development, 108, 109
chairs: high, 47, 181, 185; for toddlers, 96
charging, 191–92. *See also* credit cards
charity, 253
Chess, Stella, 108
Child, 130
child abuse, 125; allegations of, in divorce proceedings, 247–48; outrage at, 171–72; resources for, 266; speaking up about, 229–32
childbearing decisions, 153–56
childcare: resources for, 266. *See also* preschool/day care
Child Care Action Campaign (CCAC), 165–66
Child Care Aware, 159
child custody, 241–51; abuse allegations and, 247–48; books about, 251; gender-based assumptions and, 242, 246, 249; hiring lawyer and, 241; keeping log and, 246, 248; and knowing details of kids' lives, 245–46; mediation and, 240; terminology for, 249; unhappiness with arrangements for, 249–50; "winning," 250

childhood, parents' return to, 120
Children's Rights Council, 241
Chocolate Leaves, Eve's (recipe), 220–21
choices, presenting toddler with, 108, 124, 179
choking, safety concerns and, 13
clay or other molding substances, 195, 210
climbing, 14, 50, 51, 86, 116, 138
clinginess, 20, 21
clothes. *See* dressing and undressing
coin identification, 252
Coke, 182
collages, 40
college education, paying for, 131–34
color awareness, 28
communication: augmentative communication devices and, 33; physical play and, 209. *See also* verbal development
communication with partner, 80–85, 237–41; breakdown in, 240–41; differing needs and expectations in, 237–38; after divorce, 250; divorce proceedings and, 248; factors leading to problems in, 80–81; fighting and, 84–85, 239; ground rules for, 83–84; (re)learning to talk and, 82–83; listening and, 83; tips for, 81–82
communication with toddler, 67–70, 177–80; bilingualism and, 69; guidelines for, 68–70, 178–80; listening and, 69, 177–78; military deployment and, 173; signing and, 70–71; stepfathering and, 202; talking *at* vs. *with* toddler and, 68
community property, 244
comparison-shopping, 190, 252
complimenting good behavior, 108, 125, 126
compromise: with partner, 83–84; with toddler, 108, 124
computers for toddlers, 30–34, 174–77; and colored stickers for keyboard, 175–76; resources for, 266–67; rules for, 174–76; software and, 34, 176–77
concept books, 37, 102, 152, 206
confidence: toddler's development of, 209, 228; fatherhood and, 119
consequences, teaching toddler about, 27, 125
consistency, 124, 179
consolidation loans, 192
Consumer Credit Counseling Service (CCCS), 187
containers: childproof, 137; filling and emptying, 14, 26
contrariness, 87, 118, 196, 197, 228
control issues, 23; separation anxiety and, 41; and shift in balance of power from toddler to father, 198–201; tantrums and, 103, 107–8; toddler's fears and, 64
conversational skills, 88
cooking with toddlers, 99, 211, 215–21; Eve's Chocolate Leaves, 220–21; French Toast, 217; Kidsicles, 216; Liz's Eggs in the Nest, 216–17; Milkshakes, 218; Pancake Art, 219–20; Popcorn Balls, 220; Pretzels, 218–19; Quesadillas, 217–18; resources for, 267; safety and, 219
cooperation from toddlers, 139, 200, 209; contrariness and, 87, 118, 196, 197, 228
coparent counseling, 248, 249
correcting errors of speech, 69
counseling: divorce and, 248–49; marriage or couples, 84
counting, 211, 227, 252
Coverdell Education Savings Accounts (ESAs), 133
Cowan, Phil and Carolyn, 23, 82–83, 118–19, 171
creativity, 97, 120, 144, 156, 209; art activities and, 37–41; computers and, 31, 177; of parents, 120
credit cards, 191–92; divorce and, 245
criticism, 118, 125; temperament and, 126
curiosity, 118
custody. *See* child custody

D

dairy products, 183
dark, fear of, 18, 58, 62
dating your partner, 57, 81–82
Davis, Clara, 71
dawdling, 127
day care. *See* preschool/day care
death: of child, coping with, 78–79; wills and trusts and, 134–36
debit cards, 192
debt: bankruptcy and, 187; divorce and, 245; getting out of, 186–92
Debtors' Anonymous, 187
decision making, 197
De Luccie, Mary, 94
dental care, 73–75, 86
dentists, 74–75; books about, 206; fear of, 63; first trip to, 74
dependence. *See* independence vs. dependence
Dependent Care Assistance Plans (DCAPs), 165
depression, 19, 94, 130
desserts, 181
details, focusing on, 168
development. *See* emotional/social development; intellectual development; physical development; verbal development
developmental red flags, 53, 140
disability, 201; dealing with disappointment of, 76–80; positive effects on family of, 80; technology and, 32–33
discipline, 23, 123–31; gender differences and, 131; parenting style and, 123–26; spanking and, 130–31; stepparenting and, 222; tantrums and, 104, 105; temperament and, 126–31
displaying toddler's art, 41
disposable diapers, 146
distractibility level, 110, 111, 115; discipline and, 130
diverting misbehaving child, 124
dividend reinvestment plans (DRIPs), 190
divorce, 94, 201, 241–51; books about, 251; children's relationship with father after, 203; community property and, 244; counseling and, 248–49; financial issues and, 244–45; gender strategy and, 242; hiring lawyer for, 241–43; mediation alternative and, 240; moving out of house and, 243–44. *See also* child custody
doctorate, salary and, 191
doctors: father's visits to, 142; toddler's fear of, 63, 64–65
Dodson, Fitzhugh, 15, 197, 228, 232
dogs, fear of, 18, 58, 59, 62–63
dollar cost averaging, 193
domestic violence, 247
doorknob turning, 15, 51, 116, 137
double standards, 196
Down syndrome, 16, 32
drawing, 15, 37–38, 40, 86, 116, 195, 210, 226
dressing and undressing, 14, 86, 116, 167, 195, 197, 226
dropping objects, 51
durable power of attorney, 136

E

eating, 180–85; and getting child involved in meals, 184; minimizing food fights and, 181–84; new foods and, 181, 185; self-feeding and, 14, 15, 17, 72, 86–87, 195; temperament and, 185; toddler's refusal of, 18; weaning and, 73. *See also* food; nutrition
education: college, paying for, 131–34; increasing your own level of, 191. *See also* preschool/day care
educational activities, 99
Education IRAs, 133
Eggs in the Nest, Liz's (recipe), 216–17
egotism, 87, 117, 156, 195, 200
electric outlets, safety concerns and, 116
elimination diets, 75–76
embarassment at toddler's behavior, 199
emergency fund, 193
emotional sensitivity level, 109, 110, 114
emotional/social development, 10, 91; at 12–15 months, 17–18; at 15–18 months, 52–53; at 18–21 months, 88–89; at 21–24 months, 118; at 24–27 months, 139–40; at

27–30 months, 169; at 30–33 months, 197; at 33–36 months, 228
emotions: of child, acknowledging, 178; father's changes in, 170–72; giving name to, 178; imaginary friends and, 212–13; of other people, identifying, 139; of parent, talking to child about, 179; regulation vs. suppression of, 171, 172; toddler's expression of, 52, 167, 171, 177, 178, 209
empathy, 91, 171, 209
Employee Stock Ownership Plans (ESOPs), 194
energy level. *See* activity level
environmentally preferable products, 46
equipment-buying tips, 96
equivalence games, 252
erections, 88
estate planning: gifts and, 136; wills and trusts and, 134–36
estate taxes, 135, 136
Eve's Chocolate Leaves, 220–21
exercise, 185; in father's self-care, 19
expansion, father's sense of, 172
expectations: child's accomplishments and, 140–41; dealing with differences between reality and, 76–80; stepfathering and, 202; temperament and, 130
expenses, reducing, 186–92
explaining your actions, 68
exploration of environment, 97, 103
expressiveness, 209; father's increase in, 171; toddler's verbal development and, 16
ex-spouse: civil communication with, 250; new partner's relationship with, 222

F

Faber, Adele, 171, 178
Fagot, Beverly, 141–43
failures of child, responding to, 140–41
family payroll, 253
family planning, 153–56; and age difference between children, 154–55
fantasizing, 178
fantasy, differentiating reality and, 51, 66
fantasy play, 168
fast foods, 183, 192
fatherhood, resources on, 268–69
fathers: actively involved, benefits of, 9–10, 56, 90–94, 143; additional education for, 191; adoptive, 95; ambivalence in, 121–22; bad habits of, imitated by child, 169–70; child's accomplishments as mirror for, 140–41; control issues and, 198–201; costs of fatherhood and, 93; disciplining by, 123–31; embarassed at toddler's behavior, 199; emotional changes in, 170–72; fearful of being rejected by baby, 89–90; identity shift in, 118–21; intense reactions of, to child's behavior, 141; life changes made by, 254–55; limitations recognized by, 23; military deployment of, 172–74; money matters and (*see* money matters); parenting style of, 123–26, 128–29; partner's relationship with (*see* relationship with partner); physical exhaustion of, 18, 80, 93; as portrayed on television, 208; in power struggles with toddler, 197–98; self-care for, 19–20; separation issues for, 20–23, 235–37; speaking up about abuse, 229–32; and spillover between work and family life, 255–56; stepparenting and, 201–3; toddler's resemblance to, 169; younger vs. older, 198
fat intake, 183
fears, 18, 58–67, 118; of being rejected by your baby, 89–90; controlling your own reactions and, 64; discovering cause of, 43, 59; helping child deal with, 59–63; nightmares or night terrors and, 51, 66–67; parents' facial expressions and, 64; parents' words and, 64, 65; and playing through scary situations, 64–65; security objects and, 66–67;

separation anxiety and, 18, 41–43, 58; of strangers, 18, 58
feelings. *See* emotions
Fewell, Rebecca, 78
fighting with partner, 84–85, 239
financial aid, college education and, 132
financial issues. *See* money matters
financial planners, 188–89
Finley, Gordon, 95
firearms, 45–46
"first adolescence," 197
first steps, 14, 16–17
529 plans, 133–34
flexible thinking, 119–20
flirting with partner, 57
flushing toilet, fear of, 147
folk tales, 152, 206
food, 107; as behavior management tool, 130–31, 181; near computer, 174; reducing expense of, 190; safety concerns and, 47. *See also* cooking with toddlers; eating; nutrition
food allergies and intolerances, 75–76
401(k) plans, 132
403(b) plans, 132
Fraiberg, Selma, 58–59, 87, 138, 167, 168–69, 196
freezer safety, 48
French Toast (recipe), 217
Friedman, Stewart, 255
friends: of father, 256; imaginary, 212–13; of toddler, 90
frustration, 97, 118, 172; tantrums and, 102–3
Fulgum, Robert, 156

G

Galinsky, Ellen, 20
games and activities, 15, 125; for 12–15 months, 26–27; for 15–18 months, 28–29; computer, 30–34, 174–75; fun educational, 99; resources for, 272; safety concerns and, 13. *See also* play; toys
garage safety, 48
Garcia, Joseph, 70
gates, for stairways, 47
gender differences: divorce and custody proceedings and, 242, 246, 249; physical play and, 209–10; and toddler's treatment of adults, 141–43; disabled child and, 77; punishment and, 131; toilet training and, 146–49; toys and, 30, 96; verbal development and, 227–28
gender identity, 139, 232–33; toilet training and, 148, 149
genitals: adult, toddler's interest in, 233; self-exploration of, 88, 139, 232–33; teaching correct names for, 232–33
gifts, estate planning and, 136
Gjerdingen, Dwenda K., 55
gloating, 141
goal-directed activities, 196
good-bye routines, 164
Goodwyn, Susan, 70
Gordon, Edwin, 97, 100, 214
grammatical errors, 69
green babies, 46; resources for, 270
Greenhaus, Jeffrey, 255
Greenspan, Stanley, 21
grief, death of child and, 78–79
Gross, Terry, 121
group activities, 211–14
Group for the Advancement of Psychiatry, 140
Grunow, Richard, 100
guardians, 135
guilt: of ambivalent father, 122; mother's feelings of, 239
gymnastics, 211

H

haircuts, fear of, 60–61, 65–66
hair washing, fear of, 58, 60
handedness, 51, 226
hand-eye coordination, 26, 36, 86, 116, 137
hand washing, 86
Hardesty, Constance, 94
Hass, Aaron, 55
Haugland, Susan, 176–77
head-banging, in tantrums, 107
health-care directives, 136
health insurance, 191
health issues: durable power of attorney and, 136; father's health care and, 142; health-care directives and, 136; preschools and, 159–60; resources for, 269–70; toddler's first steps and, 16
hearing-impaired parents, 70

high chairs, 47, 181, 185
home equity loans, 192
Horgan, Timothy J., 241
hot water, temperature of, 45
household tasks, 80, 143, 154, 238, 239
humor, 52, 119, 228; in dealing with tantrum, 104
Huttenlocher, Janellen, 67–68, 70
hyperactivity, 234

I

identity: development of self-identity and, 228; fatherhood and, 118–21; gender, 139, 148, 149, 232–33
idle threats, 179
Ilg, Frances, 137, 138, 169, 197, 228
imaginary friends, 212–13
imagination, 27, 51, 97
imitating, 27, 52, 117, 139, 168, 214; parents' less savory behaviors, 169–70; peers, 88; tantrums, 104, 228
impulse control: of father, 171; of toddler, 97, 168, 195, 228
independence vs. dependence, 28, 43–44, 51, 58, 118, 200; experiments with physical separation and, 17–18; parents' separation issues and, 20–23; power struggles and, 197–98; separating from mother and, 91; separation anxiety and, 18, 41–43, 58, 143–44
injuries, Band-Aids and, 196
insurance, 255; auto, 191; health, 191; life, 134
intellectual development, 91; at 12–15 months, 15; at 15–18 months, 51; at 18–21 months, 87; at 21–24 months, 117; at 24–27 months, 138; at 27–30 months, 167–68; at 30–33 months, 195–96; at 33–36 months, 226–27
intensity level, 109, 110, 113; eating habits and, 185
interrupting, 177
investments: dividend reinvestment plans (DRIPs), 190; financial planners and, 188–89
IRAs (individual retirement accounts), 132
irrational requests, 178

J

jealousy, father's feelings of, 236
Jensen, Amy Hillyard, 78
Jones, Gerard, 208
juice, 182
jumping, 116, 137, 195, 210, 226
junk food, 183

K

Katz, Lilian, 84
Katzen, Mollie, 215
Keogh plans, 132
kicking ball, 27, 51, 86, 116, 167, 210
Kidsicles (recipe), 216
kitchen safety, 47–48
Kutiper, Karen, 35
Kutner, Lawrence, 9, 61
Kvols, Kathryn, 124

L

Lamb, Michael, 77, 80
language games, 196
language learning: passive vs. active, 15. *See also* verbal development
Lansky, Vicky, 225
lawyers, for divorce proceedings, 241–43
Leach, Penelope, 43
leadership skills, 97, 209
lecturing, 125
Leyden, T. J., 121
life insurance, 134
lifestyle, 93
lift-the-flap books, 36
limitations, recognition of, 23
limits: setting, 23, 104, 126, 127, 200; toddlers' testing of, 118, 197–98
Linkletter, Art, 199
listening: to music, 100; to your child, 69, 177–78; to your partner, 83
living trusts, 134–36
Liz's Eggs in the Nest (recipe), 216–17
love, expression of, 83, 238
low birth weight, 154, 155

M

malnutrition, 185
Margalit, Malka, 77
Margetts, Kay, 91
marriage counseling, 84
master's degree, salary and, 191
masturbation, 232
matching games, 99, 210
math skills, 10, 91
Mazlish, Elaine, 171, 178

McGregor, Ewan, 254
mediation of divorce and custody agreements, 240
medical issues. *See* health issues
memory, 15, 29, 51, 144, 168
men's issues, resources for, 270
mental retardation: and dealing with disappointment of disability, 76–80; Down syndrome and, 16, 32
military fathers: deployment of, 172–74; resources for, 267–68
milk, 73, 74
Milkshakes (recipe), 218
Miller, Brent, 77
Milne, A. A., 120
mimicking. *See* imitating
mind changes, 169
misbehavior: attention seeking and, 180; diverting child and, 124. *See also* discipline
mistakes: admitting, 179; learning from, 23; toddler's alertness to, 101, 117, 168, 196; in toddler's speech, correcting, 69
modesty, 233
money matters, 93, 157, 186–94; bankruptcy, 187; boosting savings, 186, 187, 192–94; college financing, 131–34; and decision to have another child, 154; divorce and, 244–45; emergency fund, 193; family payroll, 253; financial planners, 188–89; life insurance, 134; military deployment and, 173; and mother not returning to work, 254–55; preschool financing, 165–66; reducing expenses and getting out of debt, 186–92; retirement savings, 132, 192–94; stepparenting and, 222; teaching children about, 251–53; wills and trusts, 134–36; working for money and, 255
monsters, fear of, 58, 61–62
mood, 109, 110, 113, 169
"motherhood mystique," 246
mothers: stepmothering and, 221–22; work life of, 157, 254–55. *See also* relationship with partner
moving: for children's sake, 254; out of house when facing divorce, 243–44
music, 29, 97–100, 120, 210, 214–15; audiation and, 100; exposing child to variety of, 98, 100, 215; moving to, 52, 98–100, 137, 214; resources for, 270–71; singing and, 18, 52, 69, 97–98, 100, 214

N

naming objects, 88, 117, 168
naps, 18, 51, 143, 144; at preschools, 159
National Association for the Education of Young Children (NAEYC), 159
National Dissemination Center for Children with Disabilities, 162
National Information Center for Children & Youth with Disabilities (NICHY), 33
nature walks, 99
negativism, 87, 118, 196, 197, 228
neglectful parents, 123
new baby, 222–25; and easing transition for older sibling, 223–25; family planning and, 153–56; preparing older sibling for, 152, 222–23; toddler's reactions to, 223
Newman, Barbara and Philip, 141, 158, 171
newspaper reading, 199
night-lights, 18, 43, 144
nightmares, 51, 66–67
night terrors, 67
"no," 87, 180, 196
noises, fear of, 58, 60
nonsense syllables, 196
nonverbal cues, 178
notes to child, in father's absence, 173
nudity, 233
numbers, 211, 227
nursery rhymes, 69, 117, 196
nutrition, 170, 180–85; balanced meals and, 71–72; desserts and, 181; father's self-care and, 19; food allergies or intolerances and, 75–76; ideal toddler diet and, 182–83; at preschools, 159; serving sizes and, 181

O

obesity, television and, 207
object permanence, 42, 87
observation skills, 99
obstacle courses, 26
older fathers, 198, 255; resources for, 268
older siblings: books for, 152, 206–7; new baby and, 152, 222–25; walking and, 16
Oobleck, 99
opinions, asking child for, 178
oral sex, 54
outrage, 171–72
overprotectiveness, 23; with special needs child, 79–80
overweight, 131; television and, 207
ownership of objects, 87, 96

P

pain, physical, 19
painting, 38–39, 40, 138, 210, 211
Palkovitz, Rob, 92–93, 120–21
Palm, Glen, 170, 171
Pancake Art (recipe), 219–20
parallel play, 24
Parent Advocacy Coalition for Educational Rights (PACER), 32–33
parenting styles, 123–26, 128–29
Parke, Ross, 198, 209
partner, relationship with. *See* relationship with partner
Pasley, Kay, 202
passing out, in tantrums, 106–7
patience, 119, 177–78
Patinkin, Mandy, 254
peeling foods with peels, 183–84
peers: group activities and, 211–14; playing with, 53, 95–96, 139, 228; toddler's interest in, 88, 139, 169, 213; toddler's rough treatment of, 88
penis, 88, 232; genital self-exploration and, 88, 139, 232–33; holding during toilet training, 148, 149; teaching correct word for, 232–33
peripheral vision, 138, 139
permissive parenting style, 123, 129
persistence level, 110, 111, 115
pets: fear of, 18, 58, 59, 62–63; safety concerns and, 44–45
photographs, father's absence and, 173
physical development: at 12–15 months, 14–15; at 15–18 months, 50–51; at 18–21 months, 86–87; at 21–24 months, 116; at 24–27 months, 137–38; at 27–30 months, 167; at 30–33 months, 195; at 33–36 months, 226
physical exhaustion, of father, 18, 80, 93
physical play, 29, 209–10
"pie chart," 118–19
play: at 12–15 months, 23–27; at 15–18 months, 28–30, 53; at 18–21 months, 86, 94–97; at 30–33 months, 209–14; alone, 88, 96–97; fantasy, 168; fun educational activities and, 99; fun things for rainy days, 211; gender differences and, 30, 96, 209–10; group activities and, 211–14; lessons learned in, 24, 51; parallel, 24; with peers, 88, 95–96, 139, 228; physical, 29, 209–10; at preschools, 162–63; pretend, 51, 97, 158, 211, 212–13; safety concerns and, 13; scary situations and, 64–65; separation anxiety and, 42; things to avoid at 12–18 months, 29–30; of toddler with new baby, 224. *See also* toys
play dates, 96
playpens, 47, 97
Pleck, Joseph, 94
plurals, 168
poetry, 35, 102, 153, 206
poison control, 47, 48
Popcorn Balls (recipe), 220
pop-up books, 36
possessives, 168
potty seats, 145–46, 147
potty training. *See* toilet training
power struggles, 197–98
praise, 39, 108, 118, 125, 179–80
pre-divorce counseling, 248–49
premature babies, 154; first steps of, 16
preschool/day care, 156–66; adult separation problems and, 235–37; advantages and disadvan-

tages of, 157–58; books about, 153, 206; categories of, 156–57; child-teacher ratios in, 158, 159; controversy about effects of, 157; custody proceedings and, 166; easing transition to, 163–65; general cleanliness of, 160; licensing and accreditation of, 159; nutrition and health concerns and, 159–60; paying for, 165–66; program and philosophy of, 162–63; red flags for, 162; resources for, 266; safety features of, 161–62; selection criteria for, 157–63; stability of age-mates in, 157–58; staff of, 163; temperament and, 157, 160–61
pretend play, 51, 97, 158, 211; imaginary friends and, 212–13
Pretzels (recipe), 218–19
pride: of parents, 140–41; of toddlers, 169
priorities, reordering of, 120–21
prioritizing, teaching children about, 253
probate, 134, 135
problem solving, 10, 51, 91, 117, 168
promises, 179
prompting, 68
pronouns, 88, 117
pronunciation errors, 69
prostate cancer, 142
Pruett, Kyle, 91
punishment, 125; gender differences and, 131; spanking, 130–31; temperament and, 126, 127. *See also* discipline
push/pull toys, 27, 50
puzzles, 86, 116, 195, 210

Q

Quesadillas (recipe), 217–18
question asking: by parents, 43, 108, 179; by toddlers, 169, 199, 207

R

Radin, Norma, 10
rainy days, fun things for, 211
reacting to your toddler, 69
reading, 34–37, 88, 100–102, 117, 120, 138, 149–53, 204–7; advanced concepts for, 150–51; attention span and, 35, 101; books dealing with divorce, 251; books for older siblings, 152, 206–7; creating environment for, 149–50; dealing with boredom in, 100–101; early, 204–5; newspaper, 199; poetry, 35; recordings of, in father's absence, 173; resources for, 271; suggested books for, 36–37, 101–2, 151–53, 205–7
reality, differentiating fantasy and, 51, 66
recalls, product safety and, 47
refrigerator safety, 48
regularity level, 109, 110, 114; discipline and, 130; eating habits and, 185
Reich, Robert, 254
reinforcement, positive, 125
rejection, fathers' fears of, 89–90
relationship with partner, 22, 120, 237–51; actively involved father and, 10, 92, 93, 94; breakdown in, 240–41; communication and, 80–85, 237–41; dating and, 57, 81–82; death of child and, 79; disabled child and, 77; expression of love and, 83; father's needs in, 237–38; fighting and, 84–85, 239; focusing on common concerns in, 239; military deployment and, 174; as model for your child, 170; mother's needs in, 238–39; sex and, 20, 54–58, 80, 82; stepparenting and, 202, 221–22. *See also* communication with partner; divorce
relaxation, 99
remarriage, 94; stepfathering and, 201–3
repeating: what child has said, 177, 178; what you say, by toddler, 88; yourself, 179
requests, specific vs. general, 179
restaurant checks, 252
retirement, saving for, 132, 192–94
revocable living trusts, 134–36
rhymes, 36–37, 102, 117, 153
rhythm, sense of, 214
ride-on toys, 28, 50

rituals. *See* routines and rituals
Roopnarine, Jaipaul, 77
Rosemond, John, 156
roughhousing, 209–10
routines and rituals, 42, 51, 58, 196; for bedtime, 51, 66, 144, 196; military deployment and, 173; for newly blended family, 202
Rowling, J. K., 120
running, 86, 116, 137, 195

S

Sachs, Brad, 84, 85, 239
sacrifice, 93
safety concerns, 44–49; art projects and, 40; cooking with toddlers and, 219; in garage, basement, workshop, and outside, 48; in kitchen, 47–48; swimming pools and, 48–49; talking to toddler about, 65
savings: boosting, 186, 187, 192–94; for college education, 132–34; paying off debts with, 191; for retirement, 132, 192–94
scary situations, playing through, 64–65
scary stories, 62, 66
Schatz, William, 79
Schildhaus, Kim Wendee, 78, 79
schizophrenia, 156
scolding, 179
secrets, 212
security objects, 66–67, 73
self-centeredness, 87
self-control, 167–68
self-esteem: of child, 22, 125, 130, 177; of father, 76, 93
self-identity, 228
selflessness, 171
sensitivity, 109, 171. *See also* emotional sensitivity
sensory awareness level, 109, 111, 114; preschools and, 160
sensory stimulation, 29, 40
sentences, first, 168
separation anxiety, 18, 41–43, 58; sleep problems and, 41, 143–44
separation from parent, toddler's experiments with, 17–18
separation issues, for parents, 20–23, 235–37
SEP plans, 132
sequential thinking, 117
serving sizes, 181
sex identity. *See* gender identity
sex with partner, 20, 54–58, 80; in front of child, 233; potential conflicts about, 54–56; scheduling, 56–57, 82; ultimate aphrodisiac and, 56
Shade, Daniel, 176–77
shaking toddler, 125
shame, 233
shape discrimination, 15, 25, 99, 117
Shapiro, Jerrold, 237
sharing, 96, 97
shell game, 29
shootings, accidental, 45–46
Shopper, Moisy, 149
shyness around strangers, 18
sibling rivalry, 155
signing with toddler, 70–71; resources for, 271–72
silence, 100
silverware, 227; eating with, 15, 72, 86–87
Singer, Dorothy, 97
singing, 18, 52, 69, 97–98, 100, 214
sitters, 42, 66, 80; informal babysitting cooperatives and, 81–82; using television or movies as, 208
size discrimination, 15, 28, 117
sleep, 19, 107, 143–44; books about, 153; fear of, 62; middle-of-the-night wake-ups and, 144; naps, 18, 51, 143, 144, 159; nightmares or night terrors and, 51, 66–67; problems with, 143–44; separation anxiety and, 41, 143–44
smart toys, 174
smelling games, 211
smoking, 170
snacks, 184, 185; at preschools, 159
Snarey, John, 10, 209
social development. *See* emotional/social development
social life, of father, 256
software for children, 34; developmental vs. nondevelopmental, 176–77; picking, 176; resources for, 266–67
Sorce, James, 64
sorting skills, 25, 28, 211, 227
space words, 169

spacing between children, 154–55
Spangler, Doug, 131
spanking, 130–31
spatial concepts, 28, 117, 138, 226
special needs children, 201; and dealing with disappointment of disability, 76–80; positive effects on family of, 80; preschools and, 162; resources for, 269–70; technology and, 32–33
spoiling, 23
spontaneity, lack of, 80
sports, girls' participation in, 91
stacking, 15, 26, 116, 137
stairs, 50, 86, 116, 137, 195; safety concerns and, 47
Staub, Ervin, 229
stay-at-home fathers, 21, 93; resources for, 265–66
stepfathering, 201–3; and child's relationship with biological father, 203; resources for, 268
stepmothering, helping partner with, 221–22
stores, talking about money-related things in, 252
stranger anxiety, 18, 58
stress, 157, 239, 255; alleviation of, 19, 20; family, tantrums and, 104; parental, resources for, 271
Striano, Tricia, 64
strollers, 17, 137
successes of child: creating opportunities for, 180; responding to, 140–41
sunlight, benefits of, 19
supplements, 183
support groups, 82; disabled child and, 77–78, 79; divorce and, 241
swear words, toddler's repetition of, 16
swimming pools, 48–49
swinging, 116
symbolic use of words, 16–17
symmetry, 196

T

tables for toddlers, 96
talking. *See* communication; verbal development
tantrums, 52, 88, 102–8, 118, 127, 139, 197, 201, 228; breath-holding and passing out in, 106–7; causes of, 102–4; over food, 131; preventing, 106–8; public, 107; temperament and, 104, 106; what not to do about, 105; what to do about, 104–5
taxes: capital gains, 132; college financing and, 132–34; estate, 135, 136; preschool financing and, 165; retirement savings and, 132, 194
technology for toddlers, 30–34, 174–77; resources for, 266–67; special needs children and, 32–33. *See also* computers for toddlers
teeth, dental care and, 73–75
telecommuting, 190
television, 207–8
temperament, 20, 108–15, 156; ADD/ADHD diagnosis and, 234; discipline and, 126–31; eating habits and, 185; preschools and, 157, 160–61; separation anxiety and, 43; tantrums and, 104, 106
temper tantrums. *See* tantrums
tenses, 168, 228
Terry, Ann, 35
texture tour, 29
Thomas, Alexander, 108
threats: idle, 179. *See also* warnings
throwing, 15, 26, 51, 86, 116, 210, 226
time concepts, 15, 87, 138, 196, 226, 228
time outs, 104
toilet training, 88–89, 145–49; books about, 153; equipment for, 147; gender differences in, 146–49; new baby and, 223; process for, 145–46; readiness for, 139–40, 145; success boosters for, 147
tool use, 15, 28–29, 51
toothpaste, 73
touching, intimate, 233
touching games, 26
toys, 88, 228; for 12–15 months, 25–26; for 15–18 months, 28; duplicate, for play dates, 96; gender-specific, 30, 96; at preschools, 163; resources for, 272; safety concerns and, 47; smart, 174; toddler's babying of, 118. *See also* play

treasure hunts, 29
Trelease, Jim, 204
tricycles, 28, 167, 210, 226
trusts, 134–36
twelve-inch rule, 45
twins, resources for, 272
Tyson, Eric, 132

V

vacuum cleaners, fear of, 18, 59, 60
Vadasy, Patricia, 78
vagina: genital self-exploration and, 88, 139, 232–33; teaching correct word for, 233
Vaish, Amrisha, 64
values, changed by fatherhood, 121
vegetables, growing, 184
verbal development, 10, 97; at 12–15 months, 15–17; at 15–18 months, 52; at 18–21 months, 87–88; at 21–24 months, 117; at 24–27 months, 138–39; at 27–30 months, 168–69; at 30–33 months, 196; at 33–36 months, 227–28; bilingual household and, 69; gender differences in, 227–28; talking with your baby and, 67–70
videos, 207
violent children, 161
vitamins, 183
vomiting, in tantrums, 107

W

walking, 50, 51, 86, 137, 195; around neighborhood, 27, 59; first steps and, 14, 16–17; nature walks and, 99
warnings, 65, 108, 124–25, 127; idle threats and, 179
Warshak, Richard, 246
water, safety concerns and, 13, 45
weaning, 73
Whaley, Kim, 96
whining, 126
whispering, 179
"why" questions, 178, 199
wills, 134–36
window safety, 46–47
Winnicott, D. W., 97
withdrawal level. *See* approach/withdrawal level
word associations, 69–70
work, 22, 78, 81; balancing family life and, 10, 254, 255; child-related career moves and, 254; commutation costs and, 190; Employee Stock Ownership Plans (ESOPs) and, 194; mother's career and, 157, 254–55; preschool or day-care financing and, 165–66; spillover between family life and, 255–56
workshop safety, 48
writing, toddler's imitation of, 204, 226

Y

yes-or-no questions, 69, 108, 177

Z

Zweiback, Meg, 154

CARTOON CREDITS

© 2005 Frank Cotham from cartoonbank.com. All rights reserved: p. 90.
© 2005 Liza Donnelly from cartoonbank.com. All rights reserved: p. 204.
© 2005 Joseph Farris from cartoonbank.com. All rights reserved: p. 184.
© 2005 Mort Gerberg from cartoonbank.com. All rights reserved: p. 103.
© 2005 Mort Gerberg from cartoonbank.com. All rights reserved: p. 227.
© 2005 Mort Gerberg from cartoonbank.com. All rights reserved: p. 72.
© 2005 William Hamilton from cartoonbank.com. All rights reserved: p. 120.
© 2005 Joseph Farris from cartoonbank.com. All rights reserved: p. 186.
© 2005 J.P. Rini from cartoonbank.com. All rights reserved: p. 200.
© 2005 Peter Steiner from cartoonbank.com. All rights reserved: p. 2.
© 2005 Peter Steiner from cartoonbank.com. All rights reserved: p. 238.
© 2005 Mick Stevens from cartoonbank.com. All rights reserved: p. 126.
© 2005 Mick Stevens from cartoonbank.com. All rights reserved: p. 175.
© 2005 Bob Zahn from cartoonbank.com. All rights reserved: p. 150.
© 2005 Bob Zahn from cartoonbank.com. All rights reserved: p. 45.
© 2005 Bob Zahn from cartoonbank.com. All rights reserved: p. 8.
© 2005 Bob Zahn from cartoonbank.com. All rights reserved: p. 81.
© 2005 Jack Ziegler from cartoonbank.com. All rights reserved: p. 164.
© 2005 Jack Ziegler from cartoonbank.com. All rights reserved: p. 21.
© 2005 Jack Ziegler from cartoonbank.com. All rights reserved: p. 235.

About the Author

A nationally recognized parenting expert, **Armin Brott** is also the author of *The New Father: A Dad's Guide to the First Year*, *The New Father: A Dad's Guide to the Toddler Years*, *The Single Father: A Dad's Guide to Parenting without a Partner*, and *Father for Life: A Journey of Joy, Challenge, and Change*. He has written on parenting and fatherhood for *The New York Times Magazine*, *The Washington Post*, *Newsweek*, and dozens of other periodicals. He also writes a nationally syndicated column, "Ask Mr. Dad," and hosts "Positive Parenting," a weekly talk show. Armin lives with his family in Oakland, California. To learn more, please visit his Web site, www.mrdad.com.

ARMIN BROTT: OVER 1,000,000 FATHERHOOD BOOKS IN PRINT!

THE EXPECTANT FATHER BOXED SET
FATHER KNOWS BEST
ISBN 0-7892-0824-5 · $39.95

EXPECTANT FATHER
Facts, Tips, and Advice for the Dad-to-Be

NEW FATHER
A Dad's Guide to the First Year

NEW FATHER
A Dad's Guide to the Toddler Years

EXPECTANT AND FIRST-YEAR FATHER BOXED SET
ISBN 0-7892-0840-7 · $27.50

EXPECTANT FATHER
Facts, Tips, and Advice for the Dad-to-Be

NEW FATHER
A Dad's Guide to the First Year

THE NEW FATHER SERIES BOXED SET
ISBN 0-7892-0825-3 · $27.50

NEW FATHER
A Dad's Guide to the First Year

NEW FATHER
A Dad's Guide to the Toddler Years

THE EXPECTANT FATHER
SECOND EDITION
Facts, Tips, and Advice for Dads-to-Be
By Armin A. Brott and Jennifer Ash
30 black-and-white illustrations
272 pages · 6 x 9"
Paper · 0-7892-0538-6 · $11.95
Hardcover · 0-7892-0537-8 · $16.95

THE NEW FATHER
SECOND EDITION
A Dad's Guide to the First Year
By Armin A. Brott
30 black-and-white illustrations
320 pages · 6 x 9"
Paper 0-7892-0815-6 · $12.95
Hardcover · 0-7892-0806-7 · $18.95

FATHERING YOUR TODDLER
A Dad's Guide to the Second and Third Years
By Armin A. Brott
20 black-and-white illustrations
288 pages · 6 x 9"
Paper · 0-7892-0850-4 · $12.95
Hardcover · 0-7892-0849-0 · $18.95

Available from your favorite bookstore, or at abbeville.com, or by calling 1-800-ARTBOOK